Caught'ya Again!

More Grammar with a Giggle

Jane Bell Kiester

MAUPIN HOUSE

Copyright © 1993
by Jane Bell Kiester

The author appreciates comments and suggestions.
Please write her in care of the publisher (address below).

Maupin House books are available at special discounts
for promotions, fundraising, or educational use.
For details, contact

MAUPIN HOUSE PUBLISHING
P.O. Box 90148
Gainesville, Florida 32607

(904) 373-5588
1-800-524-0634

First edition

Printed in the United States of America

Library of Congress Cataloging-in-Publication Data

Kiester, Jane Bell, 1945–
    Caught'ya again! / Jane Bell Kiester.
       p.   cm.
    Includes bibliographical references.
    ISBN 0-929895-09-6; $14.95
    1. English language—Grammar—Study and teaching (Elementary)
  2. English language—Grammar—Study and teaching (Secondary)
  3. Humor in education.   I. Title.   II. Title: Caught you again.
LB1576.K48 1992   92-31482
428.007—dc20   CIP

Contents

This book is dedicated with love
to the memory of my brother,
Christopher James Bell,
who died in Vietnam
twenty-three years ago
at the age of twenty-one
before he ever had a chance
to taste all the flavors of life.

A gentle yet stubborn soul,
You touch the inner branches
Of all our trees,
Blowing oboe sounds of wind
Through all our memories.

Acknowledgements

First, I would like to rectify an omission in the Acknowledgements of *Caught'ya! Grammar with a Giggle*. Laurel Harb, dear friend (even after the omission), colleague, excellent teacher, and enthusiastic supporter of my writing career, wrote the originals of the spelling sentences provided in *Caught'ya! Grammar with a Giggle* on pages 79 to 91. We both used them for several years in our classrooms. It's collaborating with friends like Laurel that help make the teaching profession fun. Thank you, Laurel. I apologize deeply for the omission.

Once again, I would like to thank my mother, Perra S. Bell, and my husband, Charles L. Kiester, for their careful, painstaking editing of this book. Between them they catch most of my egregious errors and keep me humble. A writer could not ask for better, more willing, or more loving editors. My husband also provided me with the basketball sequence in the story of Charlie Excess and took over all my chores to give me time to write. My mother is my greatest fan. Thanks, Mom. I also wish to thank my father, James F. Bell, for his constant inspiration, encouragement, and frequent author-to-author pep-talks. Our three sons, John, Jesse, and Mark provided the examples and the laughs, and still help keep Mom's feet touching ground in the twentieth century. Thanks, guys.

Maupin House Publishing continues to be one of those rare publishing houses who believes in its authors, communicates frequently, and listens seriously to authors' concerns. Maupin House successfully marketed the first Caught'ya book with the fervor of "true believers." I feel very fortunate to be able to work with such a publisher.

We teachers get our ideas from each other. Sometimes we share so freely that we don't remember where a particular idea originated. Many teachers have kindly contributed their wonderful creative talents to this book either directly or indirectly. While each (who can be traced) has been recognized and given credit for his or her idea when it appears in the book, I also wish to list their names again here.

My first period students of 1991-1992 and I would especially like to thank the collective humor of Laura Strickland and Gail Hubbard, who submitted the material adapted into the Adolescent Karate Otter story. What a great story! Kren Kurts, Carol Harrell, and Laurel Harb are the thinly-disguised participants in the dialogue. I certainly love laughing and teaching with them. Kren and Carol induced me to the writing workshop; hence, I always shall be in their debt. Cathy Berg is ever an inspiration. Sally Larson contributed the idea for two of the writing suggestions. She also helped ease me into teaching eighth-grade English. ("They're bigger than seventh graders and just as much fun to teach.") I also want to mention Cheryl Alexaitis, Nancie Atwell, Gwen Barnett, Rebakah Caplan, Tillis Churchill, Betsy Creveling, Renée Hannen, Carol Harrell, Ken Macrorie, Stephanie McGraw, Polly Nagle, Cindy Secor, Jean Stallings, and Rosie Wysong, whose ideas, either directly or indirectly, contributed to Chapter 4. Thank you, colleagues. Your students are lucky to have such creative, enthusiastic teachers at the helm.

Because Sandra Bauldree made the mistake (thank goodness) of finding two errors (which will be corrected in the second printing) in the first Caught'ya book, she was asked to proofread the Caught'ya sentences and tests for Chapters 7, 8, and 9 of this book. Thanks to Sandra, there should be very few errors in this book, if any.

Doris Spears Farnbach, another colleague, is a grammarian, *par excellence*. She very kindly agreed to double check the Appendix. Quite honestly, I wouldn't have felt easy about printing the Appendix without Doris's input. Doris found a few skills that the editors, the traditional texts, and I had omitted; she also found a few others that needed more explanation.

Finally, I wish to thank my students. You are my guinea pigs, my shot in the arm every morning, my inspiration. Without you, life would be awfully flat and certainly would be a lot duller! I especially want to thank all the students in my fifth- , sixth- , and seventh-period classes of 1990-1991 and in my sixth- and seventh-period classes of 1991-1992. You tested the stories of Harold Weird (1990-91) and Charlie Excess (1991-92), made helpful suggestions, and, in true eighth-grader fashion, ferreted out any possible errors your teacher might have made. Teaching you was a pleasure and "a blast."

Introduction

While we English teachers cannot hope to compete either with the increasing social problems that face today's youths or with the media that saturates their lives, we sometimes can instill in them a taste for the delight of learning and writing. Eleven years ago, in a flash of I-don't-know-what, I managed to create a method of teaching grammar and mechanics that excited my fifth graders into *wanting* to write correctly. They applied what they learned to their own writing. Since then, my colleagues and I have expanded and improved upon this method in our diverse classrooms in elementary, middle, and high schools. This method worked so well that it was added to the curriculum for English in Alachua County, Florida. Two years ago, the Caught'ya grammar appeared in the book *Caught'ya! Grammar with a Giggle.*

This book is intended as a sequel to the first book. Again, there are story ideas and three sets of one-hundred Caught'ya sentences, but more has been included this time.

First, a new chapter, Chapter 2, discusses specific ways to use the Caught'ya at home. In addition, parents and tutors have been kept in mind throughout the book to help them adapt an idea to their situation.

Next, there is a walk-through dialogue in Chapter 3 designed to show you how to come up with your own Caught'ya story outline and sentences.

Chapter 4 provides suggestions for seventeen tried-and-true mini-lessons (five minutes or less) that you can use to supplement the Caught'yas and Nancie Atwell's writing workshop (1987). These mini-lessons are teacher-centered activities intended to spark young writers. They introduce the more esoteric concepts, genres, and modes used by other writers. They reinforce the English taught in the Caught'yas or provide information about concepts like metaphors and similes. They are presented in a way to try to seduce even the most reluctant writer into an enthusiasm for the written word. These discussions on techniques and skills can take place after the class corrects the Caught'ya.

Some of the suggestions for mini-lessons will work at almost any grade level from three through twelve with a little watering down for lower levels and a sprucing up for upper levels; others obviously are too sophisticated for the lower levels. The mini-lessons are not labeled for any grade level since classes and schools differ so much. It is up to you to judge those that are best for your students.

Included in Chapter 5 are a few suggestions for writing assignments that I refuse to abandon totally to the whole language approach. Perhaps the old-fashioned teacher in me still wants some control, but I feel that these few special teacher-directed writing exercises do help my students. For many students, these assignments set up an inquiry that leads to other ideas and new ways of looking at things. They also prepare students for the formal research papers they will encounter in high school and college.

Unlike conventional research papers, these writing practices with metaphors, scientific inquiry, and investigations emerge from the individual student's mind. I usually require (or suggest) one of these teacher-engendered assignments every two months or so.

Part of each of these writing exercises includes an evaluation and a critique of the assignment. Eighth graders can be brutally frank when they feel that they can express themselves freely without repercussions. In their critiques, most of the students tell me that although these assignments limit their freedom to write what *they* choose to write (unlike a writing workshop), the exercises make them really think. My students also tell me how important it is to them that in each of these papers it is *their* opinion that is sought, *their* ideas that are valued. This reaction is the reason why I continue to use these particular assignments. Other assignments that I have since abandoned did not elicit such a positive and thoughtful response.

For those who prefer to write their own Caught'ya sentences but need a story from which to begin, Chapter 6 comes to the rescue with six more story ideas. This chapter also contains ninety sentences of a delightful story contributed by two teachers in Jacksonville, Florida, about five, food-loving "adolescent transmuted Karate otters."

Chapters 7, 8, and 9 give teachers and parents another three sets of Caught'ya sentences. Each contains one-hundred sentences — enough for an entire year if they are occasionally supplemented with your own.

At the end of each of these three chapters is an end-of' the-year test which can be used to evaluate the editing skills that your students have learned over the course of the school year. The high school story includes two tests, one to use as a semester exam and the other for the end of the year.

In my classroom, I give two types of tests: a Caught'ya test and a standardized book test at the beginning and at the end of every school year. The tests given at the beginning of the year alert my students to the need for studying English. At the end of the year, the results of the tests help me justify leaving that lovely new grammar book (kindly provided by my county) sitting dusty and unused on the shelves of my classroom. The old-fashioned teacher in me still has trouble letting go.

Finally, this time, at the request of several parents and Maupin House, I have provided an annotated Appendix of the terms and the grammatical rules listed in the three chapters of Caught'ya sentences. I hope this quick reference will help those of you who did not major in English in college to explain to your children and students the "why" of things in the Caught'ya sentences.

The Caught'ya system of teaching English grammar and skills really does work. Not only does it teach the necessary skills, concepts, and vocabulary, but it does it in a way that students enjoy and remember. Even more importantly, it increases and hones editing skills that are so necessary in today's world. Since the Caught'ya takes only five to ten minutes a day to teach, that leaves the rest of the time to be spent writing (which is what we all really are supposed to be teaching).

Some school systems require teachers to spend at least ten minutes of every English class on grammar and mechanics practice. A daily Caught'ya can be that practice. For parents of home-schoolers, spending only ten minutes a day on grammar leaves your children fresh and ready to spend time writing creatively rather than doing boring exercises.

As an added attraction, teachers and parents have found that the Caught'ya forges a strong bond between them and their students. The children feel as though they can trust us with their confidences. Because of this trust, they even occasionally listen to our "sage" words of experience. The success the Caught'ya engenders raises the self-esteem of the students, translating into better grades and a more positive attitude about school. The technique is successful with low-achieving students, advanced students, and with all those in-between.

Perhaps the Caught'ya is like a daily, pleasant-tasting vitamin pill. Skills and vocabulary are ingested frequently and pleasantly in small amounts to develop good writing habits. On the other hand, grammar from a chalk-tasting, dry, traditional, textbook method is like a dose of castor oil: it leaves a bad taste despite good intentions that unfortunately are rarely realized. Traditional teaching on this subject, whether in school or at home, makes children reluctant to repeat a usage or grammar experience. The Caught'ya pill, however, produces only giggles, smiles, and more correct writing. Enjoy your freedom from grammar textbooks with a clear conscience!

Caught'ya Again!
More
Grammar
with a Giggle

Chapter 1

Revisiting Caught'ya! Grammar with a Giggle

Skim This Chapter If You Have Read the Book

The book *Caught'ya! Grammar with a Giggle* explains in detail the ten basic steps necessary to set up a successful Caught'ya program. There is no point in going into such detail in this book as well, but those of you who have not read the first book will need a brief explanation of how the Caught'ya system works so that you will be able to implement it.

If you already have read *Caught'ya! Grammar with a Giggle* and are comfortable using the system with your students, you might want to skim this chapter quickly before going on to the next chapter. This chapter summarizes the first three chapters of the previous book, and I have added a few more suggestions gleaned from another year's experience and from helpful suggestions received from other teachers in response to the first book.

Parents who are home-schooling or tutoring their own children can find additional explanation for the home environment in Chapter 2 but should read this chapter first.

The Caught'ya is an integrated approach to language skills. Essentially, it is a sentence or two of an ongoing, funny story taught from a blackboard or overhead three to five days each week. Each sentence is laced with errors that the teacher wishes to eliminate in his/her students' writing. It also contains at least one challenging word that is new to most of the class. The teacher introduces and elicits the meaning of the word(s), reads the sentence dramatically, and initiates a discussion as to whether the sentence begins a new paragraph in the story.

Students then write the Caught'ya as correctly as they can. Meanwhile, the teacher walks around the room and gives immediate, tinged-with-humor feedback to individual students, providing mini-lessons and urging or challenging a student to find the error on his/her own.

When nearly all of the students have completed the sentence and received a comment from the teacher, the teacher returns to the board or overhead. The meaning of the vocabulary word(s) is elicited and discussed again. The whole class, with the teacher presiding, then goes over the Caught'ya. Everyone uses proofreading symbols to mark errors that were missed.

When the entire sentence has been corrected communally and corrections discussed thoroughly, students count the errors they missed the first time — i.e., when they attempted to correct the sentence on their own. In the margin of their paper, the students indicate the number of their initial errors. A skill has been introduced, reinforced, or practiced, and maybe the class has enjoyed a giggle over the story or over the antics of the teacher as he or she cavorted around the room to check each child's sentence.

The evaluation of the sentences is based on whether students catch the errors and mark them on their papers when the whole class goes over the Caught'ya, *not* on the number of errors made the first time when students attempted to correct the sentence on their own. This way *every* student, no matter how weak he/she has been in

English skills, can have success with the Caught'ya. Even the student with poor skills can get an A+.

A teacher can use a Caught'ya every day or only three or four times a week, as long as the story line is not lost or forgotten. Skills can be repeated *ad nauseam* until every student in the class masters them or begs for mercy.

Students soon get used to entering the classroom and immediately settling down to write the Caught'ya. The Caught'ya routine shortens the "waste time" at the beginning of every period. Because students crave the individual feedback their teacher gives while they are working on the Caught'ya, they usually get to work very quickly.

Sometimes students help each other with the errors in the Caught'ya. You may hear whispered debates about whether a comma should be put in a certain spot or not. You may also overhear hot debates about the part of speech of a certain word.

Students who are weak in English skills especially love the Caught'ya because it eliminates any feeling of failure and frustration previously associated with language arts. Since the Caught'ya always is short, it can be completed even by those students with short attention spans. If you have an easy Caught'ya sentence on the board, it is a good idea to deliberately check the weaker students first so that you can praise them for making no errors that day.

It is important to make a game out of the Caught'ya so that students feel good about their work and are challenged to try their best. The teacher's reward is hearing two students argue over the placement of a capital letter or the necessity for a paragraph, instead of discussing the latest fight in the hall.

A parent who uses the Caught'ya as a home-school method to teach English skills can follow the same steps suggestedf for classroom teachers. A parent who teaches children on several levels can use a different story for each child or use the same story, supplying some of the answers to the younger child. Children at home experience the same success as children in the classroom.

A parent using the Caught'ya as a tutoring device can simply do one every day and have a laugh with the child. The lesson leaves the child with the feeling that learning English is fun, not something invented only to torture them. Remember, quality of teaching, not quantity, gets the point across. All of these steps are discussed again in Chapter 2 with many more suggestions for parents and tutors for adapting the Caught'ya for use at home.

It does not matter what grade you teach or how old your children are; this system works at any level as long as the children can read. Caught'yas have been successfully used by teachers for grades one through junior college. It is up to you to change and modify the details to fit the needs of *your* students.

Do not worry if you are a shy person or feel that you are not naturally a ham. Caught'yas will be successful if you are at all enthusiastic about them. If it is not your style to cavort around the classroom, a simple touch or quiet word will suffice. Modify the method to fit *your* personality. Remember, many teachers have used the Caught'ya system with great success, and all have different personalities. No two teachers present the Caught'yas in exactly the same way.

If you are still unsure of the evaluation technique, want some practice, or want to see what other student's papers look like after reading this chapter, you may wish to go to your local book store and purchase a copy of *Caught'ya! Grammar with a Giggle*.

The Caught'ya is perfect for a daily mini-skill lesson in conjunction with a whole language approach. Since, ideally, a teacher composes his/her own daily Caught'ya sentence (or changes the sentences provided in Chapters 7, 8, and 9), the skills taught can be based on the problems which each teacher has identified in his/her students' writing. The discussions engendered by the problems in the Caught'ya sentences can be part of a mini-lesson at the start of a class period in a writing workshop.

In whatever language arts system or program a teacher follows, the Caught'ya can be used as a device to settle students at the beginning of a class period and teach them mechanics, grammar, usage, vocabulary, editing, and proofreading skills in a way that carries over into their writing. Please keep in mind, however, that the most important elements are humor and the discussions about the "why" of each correction.

Ten Easy Steps to a Successful Caught'ya

1. Outline or choose story plot.

2. Decide on skills and vocabulary word.

3. Compose daily sentence.

4. Write sentence incorrectly on board or on overhead.

5. Students write Caught'ya as correctly as they can.

6. Walk around, commenting on each student's Caught'ya.

7. Go to board and check Caught'ya with class.

8. Students mark mistakes with proofreading symbols.

9. Students count and indicate number of errors.

10. Collect all Caught'ya sentences at end of week.

Step 1: Outline or choose story plot.

Beginners to the Caught'ya system probably should use one of the three sets of one-hundred Caught'ya sentences provided in Chapters 7-9 until they feel comfortable with the technique. Those of you who feel inventive can create the plot of an original soap opera. For those of you who prefer to write your own daily sentence but lack inspiration for a plot, a condition common to teachers at the busy beginning of the school year, a number of plots is suggested in Chapter 6.

If you do write your own story plot, plan it in the form of a rough, changeable outline. It is a good idea to wait to write the actual sentences of the story until after you complete Step 2 in this chapter or read Chapter 3 of this book. In Chapter 3, I illustrate how to come up with your own plot outline and daily sentences. There is also an example of a completed outline.

Step 2: Decide on skills and vocabulary word.

Here you decide which skills you wish to introduce, practice, review, or reinforce. You also need to choose a vocabulary word that you would like your students to learn. If you use one of the sets of sentences in Chapters 7, 8, and 9 of this book, you probably can skip this step. These pre-made sentences, however, are generic and may not fit the needs of your particular students. If you feel that your students need more practice in a particular skill, you may need to alter my sentences or insert one of your own that loosely follows the plot.

Check your students' writing efforts to see which skills need to be taught and which skills need more practice. For example, let's say your students need more practice punctuating quotations. When you reach a convenient conversation in the Caught'ya story, simply add more conversation. If you are working on letter-writing format, have one of the characters write a short note to someone. If your students need more practice with irregular verbs, substitute such verbs in the sentences. If you need to work on capitalizing titles, have the characters read a book or two. You might also wish to glance at the Appendix to see if there are any other skills you want to introduce to your students.

Remember, however, to insert a vocabulary word in each sentence. The difficulty of the word doesn't matter. Just write the sentence and then find a good place in that sentence to substitute a more sophisticated word. One of those little electronic thesauruses is perfect for finding those synonyms.

Step 3: Compose daily sentence.

Don't forget the vocabulary words and make each sentence flow from the previous one. You want the sentences to read like a story so you can have a daily discussion about whether a paragraph is necessary. As always, keep the range of the abilities of your students in mind.

Step 4: Write sentence incorrectly on the board or overhead.

Parents can, of course, use a piece of paper from which your children can copy. Remove all punctuation and program in other typical writing errors. Challenge your students to write this sentence as correctly as they can. For grades five and above, you may wish to ask the students to label the parts of speech of each word in the sentence, identify the subject and verb, or circle adjectives, etc.

Step 5: Students write Caught'ya as correctly as they can.

Before your students attempt to write the Caught'ya sentence on their own, read the sentence dramatically so students can hear where the appropriate punctuation should go. Elicit and then go over the meaning of the vocabulary word and discuss the need for a paragraph.

Now, instruct your pupils to write the sentence on their own paper as correctly as they can. Encourage them to read and reread the sentence after they have completed it to try to catch all the errors.

I have found that regular students like to know how many errors are in the sentence. They feel that it helps them find the errors. I sometimes oblige them for the first half of the year. In contrast, the students in my advanced English classes become nervous when they know the number of errors they should find in a sentence. These high achievers become upset if they can't find the total number of necessary corrections. I have learned from painful experience to forgo an error count for them, no matter how hard they plead.

Step 6: Walk around, commenting on each student's Caught'ya.

As your students attempt to write the Caught'ya sentence as correctly as they can, you circulate, offer individual encouragement, issue challenges, goad students good-naturedly, or provide a quick mini-lesson. Parents can hang cheerfully over their child's shoulder. This probably will drive your child nuts, especially if you are grinning happily, but it also will inspire your child to ferret out the errors.

If your classes are large, you will see only part of a sentence in the first papers you examine. You cannot wait until all your students have completed the sentence as you circulate around the many desks, or you will have pandemonium on your hands. Look at what the children have completed and simply tease them about the errors they already missed. Encourage those students who have not yet made a mistake.

This is the step children like the best. Ham it up. Make your responses funny. Poke a student gently if you "caught'im." Laugh. Be maddeningly elusive in providing answers you know your students can figure out on their own with a little more care or thought. If this is the first time a particular skill has appeared, give a private mini-lesson to those who need it. Make this interval a special one with your students even if you only spend five seconds with each child. This is where you and your children do the giggling.

If a student wrote the sentence correctly, go bananas! Make the student take a bow or shake his/her hand. Challenge that student to get the sentence correct the next day. In other words, make a big deal of the child's success. Those of you who teach high school may want to be more dignified in your praise.

It is important to note here that teachers of classes of 30 or more students *can* go around the room in less than six minutes and that students *will* wait silently while you make your rounds. Amazingly, even the rowdiest of classes usually will sit silently so that a teacher can stop by each student for a brief comment. Why? They want that feedback.

Start your daily trek around the classroom on a different side each day. If noise begins, stop. You will find that after once or twice, students learn to remain quiet. They want that daily touch and daily private moment with their teacher. They will even be quiet for it. In all my years of teaching, I've only had one class that just couldn't be quiet as we did the Caught'yas. I tried everything in my "bag of tricks." Nothing worked. I finally admitted defeat and only got to one half of that class each day.

Step 7: Go to board and check Caught'ya with class.

After your students have written the Caught'ya as correctly as they can and after you have given them your animated feedback, return to the blackboard or overhead and elicit the corrections from the class. Parents can look over their child's shoulder to jointly correct the original sentence. Parents, make sure your child has his/her own paper. Your paper is only for you.

Go over *why* each correction needs to be made. (Corrections are listed beside each sentence.) If you need more explanation, consult the Appendix. This annotated index contains all of the terms used in Chapters 7, 8, and 9.

Do not feel inadequate if you do not know some of the terms or some of the "whys" for the corrections. If you want the truth, I had to debate some of them with my fellow teachers, all of whom have taught English for years. English grammar is difficult. There are so many exceptions to each rule that it is formidable to try to remember all of them.

Step 8: Students mark mistakes with proofreading symbols.

During the group correction of the Caught'ya sentence, instruct your students to use proofreading symbols to mark the corrections on their sentences. These marks should be made clearly with a colored pencil, pen, or marker in a different hue from the one with which they wrote the sentence. In addition, for study purposes, students should write out the corrections.

Listed below are a few of the most commonly used proofreading symbols. You do not have to use all of them with your students.

Suggested proofreading symbols

¶	indent	¶̶	take out indent
∧	add words here		take out
_a_	capitalize	A̶	make a small letter
→	move word	(and / and)	reverse order
◯	add punctuation (whatever is inside circle)		

Step 9: Students count and indicate number of errors.

Students count the number of errors they did not catch when they attempted to correct the sentence on their own. They indicate the number in the right-hand margin. This has two advantages. It makes students leave a good, healthy, right-hand margin, and it provides them with immediate feedback. Remind your students to make all corrections and notations in a color different from that of the sentence itself.

Encourage, cajole, forbid, threaten, do anything to keep your students honest. Since the grade the children receive from you on the Caught'ya has nothing to do with the number of errors they made when they attempted to write the sentence on their own, it would be pointless to try to hide errors. Moreover, lying would only hinder a student from learning from his/her mistakes. What finally worked for me was to warn my students in an ominous tone that anyone who *never* missed anything on the Caught'yas also had to earn an A+ on the two Caught'ya tests I planned to give in January and June. Since no one has yet made a perfect score on the Caught'ya test I give at the beginning of the year, students understand the reasoning.

Step 10: Collect all Caught'ya sentences at end of week.

All the Caught'ya sentences for the week should be on the same piece of paper. Have your students indicate the day of the week beside each day's sentence as well as the number of errors they missed in that sentence. They should check the top of their papers to see if they have written their full name and the date of the first Caught'ya sentence; for practice, the month always should be written in full. Students who have been absent one or more days should simply write the day(s) of the week they missed and write the word "absent" by that day.

Below is a quick-reference lesson plan (without the extra comments) to use as you teach the basic Caught'ya lesson. It won't be long, though, until you no longer need it.

Lesson Plans for the Caught'ya

These plans assume that you already have completed Steps 1, 2, and 3.

■ Before school, write the daily sentence on the board, box the vocabulary word, and if you wish, indicate the number of errors below the sentence.

■ When the bell rings, read the sentence to the class with a dramatic flair, reviewing the story, eliciting the meaning of the vocabulary word, and discussing whether the sentence begins a paragraph.

■ Instruct students to copy the sentence as correctly as they can.

■ Walk around the room, giving students individual feedback. Say "Caught'ya" or something comparable if you catch a student with an error and praise or challenge a student who has caught all the errors. Remember, students may not have finished the sentence by the time you get to them. Just look at what they have completed.

■ Go back to the blackboard or overhead and check the Caught'ya sentence out loud with your class. Elicit answers from your students. Be sure to discuss the reason for each correction. Use the Appendix at the back of this book for explanations. Using proofreading symbols, correct the Caught'ya on the board or overhead. Instruct students to do the same.

■ Instruct students to count their errors and indicate them in the right-hand margin. Instruct them also to draw a line across the page under the day's Caught'ya to separate it from the next day's Caught'ya. If it is the last Caught'ya of the week, collect your students' papers.

Three Steps to Evaluating the Caught'ya

Evaluating a Caught'ya is just as important as the process of doing one. The Caught'ya is designed to eliminate the feeling of failure and to foster success in language arts. Remember, the Caught'ya is graded not on how well a student initially grasps the English language, but on how carefully that student corrected the sentence when you and the class went over the Caught'ya at the blackboard or overhead.

Parents may wish to evaluate the Caught'ya in front of their children for even more feedback. The fact that it is quick and easy to grade ensures that you will not lose your child's attention.

In *Caught'ya! Grammar with a Giggle*, I promised you "Grammar with a Giggle." Well, get ready to have a giggle yourself: a week's worth of Caught'yas takes only ten minutes a week, assuming a class of thirty-five students! Those of you who, like me, teach public school will have up to 160 Caught'ya papers a week. The following three steps reduce grading time for 160 students to less than an hour each week! I promise.

This easy grading requires that your students follow a certain format. Insist that your students put all the Caught'ya sentences for the same week on the same piece of paper. This reduces paper shuffling time. You also have to decide on the format that you like and really insist on it. You probably should stress the following:

■ student's full name in the upper right corner

■ full date underneath the name

■ a title for title capitalization practice

■ the day of the week spelled out for each day's sentence

■ an even margin on the left and a margin that leaves space on the right where the number of errors missed is indicated

■ student use of different colored ink for corrections and errors which are clearly marked so that you can tell at a glance what has been corrected by the student

Now get out your green and purple pens, and you are ready to grade the Caught'yas. The following three steps assume that you have a paper in front of you. If you do not, look at the sample paper at the end of this chapter and use it for clarification as you note the steps.

1. Check format

Glance at the paper to see if the student has faithfully followed the format. Except for uneven margins, which are worth five points each, and the failure to use a different color, which also is worth only five points, each error in the format is worth ten points. This encourages students to be careful.

■ Name written correctly. —10

■ Date written out correctly with month spelled out correctly. —10

■ Title correctly spelled and capitalized. —10

■ Number of uncaught errors indicated and circled to the right of each Caught'ya sentence. —10

■ Errors corrected in another color. —5

■ All the Caught'ya sentences for the week on the same sheet of paper. —10

■ Margins large enough and even left margin. — 5 each margin

Mark all errors clearly in a pen that is a different color from the two hues that your student used. It is always helpful to keep an array of colors handy as you grade.

2. Check content of one Caught'ya.

Choose one of the week's Caught'ya sentences. This is what really saves you time. I assure you that if you read all of the Caught'ya sentences each week for each of your students, the final grade would be about the same as if you read only one.

For six years I graded every sentence of every child every week, but it got to be such a chore that I grew to dread the weekends. I struggled for about three or four years when I noticed that if I increased the number of points per error and graded only one Caught'ya per student per week, the grade almost always came out the same. When another teacher independently came to the same conclusion, we talked it over, pooled our collective guilt at not reading every sentence, and chucked it out our classroom doors.

Do not tell students which Caught'ya sentence you plan to grade. This makes them careful with all of the sentences. Do not always choose the most difficult sentence. This way you will always keep your students guessing.

After you choose the Caught'ya you wish to grade for the week, focus on it. Ask yourself the following questions:

- Did the student write the sentence correctly the first time when you went around the room poking students?
- If not, did the student clearly mark the errors with the proof-reading symbols you want him/her to use? Did the student catch them all? Did the student mark the corrections above the errors?
- Did the student catch *every* error either the first or the second time?
- Is the number of errors indicated in the right-hand margin? Did the student use two colors?
- Are all words (including vocabulary word) spelled correctly?
- Is the sentence copied correctly from the board or overhead?
- Have any words been left out or added?
- Are there any extraneous capital letters?

Take ten points off for each error you find that has not been marked by the student or does not have the correction written in above it. Each tiny error is worth ten points. You will be surprised at the results. Even your poorest student can earn an A+. In fact, I find that my regular students often get higher grades than my advanced students. Although they may miss more the first time around, regular students are more careful about checking each sentence. They tend to be less arrogant than the advanced students, and the chance to earn an A+ in language arts is exciting to them.

After you have added the number of points lost for format of the entire paper or for errors not caught in the one Caught'ya you checked, subtract the total from 100. Put that grade at the top of the student's paper with an encouraging or positive comment. Since you grade only one sentence per week per child, you have the luxury of making a brief, private comment to each child. This is so important!

Parents, you might want to make the comment in writing as well as orally. Children love private notes that are written just to them. Your comments will mean so much more in written form. Since you have only one or two papers to grade, your positive comments can be longer. You might even want to start a daily written dialogue with your child on the Caught'ya paper and invite your child to respond in writing to your comments.

3. Reward the students.

One of the reasons that the Caught'ya system is so successful is that it makes students feel good about themselves. There is always something positive you can say (no child will miss every single error). Students also like a tangible reward that they can parade in front of their peers. This really raises their self-esteem.

Teachers of students with learning or behavioral problems have repeatedly told me how well the Caught'ya technique works. The learning-disabled students I teach love the Caught'ya system because they can experience success.

After trying other less successful methods of publicizing student success, I experimented with a Caught'ya "lottery" in my classroom. This did the trick.

The lottery is simple. When I pass back the graded Caught'ya papers, I also give a quarter of a three-by-five file card to each student who earned an A+ on his/her paper. I announce the A+ students publicly with a challenge, a grin, or some comment designed to bring notice to the child to be rewarded. The weekly A+ winners then write their names, the date, and the class period on the card. Each walks to the front of the classroom in full view of the rest of the class. Relishing the moment of public recognition, the student deposits the card in a box. Twice a year, I open the box and draw out a card from each class. Those students receive a prize: a small stuffed animal, a game, a candy bar, etc. Weekly drawings for small prizes work well too.

The "lottery" is an easy, painless, no-work-for-the-teacher way to encourage and to reward students. You would be amazed if you could see one of my slower students proudly prance up to the box to put in a card. The look of sweet triumph on the faces of students who do not experience much success elsewhere in their lives will convince you of the effectiveness of the material / verbal / public recognition.

If the idea of a raffle offends you, you can easily devise some other method of reward which allows the A+ students to parade their success. You will find, too, that after a month or so of doing Caught'yas, well over half of your students consistently will earn one-hundreds on their papers.

Parents, you can easily reward an A+ Caught'ya paper with whatever you know appeals to your child. It also might be a good idea to keep a chart of your child's progress posted prominently. This way your child can display prowess in English in front of friends.

An example of a corrected student paper follows. *My* marks and comments are inside the dark black lines. The sentences are from the high-school story about Charlie Excess. Note that there is one format error.

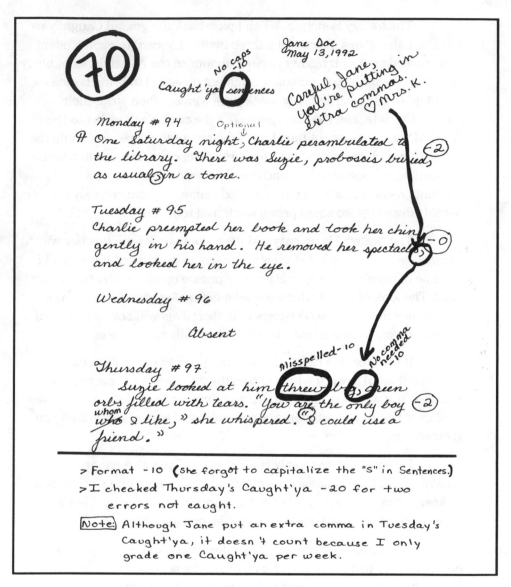

A sample student Caught'ya paper. The thick, dark marks are mine.

Notes:

1. Format −10 (She forgot to capitalize the "s" in Sentences in the title for the week.)

2. I checked Thursday's Caught'ya and marked −20 for two errors not caught.

3. Although Jane put an extra comma in Tuesday's Caught'ya, it doesn't count because I grade only one Caught'ya per week.

Chapter 2

How to Do a "Caught'ya for Two"

**Parents and Tutors,
This One Is Especially for You**

Every year, at least a dozen parents ask me to suggest ways to help their children retain skills over the summer. When I received the requests this year, however, it rang a chime because one parent asked me how she could continue my daily Caught'yas at home. My answer was to give the parent a photocopy of a set of Caught'ya sentences and instruct her to keep a journal with her child. At this point, I immediately began taking notes for this second book with parents in mind.

After I decided to devote a chapter to parents, I was asked to speak to a convention of Florida parents who home-school their children. Many of the parents liked the technique. With a few alterations, Caught'yas can be as effective at home as in the classroom — as long as you laugh and tease your child while you do the Caught'ya.

When parents request help for tutoring purposes, I never have a problem suggesting a daily family writing time and daily two-way journals to talk about books that the family is reading (see Atwell, 1987), but they

19

inevitably ask for a book reference as well. Perhaps I am arrogant or ignorant, but I have yet to find a book except maybe *Daily Oral Language* (McDougal, Littell, 1989) that would do the trick. That book has its drawbacks as well; the daily sentences are not in a story and are somewhat dull, and there are no vocabulary words within the context of the sentences. Since there is no story, no daily paragraph discussion can be held.

Any traditional grammar text turns children off — especially in the summer. Because of the bad gag reflex that those drill-oriented texts seem to trigger among the young, they actually may harm the children's writing more than an absence of instruction. Besides, for the past forty years most of the research has shown that those traditional texts with their dry, chalky examples and technical, yawn-making explanations do not achieve the end result sought in the study of grammar — namely to write correctly. (Elgin, 1982) I recommend that such texts be used only as references when a budding writer feels the need to explore a specific point in depth.

Children rarely make the connection between error-free writing and grammar textbooks. In twenty years of teaching, I certainly have never seen it. As Nancie Atwell points out in her book *In the Middle* (1987), correct writing is learned only through writing that has relevance for the student.

Because class sizes in public schools today are so large, and because a teacher often must teach to the middle and risk losing the interest of students on the extremes of the spectrum, home tutoring and home schooling have become more important in recent years. Public school is designed for the "norm." Certainly none of my three sons fits this "norm." I suspect many parents experience the same frustration.

Even though the county where we live has an excellent public school system, I felt I had to supplement its teaching for all three of my sons. All are bright, normal, active boys. The curriculum just wasn't always designed to stimulate their individual interests. My husband and I tutored each of our sons at some point in his school career. All three have since gone to college where they have done very well.

Currently, however, I am happy to note that more and more schools are adopting individualized writing and reading workshops, abandoning traditional basal readers and grammar textbooks. During a reading workshop, children read what they choose to read and talk about it in a journal in which they keep an open dialogue with their teacher. Under this system, a teacher can better meet the needs of the individual student.

Indeed, those of you who are home schooling have two great advantages over those of us who teach public school. One, you have only one or two students and can give them lots of individual instruction. Two, you have time. A lack of time is an English teacher's greatest enemy, not the difficulty and the complexities of the English language.

I invented the Caught'ya system of grammar and skills teaching because I was frustrated by this lack of time. You parents can use Caught'yas as a springboard for really productive writing and reading workshops with your children. While a Caught'ya takes less than ten minutes a day to do, public school students still have a mere thirty minutes or so to plunge into their writing. Then the bell rings, and they have to abandon whatever they are working on, even if they are in the middle of a sentence. Without a bell-bound schedule to follow, a parent can schedule an hour or two a day for writing.

What you do lack at home is peer response. You lack the "public" recognition of your child's peers when your child correctly edits the Caught'ya sentence. When your child writes, he or she gets only adult feedback instead of being able to confer with contemporaries. While I feel that this is a definite lack, the advantages of the flexibility of time and increased individual, adult attention is a counterbalance.

I invite you to abandon that traditional grammar text (along with most of us who teach English in the schools today) and enjoy a giggle or two as your child writes his/her way to good English.

The Caught'ya for Two or Three

First, read Chapter 1 to become acqainted with the ten steps of the Caught'ya. Each step is listed again below with some hints that should make Caught'yas-for-two more successful.

Step 1: Outline or choose story plot.

You will probably want to alter the ready-made stories since they are about classroom situations. There are suggestions for changing each story in the "Important Notes" before each set of Caught'ya sentences in Chapters 7, 8, and 9. Children of all ages love to hear about themselves or about other people like themselves. A parent can make up a little story starring the child, filled with familiar situations and places.

Jackie Patton, a special education teacher at my school, made up an animal story that her own children love. Wally the Mole visited her house, interacted with everything and everyone there, and decided to go back to his old home underground where things were less complicated and certainly much quieter. She told me that she strung this story out for months. You could use any animal and make up a similar story. Younger children love it.

Parents of children nine and older might want to enjoy the fun of brainstorming with their child to write a story. Children's minds are often much more original and fertile than ours. You can outline the story together. You do the writing. Go wild. Be humorous. Enjoy yourselves.

The original version of the "Magic Purple Umbrella" story used in *Caught'ya! Grammar with a Giggle* began with a bedtime tale I told one of our own children when he was little. It was all about a boy with his name who was given a magic purple umbrella that took him all over the world. These trips included frequent visits to a beloved set of grandparents. Jesse loved hearing fictional and fanciful adventures about himself. He especially loved meeting his grandparents in odd situations and hearing words purportedly coming out of his own mouth.

Step 2: Decide on skills and vocabulary word.

Decide on the vocabulary word in the same way a classroom teacher does. Look at your child's writing, find the weaknesses, and include them in Caught'ya sentences until such problems disappear.

Step 3: Compose a daily sentence.

This step does not differ from that for the classroom teacher. It might be stimulating, though, to compose the sentences with your child. You must retain control while still making sure that you include the skills your child needs to practice. The last section of Chapter 3 includes a walk-through of sentence composition.

Step 4: Write sentence incorrectly on a piece of paper.

Instead of writing the sentence incorrectly on the board or overhead, write it on a piece of paper. You can use a set of 5" x 8" file cards, one for each Caught'ya sentence. You then can refer to them later on in the year, just to see how much has been learned. You might want to make a copy of the incorrect sentence on the front *and* on the back of each card. One side would include only the incorrect sentence; the other would contain the corrections made as you went over the Caught'ya with your child in Steps 7 and 8.

Step 5: Students write Caught'ya as correctly as they can.

Parents, warn your child of difficult skills that appear in the Caught'ya. Tease, challenge, be obtrusive, but don't provide any answers at this stage. Instruct your child to keep a week's worth of Caught'yas on one piece of paper.

Two or more children of different ages or grade levels still can use only one Caught'ya sentence. A Seventh Day Adventist teacher in Ohio who used the first Caught'ya book told my sister-in-law how she managed with one Caught'ya sentence for students ranging from grades one through four in the same classroom! This teacher had planned to do Caught'yas only with her third and fourth graders. The younger children felt left out. She simply went around to the younger children and, on their papers, she wrote the corrections that she knew they couldn't understand.

First graders, for example, can probably work on beginning a sentence with a capital letter and using end punctuation, but there is no reason that they can't learn this from the Caught'yas and feel good in the process as long as those are the only errors they have to correct.

With only one or two children in the class, a parent easily can lean over the younger child and supply commas or whatever the younger child is not old enough to grasp. The younger child then feels included, and the parent does not have to work with two stories and two sentences. Each child can do well.

Step 6: Comment on the Caught'ya.

Hang over your child like a hungry vulture. Drive him/her crazy. Make a big deal of correct answers. Torment verbally in an amusing way when a mistake is made. I am known for my raucous, annoying cackle. My friend Laurel has perfected the enigmatic smile. If your child is the type who likes to work in privacy, then sit like a cat, a little distance from your child. Keep your tail swishing and look as if you are ready to attack your prey. When your child announces that he/she has completed the sentence, pounce with all humor unsheathed.

Step 7: Correct the Caught'ya with your child.

Sit next to your child and, with your copy in your hand and your child's copy in his or her hand, go through the same procedure as the one described in Step 7 in Chapter 1. Mark up your copy with a different colored pen or pencil. Use the proofreading symbols listed in Chapter 1. Instruct your child to do the same with his or her copy.

Step 8: Students mark mistakes with proofreading symbols.

This does not differ in any way from the original Step 8. You have to decide how many proofreading symbols your child can use comfortably. Post a chart in the home-school area in your home to provide a quick reference for your child. At this stage, do not look at your child's paper.

Step 9: Students count and indicate number of errors.

No change here.

Step 10: Collect Caught'ya papers at end of week.

It might be a good idea to make your child keep a notebook or folder for English work and writings in progress. This helps teach organization. At the end of each week, collect the Caught'ya paper and grade it.

In grading the Caught'yas, a slightly different approach from that of the classroom teacher might work better. Reduce the amount taken off per error to five instead of ten and grade all the Caught'ya sentences for the week. Then follow the same procedure for evaluation described in Chapter 1.

Step 11: Post results in a public place.
(Extra step for home-schoolers.)

Because home-schools lack peer response, parents have to provide it artificially. You can post A+ papers in a prominent place where friends can see them. You can also use the graphing skills you teach in math to create a bar graph in vivid colors of your child's progress with the Caught'ya sentences. Make it colorful and post it in a prominent place where visitors might see it and ask about it. Some commercially made, delightful pictures of animals and dragons whose heads and tails hang over a bulletin board are available to help draw attention to posted papers. These aids are available at any book store that provides supplies for teachers.

––––––––––

Good luck! The rest of the time you have allotted for English can be spent writing and reading. See Chapter 4 for suggestions for mini-lessons and Chapter 5 for writing suggestions. In Chapters 4 and 5, I wrote notes to you only if the suggestion needs adapting to be successful in a home-school situation. You will notice that most of the mini-lesson and writing suggestions, however, need no adjusting.

Chapter 3

Coming Up with Your Own Stories and Sentences

(A Dialogue with a Plot in Mind)

The classroom was unnaturally quiet. Not even the air conditioner thrummed. No feet shuffled in the hall beyond the open door. No voices squeaked and rumbled at each other. The walls and bulletin boards looked depressingly naked. Piles of books snaked unevenly in front of empty bookcases. No papers cluttered my desk. It was pre-planning — before the teachers even knew which students were to be theirs for the year.

Suddenly, laughing adult voices echoed in the hallway. The voices approached my room and rounded the doorway. Several gossiping teachers, catching up on mutual summer news, walked in and squeezed themselves into two of the four student desks I had set up in a circle. A few minutes later another teacher ambled into my almost empty classroom and angled herself into a third student desk mumbling something about a diet. I slid into the last desk and joined in the conversation.

"Well, did you ever get away, Jane?" queried Karen.

"Yes, we finally coordinated our deadlines and drove to Ohio to visit with family," I answered. "It was a nice change. I always enjoy Chuck's family."

"Yeah, that's what we did too," chimed in Carolyn. "We always seem to visit family for our vacations, but I got another course out of the way!"

"Wow, when will we have to call you Dr. Harman?" queried Laura.

"It'll take me another two years," answered Carolyn.

"And a few gray hairs too, I'll bet," I remarked. "Teaching all day, going to class at night, and raising two kids has to take its toll."

"You bet!" agreed Carolyn. "I've been thinking about taking a sabbatical next year."

"Wise move," murmured Karen.

"Poverty move," laughed Carolyn.

"O.K.," said Karen in as businesslike a manner as she could muster for nine o'clock in the morning on the second day of work after a lazy summer in her cabin in the mountains of North Carolina. "Let's get this show on the road. I'm starting to feel antsy, and Friday is just around the corner. My room looks like a pre-Columbian garbage heap, and my bulletin boards stared at me vacantly this morning, begging for a cover."

"All right," I said, "I've got an idea to start us off. How about this idea? The title of the story will be 'Tales of a Middle School Weirdo.' The story can open with the description of a poor transfer student who wears glasses, has a face full of zits, and is tubby to boot."

"All middle schoolers are weird," threw in Carolyn. "Why is this one different?"

"Let's hear the rest of this plot. It's probably really bizarre like the one she came up with before," grinned Karen.

"It wasn't that strange," I retorted, mockingly indignant as I drew myself up as best I could in the restricting student desk that had not been made with forty-six year-old bodies in mind.

"Remember the one Carolyn came up with about the two nerds and the cool surfer dudes? Does this one bear any resemblance to that?" asked Laura, always the diplomat.

"Of course," I replied. "All the plots are basically similar. Love, rejection, parties, fights, obnoxious parents, and so on — just what our students like to read about."

"Yeah," said Carolyn, "but they thought Gerald the Nerd was too dorky for words. Remember that story?"

"How could I forget," I said. "We did that story the year I had that difficult fourth-period class. I did everything but stand on my head, and they didn't come around until February or so. They liked the party, though. They never got the idea that the teachers in the story resembled us. What a class!"

"Let's do that part again," said Karen. "My students liked that idea. They took a while to identify all of us, but they enjoyed the similarities."

"O.K.," I replied, "My other classes liked that, too. It was just that one class . . ."

"Oh, I had the same bunch fifth period for reading," said Carolyn. "They were humdingers. What a combination of students. They sparked each other to new heights in the art of teacher-baiting. Remember Iris and her famous, never-silent mouth?"

"How could I forget her?" I groaned. "The rest of the plot is that this kid with the zits, glasses, and chub is also a good student because his mom will maim him if he brings home anything under an 'A' on his report card."

"Let's have a black hero this year. We had a white one last year," said Laura.

"Shall we make our protagonist a hero or a heroine?" asked Karen. "I opt for another male since the boys are the hardest to interest, and eighth-grade girls love reading about boys."

"O.K.," I agreed. "Black, he is. Male, he is. What about a brother in college? We even could have a custody battle in the background. I had so many students last year who were going through that."

"Good idea!" responded Karen.

"Now," I continued, "what about us?"

"What about us?" asked Karen. "We're fine. It's just our bulletin boards that are in trouble."

"No, what about the thinly disguised descriptions of us? What should our names be?"

"I want to be Ms. Hard," interjected Laura. "That sounds like my name and it's what the kids tell me I am."

"I'll be Ms. Klutzer," I smiled. "I'm always dropping things."

"I'll be Ms. Haggle again as I was in the story about Gerald. It fits my style," said Carolyn, "but who can Karen be?"

"How about Ms. Carp?" suggested Karen with a grin. "That's what I do until my students turn in their projects."

"Something's fishy," I dead-panned.

Karen gave a mock swat in my direction, the corners of her mouth turning upward. "We'll all be very unsympathetic to poor what's-his-name with the zits, mom, chub, and glasses."

"Harold."

"Percival."

"Lawrence."

"Leonardo."

"Nah, that's one of the Mutant Ninja turtles," said the one member of the group who still had young children at home.

"Well?????"

Laughter and chuckles echoed in the empty room.

"Wait, wait," I cried. "You haven't even heard the rest of my thrilling plot. Our alleged weirdo what's-his-name is invited to a party by the popular crowd so that they can make fun of him. Everyone drinks beer except our hero, and somehow he saves them from getting into trouble. Then one day a mean substitute comes to school. This sub picks on the 'cool' dudes and the popular babes. Again our weirdo comes to the rescue. There needs to be something else in here, but my brain wasn't that fertile this summer. Somehow, he loses weight and gains his deserved prestige, and everything ends happily ever after. Tah dah!"

Silence and furrowed brows greeted my crow of creative invention.

"Well?"

"I like it," said Laura.

"Let's throw in something about sports. Let's make him a whiz at soccer," suggested Carolyn.

"Nah!" I said. "I'd prefer to have him non-athletic. It might help those children who aren't gifted in sports identify with him and feel less pressure themselves."

"Good point," agreed Carolyn.

"How about if the popular babes help him lose weight?" added Karen.

"Make sure the lunchroom smells awful," I interjected. "That always grabs the kids."

"Let's go with it and add another party," said Carolyn.

"Yeah," echoed Laura, "let's fill in the gory details and write it all down. I'll do the writing this year."

"Are you sure this one isn't too much like the Gerald story?" I asked.

"Nah," reassured Karen, "they'll never know the difference. It's different enough. Besides, it has all the ingredients of a true teenage soap opera. We'll add a love interest and, voilà."

"We could take one of the novels we teach and adapt the story a bit," I said, still unsure if my "brilliant" idea would work. "I used a revised Romeo and Juliet with my advanced eighth graders last year."

"No, I like this story," said Carolyn. "It has all the elements that appeal to Westwood's students."

"Let's add a 'cool dude' whose grades may flunk him. Our hero can tutor him," I suggested.

"And have our weirdo give an awesome party," threw in Laura.

"I don't like the idea of booze at a party. That might anger some parents. How about cigarettes? You know there's always a group of students each year who try to sneak into the woods to smoke each morning. It's a more realistic vice for our students. We can have someone catch something on fire, and our hero can save the day. He might even take the blame which could speed him on the road to having his peers think of him as a part of the 'in' crowd," Karen added in a fit of creative genius.

"Ah, the gifted teacher adds her gifted ideas," I chortled. I got another pained look from my friend. "But I like it. I like it."

"O.K., you guys, we still don't have a name for our hero," said the practical Laura. "We can't get too convoluted a plot," she added. "After all, we have to tell the whole story in one-hundred or so sentences."

"Do we want to do three a week or four a week this year?" I asked.

"Let's do four. The sixth-grade teachers said that this group really needs the work," said Laura.

"That means that we need about 120 sentences."

"Write this down," I ordered. "'Tales of a Middle School Weirdo.'"

"What about 'Tales of a Four-Eyed Blimp?'" laughed Carolyn.

"All right, you clowns, let's compromise on 'Tales of a Four-Eyed Weirdo,'" said Karen. "After all, we already decided he's going to lose his puppy fat."

"We still don't have a name for our blimp," I wailed.

"It's your turn this year, Karen," said Carolyn. Jane had her Hairy Beast. I had Gerald. Now it's your turn. Laura can do next year's if we decide to use a new story instead of using an old one."

"I dub our chub Harold," said Karen. No student has had that name in years. We'll make his 'cool' nemesis named Conan."

"Oh, no," I groaned, "here we go again."

"Wait a minute. I wanted that name for the school librarian. 'Conan the Librarian . . .'" said Carolyn with a swallowed grin.

As three collective moans surrounded this statement, we then began in earnest to formulate the plot for the year's Caught'ya sentences. The next hour was busy and productive, occasionally punctuated by chortles and groans. Laura wrote furiously, often stopping to cross out or erase. At last we had a workable outline that looked like this:

Tales of a Four-Eyed Weirdo

I. Describe Harold and his problems.

   A. Transferred from another school to our school.

   B. Horn-rimmed glasses, portly, black, short, zits on face, but nice kid; liked by adults, considered a "nerd" by his peers, bad at all sports he has tried so far, always the last to be picked for a team.

   C. Teased unmercifully by peers.

   1. Tripped.

   2. Called a "Four-Eyed Weirdo."

   3. Ignored in lunchroom. Girls tease. Studs disdain.

   4. Stuck with a bottom locker, and no one will share a top one with him.

   5. Kids do not flock to nearby seats in classes.

   6. Etc., as the creative muse strikes the writer of the sentences.

   D. Home life.

   1. Has to get A's and B's, or Mom will maim.

   2. Brother in college whom everyone looks up to (handsome to boot).

   3. Parents just got a divorce, and they are battling over him.

4. During period of adjustment, Dad ignores and Mom overprotective. Big brother lords it over him. Not a happy camper!

II. School setting.

  A. Teachers

    1. Ms. Carp — bizarre, fishy sense of humor, has a deadly stare, known for giving quotes to paraphrase for punishment of talkers, gives unbelievably hard assignments designed only to torture, has a real rug in her room; known for her statement, "There's no such thing as perfection."

    2. Ms. Hard — smiles out of the corner of her mouth, hard grader, unmoved by any excuse for lack of homework, gives tons of homework and wears yellow a lot; known for the line, "Come out in the hall. I want to talk to you."

    3. Ms. Haggle — short, nippy, constantly nagging students to get in homework; always looks neat and composed, loves to stand behind students as they work; occasionally known to scratch fingers on the blackboard; also renowned for her long sighs with hands on hips and the statement, "You can do better than that."

    4. Ms. Klutzer — short, somewhat chubby; always has a smile on her face (but don't trust it); gives enough homework to make you gag; nags, has a funny laugh, and eyes in the back of her head; always dropping things; backs up to the chalkboard and gets chalk all over her rear; calls parents at any excuse; famous for her rotten dancing during class and her pervasive voice saying, "This is going to be so much fun. . . . "

  B. Students

    1. Conan — a really cool dude, flunking but bright, more interested in impressing his peers with his manliness than getting good grades; wears lots of fake chains.

2. Various other cool dudes led by Conan.

3. Belinda Beautiful — gorgeous babe with long blond hair, queen of the snobs who always dresses in designer clothes.

4. Lots of other beauty queens whose noses are stuck permanently in the air.

5. Gnarly Nerd — a nice wimp of an A student who befriends our hero; wearns no glasses but does have a plump problem.

6. Classy Cassandra — the most beautiful girl Harold has ever beheld; shy, good grades, cool, lusted after by all the cool dudes, but she is not interested in their sort; a good student.

7. Cassandra's two or three friends, all like her; nice but aloof.

III. Party of Beautiful Belinda

A. Harold invited in order to have something at which to laugh.

B. Harold goes and finds all kids, except Gnarly, smoking cigarettes to be cool.

C. Harold refrains from smoking, and kids tease. He and Gnarly become the butt of all the jokes.

D. Harold spies Cassandra, sitting on the couch and wants to talk to her.

E. Conan and friends beat up Harold and Gnarly.

F. A cigarette butt thrown in trash can starts a fire, and nearby curtains catch as well. Harold grabs baking powder, puts out the fire, and when the irate parents return home, takes the blame in order to save his lady love, Cassandra, from possible trouble.

G. Kids soften a little toward Harold.

IV. Mean substitute

A. A kid's nightmare of a sub appears in English class one day. (Writer, use your imagination here.)

B. Sub corners Conan because he doesn't have his homework (as usual) and is combing out his hair.

C. Before sub can send Conan to the Dean, Harold steps in and slips Conan his homework so Conan can pretend to find it. The class stares in shock.

D. Since substitute teachers are always "fair game" for middle school students, Harold comes up with a plan: the entire class will drop its books at his signal. This really works to unnerve the sub.

E. Afterwards, Conan, threatened with flunking the grade, asks Harold to help him change his study habits. Maybe it's not so cool to get "F's" after all.

V. Harold becomes a "happy camper."

A. Harold's dad realizes his son's worth and suggests that they spend the summer together.

B. Harold's mom is so pleased with his grades that she lays off heckling him for a while.

C. Harold's big brother helps him with his algebra.

D. Harold and Gnarly make friends with Conan.

E. Belinda and crew take Harold and Gnarly in hand and at lunch in the horribly smelly lunchroom, help them both stick to their diets. The girls even bring lunch for the two rapidly reducing chubs.

F. Cassandra falls for Harold!

G. Harold's mom lets him give a party, and he is a hit.

H. Even the zits go away!

Laura read the completed outline to us. We spent a few minutes laughing over a possible description of the substitute and decided that whoever wrote the sentences for that section would have the pleasure of describing the ogre.

"If you all will bow down before me, and Karen will lend me some of that orange craft paper I saw in her room this morning, I will write the sentences for the first nine weeks," I magnanimously offered.

"I don't know about the bow, but you're welcome to some of the paper," said Karen. "I'll take over from Jane."

"That'll put me after the winter holidays for the next nine weeks," said Carolyn. "That suits me just fine as I plan to take that nasty course in law this fall to get it over with."

"I'll happily finish up the year," offered Laura.

"So be it," I said, taking the outline from Laura. "I'll run off a copy of this outline today for each of you and by Friday get you a copy of the sentences for the first two weeks. Does anyone have anything to add to last year's skills list? Anything that your students needed extra work on? I plan to add more 'wells' and 'goods' this year. My students never mastered that last year."

"How about we think it over and get our ideas to you by tomorrow," suggested Carolyn. "I want to look over some old papers."

"I'll talk to the sixth-grade English teachers to see if they have any suggestions," offered Laura. "I know my one sixth-grade English class last year could have used much more work with quotations. We worked hard on the strong verbs, but most of the kids never did master the delicate art of quote punctuation. Today, I'll look over a sampling of papers in their writing folders from last year. I'll get a note to you by tomorrow, Jane."

"Great," I said. "I'll start composing."

"I'll start bulletin boarding," murmured Karen as she rose from the cramped desk and headed purposefully out the door.

Although the above dialogue is a fictional version of a planning session and the names have been slightly changed to protect the guilty, my fellow teachers at Westwood Middle School and I have come up with plots for our Caught'ya stories in similar work sessions. It is fun to brainstorm with friends when you can be a bit productively silly at the same time. You can also write outlines around the kitchen table in the evening in conversation with your spouse if you prefer. The creative muse can strike anywhere.

For this book, in fact, I came up with the story outlines by myself (usually in the shower, hot tub, or when petting my dogs), but it is infinitely more fun to do it with one's fellow teachers. Two or three teachers compose best together. As you can see from the above dialogue, however, four teachers can work very well if they are compatible and somewhat focused on their goal. Any more than four and you might end up spinning story wheels.

If you use this communal method of making an outline, you also can share the writing of the sentences as did the teachers in the dialogue. Simply divide the thirty-six weeks in the school year with your fellow conspirators. If you work with one other teacher, you can split the year in half or each, in turn, take a six- or nine-week period. While writing the sentences doesn't take that much time, it is another task to add to your long list of things-to-do.

The list of skills to which I referred is more like a chart that a few teachers and I made up one year. In order to coordinate the language arts for our grade level, we made a chart of the grammar and mechanics skills, novels, poetry, stories, writing practices, etc., we wanted to be sure to cover in a given year. We all staggered times of the year that we used certain things in order to share the books and supplies, but we always tried to include most of the things on the chart.

A two-period block of reading and language in the sixth and seventh grades and use of reading and writing workshops simplifies coordination at my school. Each year we find that each class (as a whole) lacks different skills from the last year's class. For example, some years we need to stress basic punctuation, while other years the majority of the students already have mastered those skills and are ready for more sophisticated ones.

For clarity, I have listed in an Appendix the skills (annotated and elaborated upon for non-English majors) from our chart and also from several traditional grammar texts. The list easily can be simplified for lower grades. Use only the ones your students need and are ready to learn. I usually mark a star next to the skills I know I must stress. As the year progresses, and I know my students better, I pass along to the teacher who is the current writer of the sentences, the information that more practice is needed in certain skills. If I use a story written in a previous year, I modify the sentences to reflect the needs of my current students.

Plot

If you have to write the story line on your own, don't despair. As long as you include certain basic details and make the protagonists of the story the same age group as the pupils for whom you are composing, you can't go wrong, and the story practically writes itself. Since you aren't publishing your story and since, therefore, you are not infringing on a copyright, you can modify a plot from any children's book that suits your fancy. You can take part of a plot or pirate one entirely. Your students will not be bothered by similarities since you are writing sentences that differ from the original ones.

Those of you who teach in a church school or at home have an automatic source that will work very well. Take some of the popular Bible stories and use those plots. The morals clearly emerge, and the stories provide plenty of action.

Other good sources of story lines can be either the stories your parents told you when you were little or the stories you spun for your own young children.

Don't feel bad if your plot isn't the most original in the world. Mine certainly aren't. In fact, one reviewer of the first Caught'ya book called them "pretty bad." While she wasn't reading the stories from the child's point of view, she had a point. The stories are silly—just what wakes up bored language arts students. The plots don't have to be scintillating, just packed with action and filled with events and descriptions that will appeal to students. You may want to use one of the plots suggested in Chapter 6 of this book until you feel comfortable using one of your own.

Outline

Once you have decided on the basic plot, it is fairly easy to make a simple outline like the one in the dialogue. If you cannot come up with some of the details as you write the outline, simply make a note to yourself to invent those details as you write the actual sentences of the story just as Laura did with the description of the substitute teacher. The outline is only the bare bones of your story. It reveals the direction you'll travel when you actually sit down to write the daily sentences.

As you well know, certain events and actions appeal to young people. Those I have noticed are listed below. I'm sure you'll be able to add others.

Things to Include When Formulating Plot and Outline

Ages 7 - 10 — Elementary School

- names of the children themselves so that they can identify with the characters
- details of the children's own lives
- animal stories where animals are personified
- a case where the child knows best and advises the adult
- a kid-saves-adult story or a kid-changes-adult story
- close friends doing things together
- travel to faraway or imaginary places
- an adult who provides a supporting perspective for the children.

Ages 11 - 14 — Middle School

- fights
- "wild" parties
- adults as villains, kids as heroes
- underdog triumphing
- unpopular kid becoming popular
- humor and silly stories
- kids handling difficult situations well
- love triangles
- "gross" details of anything

Ages 15 - 18 — High School

- kids acting like adults and being in charge of their own lives
- parents who seem like villains and really turn out to be nice
- any adventure with teens as protagonists
- love affairs and love triangles
- boy meets girl and vice-versa
- friendship and understanding; getting praise from adults
- anything humorous and fanciful
- teenagers being in charge of situations and handling them well.

Writing the Actual Sentences

Now that you have your plot and basic outline, you can begin to write the story. A word of caution: do not write more than two or three weeks' worth of sentences at a time! When I pre-write all the sentences, changes are often needed to cover the specific problems I encounter in my students' writing. This means that I waste time redoing work previously done.

The beauty of writing the actual sentences during the course of the year is that you really can tailor them to the immediate needs of each particular class. This works well in mixed-ability classroom or home-school situations.

For example, two years ago, when I used those pre-written sentences from the *Romeo and Juliet* story with advanced eighth graders, I toned the skills to eighth-grade level by eliminating some of the errors when I wrote certain sentences on the board. I added more practice in verb-tense agreement which my students needed. The eighth graders learned a lot of English, and they were kept amused, yet I wished that I had been able to fit into the story more practice on the agreement between antecedents and pronouns. My students showed me from their writing efforts that they really did not understand this piece of syntax.

I added *ad hoc* what I could, but the story was written and antecedent / pronoun agreement was too specific a skill to insert without changing a great deal of the plot. If I had written a week or two of the sentences at a time, I could have changed the plot enough to write in the skills practice that my students needed. In a story in which the final sentences have yet to be written, nothing is lost by altering the plot.

Basic, common skills like punctuation, spelling, verb-tense agreement, etc. are easy to include in a pre-written story. Just try to put in a misplaced modifier, however, if nothing in the story lends itself to it!

So, how do you begin to write a Caught'ya? Do not approach the actual writing of sentences as if you were writing a short story. Below, I model the thought process by which I composed the sentences for the "Four-Eyed Weirdo" story included in Chapter 8. Doing it this way might give you a clearer picture about Caught'ya sentence composition.

First, I refer to the outline. It starts with a major description of the looks and life of the protagonist. That's easy enough. What skills do I want to stress? Since this supposedly is the beginning of the year, how about a review of skills that can be stuffed into the sentences? These could include an introduction to as many of the nine comma rules I can comfortably fit in, as well as verb-agreement practice — two all-time mistake-generating skills. I'll throw in some homophone errors like "their, there, they're" to start my students out right and to see where their problems lie.

My trusty thesaurus is open, ready to supply the vocabulary words (remember, one per sentence). I think I want to do four Caught'ya sentences a week, so I need four sentences for the first week.

Sentence 1

This is just an introductory sentence, so it is easy.

> Once there was a four-eyed weirdo from Baltimore, Maryland, who, against his will, moved to (your town, your state).

Good. That sentence includes a new paragraph, a hyphen, and two different comma rules. It practices capitalization of four proper nouns, introduces the dread "their, there, they're," promotes a discussion of the "i" before "e" except after "c" spelling rule, and it can lend itself to a discussion of the correct usage of "who" and "whom" if I feel that my students are up to it.

This is a great start, but where's the vocabulary word? How about "will"? I can substitute "volition" without even having to pour through the thesaurus! Now the sentence reads:

> Once there was a four-eyed weirdo from Baltimore, Maryland, who, against his volition, moved to (your town, your state).

Wonderful! Now, if I take out all the punctuation and capitals, I have the board sentence. Here comes another debate. Will my new students know about hyphens? Last year a few of them did. No, I'd better keep the hyphen in the otherwise unpunctuated sentence at least the first time that it appears.

On the other hand, I want to withhold help to find out what my students do and don't know. I'll find out very quickly how many of them know that they need to put in a hyphen.

As it will be the first week of school, I'll want to use this sentence as a sort of pre-test. I think I'll misspell "there" and "weirdo" to promote spelling and usage discussions. I shall, however, leave "who" correct and maybe discuss the use of "who" and "whom" when I go over the sentence — if I feel that my classes are still paying attention.

While I realize that this sentence is probably beyond the ability of most of my students to write correctly on their own at the start of the year, it can serve as a humbling lesson for the arrogant ones who think they know everything, and it won't discourage the weaker students if I emphasize how difficult it is. I can challenge my classes that first day, promising a small prize to anyone who can get the sentence entirely correct on his/her own. That ought to get their attention. The sentence I'll put on the board the first day of school will read:

> once their was a four eyed weirdo from baltimore maryland who against his volition moved to gainesville florida

Sentence 2

Still following the outline (I can always modify it if necessary), I need to further describe my hapless hero. Hey, "hapless" is a good vocabulary word. Since I don't have a last name yet for the four-eyed hero, and most students never spell "weird" correctly, I think I'll use that as Harold's last name. That way it will be repeated all year and students will always have to debate whether I am spelling it correctly; they will have to think every time they encounter the word. Oh, nasty me!

No new paragraph is needed. This should generate a good discussion. I want to include a few more comma rules if I can. It's probably not a good idea to play with the tense of the verb at this stage. I'll wait until I establish it more clearly. How about another hyphen or a "who" or "whom" to see if the class listened yesterday? No, I can't fit them into the sentence. What about putting in one of the dread "their, there, they're" again? Let's get *that* bugbear out in the open early and often.

The first day of school Harold Weird, a chubby kid with horn-rimmed glasses, fat tummy, chocolate brown skin, and zits on his round face, appeared at the front door of (your school).

O.K., so I didn't fit in a "their, there, or they're." I'll keep trying in later sentences. It's hard with only one character in the story so far. Now I need a vocabulary word. I'll put "hapless" before Harold's name. That should do the trick.

What have I covered? A discussion of the need for a paragraph; an appositive; commas in a series; another hyphen; a discussion of why there is no comma between chocolate and brown (the adjective before the noun is a color adjective); a discussion of plurals of nouns that end in "ss," "ch, "sh" etc., and capitalization of two proper nouns should be enough for one day.

I can also check to see if my students learned how to spell "weird." I'll make a note to myself so that I won't forget to reiterate to students that the story is in the past tense and to introduce the idea of strong verbs ("appeared"). Here's the sentence I'll put on the board.

the first day of school hapless harold wierd a chubby kid with horn rimmed glasses fat tummy chocolate brown skin and zits on his round face appeared at westwood middle school

To help them along, I think I'll tell my students that there are five commas in that sentence. If I used this sentence with seventh graders, some inserted commas in the otherwise uncorrected sentence could help. I also would leave in the hyphen.

I need to add a silly note and an extra paragraph here. As I edit this draft — it is now December, and the first draft was written in July — I must note a problem that I encountered with this sentence when I used it with my eighth-graders in August. This year, horn-rimmed glasses are the "in" thing among the thirteen-year-old set in Florida. The students promptly voted to change Harold's horn-rimmed glasses to plastic pink-and-blue ones for the duration of the year. These were sufficiently "gross" and "dorky" for Harold to wear. The generation gap strikes again in English class!

Sentence 3

I need to continue the description, but what skills did I leave out? How about punctuation in a quote or more comma rules? No, I can't have a quote since poor Harold is the only character at this point and, with all of the problems he has in his life, I probably shouldn't make him talk to himself as well. Could I slip into the present tense to see if students notice? Let me think. . . .

> Poor, hapless Harold was bad at every sport he had tried so far in his thirteen years of life.

This is good. I have now given the students two long sentences. It's time to give them a bit of encouragement. I've introduced another comma rule. There will be another proper noun to capitalize, a verb tense shift to change, a number to write out (any number with two words or less), and another paragraph discussion.

I still need a vocabulary word. I'll check my handy thesaurus. How about the word "bad"? That's always a good one. Students use it frequently, so they might latch onto the synonym and use it. Among the many synonyms listed in the thesaurus are "vile, evil, wrong, corrupt, rancid, decayed, in ept, putrid, defective, inferior, imperfect." How about "vile"? I've always liked that word. "Putrid" might even be better. Nah, I prefer "vile." "Inept" would probably be more accurate, but the word "vile" would catch students' attention with its intensity. After double-checking the meaning, however, I find that "vile" refers to traits and personalities. "Inept" it is.

Here's the sentence I shall put on the board. I've put one of the verbs in the present tense. I always begin each student sentence flush with the left-hand margin. This tells the students that they have to debate whether there is a paragraph. Daily practice makes correct paragraphing miraculously appear in student writing.

> poor hapless harold is inept at every sport he had tried so far in his 13 years of life

Sentence 4

Now I can really move along. I'd like to introduce the idea of the compound sentence and the seven coordinating conjunctions (and, or, nor, for, so, but, yet) and the comma that goes with such a sentence. Anything else that crops up will be fine. Let's see. The outline says to continue the description of poor Harold, and I'm still at "B." I think I'll skip to "D" and discuss his home life. That should give me a compound sentence.

> Unfortunate, hapless Harold also had to get "A's" and "B's" on every report card, or he would be dead meat at home.

This will work. I've repeated a comma rule, got in a compound sentence, repeated a vocabulary word, and provided the usual discussion of the need for, or lack of need for, a paragraph. (No paragraph is needed here as the topic continues.) The sentence is simple enough to give most students some success. Maybe some students can write it without errors even if it is the first week of school — a great confidence-builder.

When the class and I go over a sentence like this, we discuss the whys and wherefores of compound sentences and repeat the coordinating conjunctions in sing-song voices so that students inadvertently memorize them. I make a note to myself next to the sentence to remember it. I'll check to see if they remember those conjunctions every time we have a compound sentence. If I have an advanced class, I might even switch the "also" and the "had" to promote a discussion of interrupted verbs. This probably would be too much for regular students, but you never know.

I still need a vocabulary word. I've looked up the word "unfortunate" in the thesaurus and don't like any of the choices. How about making the sentence more interesting by substituting "diseased pachyderm meat" for "dead meat"? This certainly is accurate since Harold is corpulent, and the image of diseased pachyderm meat may draw a groan or two from students as they visualize it. I'll help students along if they have trouble with the picture.

Using such a disgusting vision also would be good to establish the fact that my students are not dealing with a totally normal teacher.

They actually may sit up and take notice. It will also stir up interest for future sentences.

All right, here's my board sentence. I think I'll help students with some of it this time. I'll supply the quotation marks for "A's" and "B's," but I'll have to make a note to myself to discuss why the quotation marks are needed so that they can be left out in later sentences. We also can discuss the plurals of single letters.

> unfortunate hapless harold also had to get all "A's" and "B's"
> on every report card or he would be diseased pachyderm meat
> at home

That sentence practically wrote itself! Now, are you other teachers and parents ready to start your own sentences? Enjoy a giggle or two as you compose the rest. Please remember that humor is the most important ingredient. It sells more correct English than any other device I've ever encountered. I wish you the best of luck and the funniest of stories.

Chapter 4

Mini-Lessons

Introduction

Finding things to do with one's students in order to cover the curriculum is not a problem for most teachers who have been in the classroom for a while. In fact, it is harder to find the time to do all those wonderful things we have seen in other classrooms, heard about at workshops, read in books, or thought of ourselves in a creative moment than it is to find the activities to fill that time. This chapter, plus the one that follows, I hope, will give you an idea or two which you might want to pursue with the class time you now have, time that formerly may have been spent in skills practice and drill from a traditional textbook.

For the past decade in my career as an English teacher, I have used the grammar book that my county so kindly provided only as a reference for me or for an individual assignment for a child who persisted in making a particular error. During that time, I have not

47

assigned my students any skills exercises or drills. To teach correct English, I use only the Caught'yas, fun mini-lessons, writing, and consultations with individual students concerning the errors on drafts of their writing. For me, abandoning the traditional grammar textbook was like regrowing long-clipped wings. My students agreed with me.

Now that I had all this class time, I found myself instituting a mini-lesson right after the Caught'ya. I didn't do it every day. I didn't even do it on a regularly scheduled basis. My students told me what they needed by their responses to the Caught'yas, by the errors in their writing, or by their interest in a particular type of writing. Sometimes I simply introduced a new genre to my students or a device that might improve their writing.

This chapter includes seventeen mini-lessons. If you use Nancie Atwell's writing workshop mentioned later, you will need more than seventeen, but this will give you a start. Mini-lesson #1 is really a suggestion for many lessons. You can use any or all of these suggested mini-lessons to supplement the Caught'yas and whatever writing you and your students do for the majority of the class time. Don't plan to do one every day, or too much time will be spent on teacher-directed lessons and not enough time on writing.

Mini-lessons add only five minutes or less to the time spent on the Caught'yas, but they do teach some aspects of the grammar that are difficult to teach in the Caught'yas, and they do introduce and reinforce techniques and styles that students will want to incorporate into their writing. If you do Caught'yas only three to four days a week, it is handy to teach the mini-lessons on the other days.

You will probably notice that most of the mini-lessons concern themselves with form rather than content. Details of the literary mini-lessons that I use with my students are not included because although they are mapped out in advance, they usually are spur-of-the-moment-taught lessons designed to excite students at the brink of discovering a new literary genre or technique. I use them when I feel that students are ripe for them.

Almost all of the suggested mini-lessons will take more than one session to implement. Most need to be carried out on a daily basis for a few days, in short, three-minute doses.

Although they have been tested on seventh and eighth graders, these mini-lessons (watered down or beefed up) will work with younger or older students. They are not limited exclusively to the middle-school student. Teachers at other levels use them successfully.

Please note that the mini-lessons are listed in the order in which I typically use them in my classroom rather than in alphabetical order. You would not want, for example, to teach about strong verbs before your students have memorized the parts of speech.

Mini-Lesson Suggestions

1. Literary Mini-Lessons

I usually prepare these lessons way ahead when the idea strikes (or when another teacher shares an idea with me) and keep notes with my lesson plan book. You can keep the developed topics on a three-by-five-inch file card on the current page in your plan book. When you turn the page each week, glance to see what you've prepared that has not yet been used. In this way, you won't forget what is available.

A good part of effective teaching is seizing the right moment to teach. I try to use the mini-lessons that I have previously prepared at the right "teachable moment" in "spur-of-the-moment-taught" lessons designed to excite students when I feel that they are ripe for them.

In literary mini-lessons I read passages from books, play tapes of stories and of famous poets, read poems, and generally expose the students to the world of good writing. I even read to them from my rather dubious efforts at poetry or fiction to demonstrate the improvements that can be made by rewriting. We discuss voices in which to write, literary tricks such as alliteration and personification, scene setting, character development, and the importance of good descriptive writing.

Many students have great difficulty fleshing out their writing. They assume that the reader knows everything that they know. Reading first drafts of some students often is like solving a puzzle. A major, often repeated mini-lesson in my classroom concerns scene setting, character development, and fleshing out of what I call "bare bones" writing. Use examples of your own and your students' writing to engender discussion. The overhead is a very useful tool in these lessons.

2. Parts of Speech

You can explain almost all other grammar from just eight parts of speech. Start early in the year and ask students to identify the parts of speech in the Caught'yas. This should work from grades five on up. Lower grades can concentrate on learning and recognizing only the four major ones: nouns, adjectives, verbs, and adverbs.

I like to post the eight first letters of the parts of speech prominently in the room. (If you only plan to teach four parts of speech, you can use NAVA or something similar.) I arrange the letters so that they look like a word such as "NIPPAVAC." Some years, however, I have used "PAVPANIC." Whatever mnemonic you use, make the letters big. Don't tell your students what the letters of the "word" might indicate. Do, however, tell them about mnemonics in general. Let them stew for a few days. Build up the suspense. Ask them to figure it out. This sets them up for Mini-Lessons 3, 4, and 5.

Finally, when you feel that your students will crack or one smarty has figured it out, you can tell them what each letter of the "word" signifies. Then chant and chant and chant the eight parts of speech until students want to throw up or attack you: "Noun, interjection, pronoun, preposition, adjective, verb, adverb, conjunction."

Recite the parts of speech daily for a few more days until you are sure that your slowest student can recall them at will. At this point, your students are ready for the real meat of the lesson. Introduce one part of speech, explain what it is, go over its uses, and elicit examples from the class. One part of speech every few days is enough. Teaching all of the above should take about a dozen mini-lessons, each of which consumes one to five minutes of the class period.

3. Applying Parts of Speech

Now that students have learned the parts of speech and have memorized the prepositions and conjunctions, it's time to apply that knowledge. After presenting explanations and examples, start asking your students to identify one of the eight parts of speech in the daily Caught'ya. You can do this orally when the class goes over the sentence with you at the board, or you can instruct students to underline the examples of the targeted part of speech when they attempt to correct the sentence on their own.

Go over only one part of speech at a time. You have an entire year and only eight parts of speech to cover. Take your time and make sure that your students are comfortable with each part of speech before you move on. Done on a daily basis in small doses, this adds only a minute or so to the Caught'ya time, and your students don't even realize that they are being stuffed with grammar. Quite a few students have asked me at the end of the year — after finding that the dreaded 200 question final exam was extremely easy — how they knew all that grammar and usage when I never taught them any of it during the year. Small doses is the key. They never know what hits them!

4. Prepositions

When we get to the prepositions, my students memorize them. (You can boogie with hand signals to the prepositions. The Appendix lists the most common ones.) We memorize them slowly, reciting them daily, until everyone knows them. Recitation adds approximately fifteen to thirty seconds to the Caught'ya time. Learning the prepositions takes about a month of daily repetition.

It is a good idea to give a test at the end of the month. On it you can write the first two letters of each of the forty-four prepositions your students have been repeating. Students must show mastery by writing the rest of the words. If you and your students chant the prepositions daily, you will find that the average grade on this test is a high "A."

Younger children can learn fewer prepositions. I have found that students "own" prepositions when they have them memorized. They then find it easier to remember not to capitalize them in titles and to use them correctly and appropriately in their writing.

5. Coordinating Conjunctions and Compound and Complex Sentences

Have your students memorize the coordinating conjunctions—and, or nor, for, so, but, yet. This takes only one day of repetition. Then, every time you find a compound sentence in the Caught'ya, you can have your students recite the conjunctions again as well as explain what a compound sentence is. Similarly, you can explain complex sentences once you have taught the subordinating conjunctions (see next mini-lesson). If your students write fragments of sentences rather than complete sentences, throw some fragments onto the overhead and discuss them.

Once the coordinating conjunctions have been learned, students also can be taught how to use them: do not begin sentences with them, do not capitalize them in titles, but do use them to look for a compound sentence that requires a comma.

6. Subordinating Conjunctions

After you have used a few Caught'yas with complex sentences, introduce what my colleague Sally Larson refers to as the "white bus words." I pass out Sally's ditto with a picture of a bus on it. The letters A — W-H-I-T-E — B-U-S are spelled out vertically from top to bottom with blank spaces beside each letter. One day we fill in the subordinating conjunctions in the spaces:

A – after, although, as

W – when, whenever, where, wherever, while

H – how

I – if

T – than

E – even though, even if

B – because, before

U – unless, until

S – since, so that

We then spend a week or so repeating the conjunctions to learn them, finding complex sentences in the Caught'yas, and discussing both. My students often call subordinate clauses "white bus clauses." Sometimes I even give students a blank copy of the "White Bus" ditto for a test. I also ask them to write three complex sentences at the bottom of the sheet. Almost all of my students earn an A+ on this test. Please note that complex sentences are really too sophisticated for most children under twelve, but there is no reason that younger children can't learn that there is rarely a comma before the words "because" and "since."

7. Strong Verb Practice

Longer exercises in strong verb practice are mentioned in the writing suggestions under "General Suggestions #8" in Chapter 5. However, strong verb practice also can be taught as a quick mini-lesson if you find that your students use only "am," "is," "are," "was," and "were" as verbs in their writing. Since the use of strong verbs is essential to good writing, you can teach the use of strong verbs first in a few mini-lessons and then reinforce the lessons by using the longer paragraph writing suggestion mentioned in Chapter 5.

After the concept of "dead" verbs and "strong" verbs has been introduced, it is a good idea to institute strong verb practice on a regular basis. I like to do this exercise with my students twice a week for about twenty weeks of the school year. After a month or so, the use of active verbs always increases dramatically. Students become aware of every "is" and "was" that they write. This activity can be used at any grade level. It is based on Rebakah Caplan's idea in *Showing Writing* (1980).

Here's how I do it. Once or twice a week, after the Caught'ya or even instead of the Caught'ya, I put a silly sentence on the board. This sentence has a "dead" verb in it and is usually about an English teacher, her life and her animals. A typical sentence reads: "Mrs. Kiester is very strange." Or, if I want to discuss predicate nouns, "Mrs. Kiester is a very strange teacher." Students are instructed to copy the sentence, find the "dead" verb, replace it with a "strong" one that *shows* that Mrs. Kiester is strange instead of merely stating it, and rewrite the sentence, retaining the meaning of the original.

Students spend a few minutes writing their revised sentences. Each student then underlines the strong verb in the new sentence, and we all share the results. They are hilarious. A typical example is: "Strange Mrs. Kiester *leaps* from tall tables to teach us about verbs." This sentence not only tells that this teacher is strange, but it also gives an example. As the year progresses, the board sentences become more and more complicated because I forbid the use of such verbs as "make," "made," and sense-verbs like "feel," "see, hear, touch," and "smell." A few students find this to be an excruciatingly difficult exercise, but frequent practice changes their minds.

By the way, it is a good idea to instruct students to put all Strong Verb Practice sentences on the same sheet of paper. After ten sentences (I keep track in my plan book), you can give students a few minutes to check over their sentences, correct any errors, and make a good, neat copy. You can then collect the sentences and grade them. This gives you a grade and keeps the students on their toes.

Examples

Board sentence - The boy was angry.

Student paper - The boy was angry.

> The boy's anger raged uncontrollably.
>
> *or*
>
> The boy **tore** out his hair and **yelled** at his dog in anger.

Board sentence - Mrs. Kiester is chubby.

My students love sentences like this that exaggerate my traits. I also have topic sentences that make fun of my large, wimpy dogs, my out-of-style clothing, my outdated attitudes, or my propensity to dance around the room reciting poetry or prepositions. In other words, use yourself as a humorous target.

Student paper - Mrs. Kiester is chubby.

> Mrs. Kiester's chubby stomach **hangs** over her size eighty skirt. (No, really, Mrs. Kiester, you only **wear** a size sixty.)
>
> *or*
>
> Mrs. Kiester **cannot squeeze** herself into a student desk because of her weight problem.

I'm sure you get the idea. These sentences are good practice in the agreement of verbs. Students must notice the tense of the board sentence and write their sentence accordingly.

I follow up these exercises by requiring students, as a part of proofreading, to put checks over all main verbs in the next-to-last draft of papers. If they do not have enough "strong verbs," they know that they need to rewrite some sentences. They also check for inappropriate verb-tense shift.

8. Sentence Diagramming

Another thing to add in very small doses is sentence diagramming. Many teachers hate diagramming, but I have found by experience that it is a real help to those left-brain students who just can't envision the structure of sentences when they try to write correctly. Thus my objectives in teaching sentence diagramming are to help those students and, in the process, to not turn off those right-brained students for whom diagramming is worse than torture by grammar book. Diagramming also is a wonderful tool with which to teach students to think.

Show your students how to diagram a sentence (a little bit each day). Again, small doses work best. After a few weeks of this, ask your students to diagram part or all of the Caught'ya sentence. (The days you do this, leave no errors in the sentence on the board. To have errors would be too much.) With only one sentence to diagram every once in a while, students can catch on without too much resistance or pain.

Note: Those of you who teach younger children, of course, would not want to cover all of the parts of speech and certainly don't want to attempt any complicated sentence diagramming. Fourth graders, however, can learn to diagram the subject and the verb. Fifth graders can add adjectives and adverbs. In sixth grade, students certainly can add prepositional phrases. Middle schoolers and high schoolers need the reinforcement of diagramming. Students do need to learn the terms and their relationship to other words in sentences before they begin to learn a foreign language. In my French classes, I find that those students who know and understand the use of the parts of a sentence have a big advantage over those who do not.

9. Direct and Indirect Objects

The best way to teach about objects is through sentence diagramming in which students can see the purpose of direct and indirect objects. In many languages other than English, direct and indirect object pronouns become extremely difficult to learn since they come before the verb. It really helps, therefore, to know the terms and their uses in English.

When you want to work with objects, insert a few in the Caught'yas and ask students to find them. You will find that when you go over the Caught'ya with your class, the discussion lasts a little longer than usual. You also can talk about transitive and intransitive verbs in the same way.

10. Similes

A high school teacher, Betsy Creveling, introduced me to this idea in a workshop. She uses this with her high school students, but it works very effectively with seventh and eighth graders as well. I don't see why it wouldn't work at any level, including first grade, if done orally. This mini-lesson takes a little longer than the others, but it is well worth the extra time.

Buy a packet of Burnt Peanuts. They look really disgusting, like little orange rabbit pellets that are covered with uneven bumps. Put about five on each desk and instruct students not to touch them (Stir up their interest!)

After a brief discussion about the five senses and about similes, have the students write a simile for each sense while examining the Burnt Peanuts.

For example:

Sight – The candy looks like orange rabbit pellets with funny bumps.

Sound – When I bite on it, it sounds like seaweed cracking under my feet at the beach.

Smell – The candy smells sickly sweet like sugar coating my nose.

Taste – It tastes as if my Mom burned a dog biscuit with a peanut on it.

Touch – It feels hard and lumpy like a stale piece of cookie.

You can extend this lesson to another day and assign your students to write a paragraph, or you can stop with the similes.

Students like to share these similes as they are often very funny and extremely imaginative. One year I collected the similes and read a few a day for a while. Students loved this.

11. Using Student Sentences

A delightful fifth-grade teacher, Kathy Vance, used this with her students last year. I like to implement her clever idea every now and then to iron out some of the difficulties I find in my students' writing.

First, ask each student to write a paragraph about himself / herself without identifying the subject. Collect the paragraphs, pick one with English problems, and write the first sentence on the board. This sentence is treated just like a normal Caught'ya. Then, after the corrections have been discussed, students can guess who the mystery person is. If the student's identity is not guessed, continue with a sentence a day from that student's paragraph on subsequent days until the entire paragraph has been used or until the identity of the mystery student has been guessed. Kathy says that her fifth graders never get tired of this.

My eighth graders like it too. I don't see why this can't also be used at the high school level as well. All children like to read about themselves.

A home-schooling parent might want to have the child describe a family member or a friend. You can be the one to guess the identity of the person being described.

12. Vocabulary Practice with a Twist

This idea was presented at a workshop several years ago. Unfortunately, I have never been able to find out who created the exercise. Students (and adults) find this ingeniously simple exercise extremely difficult, but it provides wonderful practice in vocabulary, in word awareness, in thinking, and in using the thesaurus. This is probably more appropriate for high-school aged students, but done as a whole-class exercise, it will work with younger students. Most children love the challenge.

About halfway through the year, after students have had fifty or so vocabulary words in the Caught'ya sentences, divide them into groups of three or four and have them briefly (very briefly) tell a common fairy tale. There is only one rule. Each word may be used only once, excluding words used in the title. Read to your students the example provided below, to illustrate how to manipulate the words. The exercise can be worked on in class for a few minutes a day until it is completed. This way, students can go home and check for synonyms. Remember, this is harder than it looks!

The Three Little Pigs

Once there were three little pigs. Each wanted to build a house. Squeaky built his with straw. Oinky chose wood. Grunty used brick. Along came Mr. Wolf. The hairy canine threatened our friends. He said, "I'll huff, puff, and blow your home in."

First porker perished. Second swine succumbed. Third greaser called bluff, boiled furry mammal, lived, telling this kinky tale.

13. Poetry

A. Memorize it with your students. Pick a poem, say it daily with your students for a month or so after you do the Caught'ya, and commit it to memory. Then, when you feel that most of your students know the poem by heart, have everyone (teacher too) recite it in front of the class for a test grade. Very few students earn less than an "A." This lesson is discussed in much more detail in "General Suggestions" #4 of the suggested writing assignments in Chapter 5.

B. You also can spend a few minutes some days reading a poem. Decide which literary form, idea, or device you wish to impart to your students and find four or five poems that include what you wish to teach (for example, sonnets, metaphors or alliteration). Each day read only one poem to your students, eliciting what the metaphor is, or why the poem is a sonnet, etc. Make sure that you choose poems that you love since your enthusiasm continues to be the key to learning.

When you feel that your students understand the concept, challenge — not assign— them to find a poem with a similar device. On subsequent days your students can read their poems, one a day.

Most school librarians will provide you with a cart full of poetry books for use in this exercise. Search out all your old poetry books at home, box them up, and lug them into your classroom.

Please note that this activity also can be used solely to teach students to appreciate poetry. You'd be surprised at the poems that the children find. I suspect that they are influenced by their parents. Last year, when I did this activity with my eighth graders to work with metaphors, one of my weaker students really got excited and came in with poem after poem by Emily Dickinson. She had been named after that poet!

Parents can take their children to the public library to search out poetry books. Looking up the books in the card catalogue will provide still another mini-lesson. Children will be impressed at the vast selection of poets.

14. Active vs. Passive Voices

Frequent use of the passive voice makes writing, especially scientific writing, unclear and poor. This again shows the need to use "strong," active verbs.

Write a passive voice sentence on the board and ask students to rewrite it in the active voice. This simple exercise can be very effective, especially when that sentence comes directly from a student's paper. You can store up these sentences on a piece of paper which you keep nearby as you read student themes and stories. Repeat this little exercise once a day for several days or as often as you feel that your students need it.

15. Bibliographies

This is something that is so simple, yet most students agonize over it and invariably get the form wrong. Consult your school's social studies teachers for the preferred format for research papers, then type it up for your students. At periodic intervals throughout the year, test your students on the correct bibliographical format. My students never know when I shall hand them a book (any handy set of paperbacks will do or even that grammar book you no longer use!) and ask them to write it out as if it were to appear in a bibliography. A spot exercise like this, repeated a half a dozen times or so throughout the year, helps students learn the format.

When I use the individualized spelling exercises described in the first Caught'ya book, I also require that my students list, in bibliographical form, the dictionary they used. Frequent practice makes perfect bibliographical form.

16. Who and Whom

After explaining the differences in the Caught'yas, it is a good idea to keep an eye out for "who" and "whom" errors in the local paper or in magazines. Cut out the offending error and share it with your students. Then challenge them to find similar errors in books, in newspapers, or in advertisements. The lure of extra credit spurs students to search at home for errors in the use of "who" and "whom." Share only one or two a day.

When I have a class that indicates through errors in writing that it needs more help in this area, I have a ditto that asks students to fill in the blank with either "who" or "whom." We always take time (a few questions a day) to go over the answers.

Those of you who teach younger students may simply want to introduce this idea so that youngsters will be familiar with it when it is taught in more detail at a higher grade level.

17. Making Students Think

This is often the most difficult concept that we try to teach. Students are so used to parroting back information that they usually have not learned to think for themselves. Children like to follow the herd, to be like everyone else. How else would all those fads sweep our youth, taking our money?

Spend a few minutes one day talking about vague, general statements, exaggerations, contradictions, and questionable assumptions. Set the stage. For a homework assignment on subsequent days, ask students to find examples of each such statement from conversations with their friends. One statement a day will suffice. Collect the results and share them, a few each day, in class.

If you wish more follow-up, discuss a TV advertisement to elicit thoughts about distinguishing fact from opinion, recognizing biases and propaganda techniques, and drawing reasonable conclusions.

Offering an analogy a day to your students is another quick way to promote thinking. You can find examples of analogies in many books. An example of a simple one is: hot is to cold as hard is to soft. You can make them more difficult each day and even offer a prize to the person who finds the most creative solution.

I even found a book that contained analogy crossword puzzles. Every year we take a week's break from writing in the classroom, get into our response groups, and work on a few of these diabolically difficult puzzles. Unfortunately, the book that I use is out of print, but there must be others out there that contain such puzzles.

Chapter 5

Writing Suggestions

Introduction

Before I was introduced to Nancie Atwell's writing workshop described in *In the Middle*, I used only teacher-directed writing exercises. In fact, although I usually gave students a choice between two topics, I never gave them the freedom to choose their own topics and to work at their own pace. Today I cling to only a few of these teacher-made topics — those designed to introduce students to a genre, to help force them to think deeply, or to satisfy my county's requirement to write a research paper.

I like to begin the year with teacher-made topics to establish proper modes of responding, to establish my requirements for major contextual revision and careful editing, and to give students a few ideas they might wish to pursue when they are coming up with their own topics.

The ideas included in this chapter have all been student tested and have engendered positive results. Since any teacher-directed activity must be endured by students, it is the latter's feedback and success (or lack of it) that determines, more than anything else, whether I deem such an activity worth repeating. I take my students' comments seriously and seek their input. The suggestions have been divided into three categories: General, Elementary, and Secondary. The general ideas can be adapted to any level of students.

It is important to give students a say in their own learning process. My seventh and eighth graders usually respect my efforts on their behalf and respond seriously with much thought and introspection when they are asked for their opinions. When I taught fifth grade, the students responded similarly. It was my students who taught me always to give a choice in writing assignments as well as the desirability of offering the creative freedom of writing workshops. The students are not the only ones who are learning.

General Suggestions

1. Ms. Atwell's Writing and Reading Workshops

Nancie Atwell has influenced and revolutionized the teaching of many English teachers all over the country in the past few years. The ideas from her book, *In the Middle*, published in 1987, have changed the whole focus of English classes from teacher-centered to student-centered.

Like any effective teaching method or system, Ms. Atwell's idea is one that you can personalize to suit you, your classroom situation, and the demands of your school system's curriculum. As you read Ms. Atwell's book, you will find it easy to modify the idea to fit the needs of your students.

Every teacher I know who uses Ms. Atwell's writing and/or reading workshop personalizes it in some way. Some do it for part of the year while others combine it with computer time in a computer laboratory. Still others modify the method of recording progress, the way of doing the Status-of-the-Class Conference, or come up with another method of keeping track of student progress. Some teachers set a deadline for second drafts. One sixth-grade teacher I know reads all rough drafts himself. A bunch of teachers at various grade levels use a Caught'ya every day as a prelude to writing. One teacher even requires her students to complete a certain number of pages in a grammar text each six weeks of writing workshop. We teachers certainly are an individualistic lot.

At my school, other teachers and I like to use Ms. Atwell's method for five to six weeks at a time three or four times a year. We require that during that time, at least one piece of writing be taken all the way through the writing process — a minimum of at least three drafts, responses, self-edit, peer-edit, teacher edit. This way we can build the anticipation among our students for choosing their own topics and genres for writing. It also allows us to insert the teacher-directed assignments (always giving a choice) in between, making for much variety in our classrooms. Our students respond very well to this. Each break from the writing workshop sharpens our students' appetites for another workshop.

Home-schooling parents will find Ms. Atwell's reading and writing workshops ideal. They are totally individualized systems that use the adult as a resource. Since your time for lessons is flexible, your child doesn't have to abandon a piece of writing when a bell rings. Children really become excited about writing and reading when it is they who choose what they read and what they write. I have been told that this method has been successful as low as a third-grade level.

2. Descriptive Writing - The Moldy Bread Contest

Finding topics that excite students to write really descriptive paragraphs is difficult. A teacher in North Carolina, Renee Hannen, heard about this odd idea some years ago at a workshop. In her own inventive fashion, Renee took the basic idea and expanded it into the following. She says that, although the other teachers in her school think that she is "bizarre," her students love this assignment and produce some fine descriptive paragraphs as a result. Renee and her students also have a lot of laughs along the way. I ran a moldy bread contest this year for the first time. It was one of the major "hits" of the year. Even the principal got into the act!

First, collect pictures of mold from science teachers, magazines, friends, and students. Then research the subject at the library. After a single year, I already have a bunch of pictures and several sheets of information.

Armed with your research, begin the unit. Tell your students about a contest — a moldy bread contest. Inform them that some "really important scientific people" (a science teacher, a neighbor) will judge the event. This gets students excited. As the first lesson begins, write the word "mold" on the board and instruct your students to write everything they can about the subject — which is virtually nothing. Students usually offer nothing more than vague, pejorative adjectives such as "grungy," "nasty," and "gross."

Then share your wealth of information about mold with your students, show them pictures of various types of mold, and introduce the writing project. This project takes four weeks, but only four days of class time is needed. Thus, a teacher can do this concurrently with a writing workshop or with some longer writing assignment.

Tell your students that they are going to become mold experts, each nurturing a piece of bread until it becomes very moldy. The contest will be held three weeks from the day you introduce the unit, with three winning categories: grossest, most colorful, and smelliest. During the unit, students keep a diary of the progress of the mold on their piece of bread, and they write four short papers that describe the mold at each stage.

This unit is best begun on a Friday. On the first Friday, when you introduce the unit by sharing your "extensive" knowledge on the subject of mold, instruct students to go home and pick out a piece of bread. Any type of bread will do. Students should place the piece of bread anywhere they think will be conducive to mold production — inside, outside, under their pillow, under the dog's dish, etc. There are no rules about where the bread is to be placed nor on what can be added to the bread to make the mold grow more quickly and more colorfully. Some students add a different substance to each corner of the bread in an attempt to produce a variety of colors.

Students, however, must inform their parents about the piece of bread so that parents don't discover a moldy incrustation and throw it out. For our project, I sent a letter home to parents to warn them not to dispose of their child's mold and to solicit volunteer parent judges.

Students must check on their bread every day. They also need to keep notes on its changing appearance as it rots. These daily, short descriptions can become part of a diary. Students are also instructed to not talk about the progress of their mold. This restriction builds the suspense.

On the second Friday, students write a complete description of their bread and its mold. They use the daily notes as a basis for this description.

This assignment is repeated a week later. They share descriptions. By now they realize that their descriptions need to be really vivid in order to be different from those of their classmates. The fourth Friday students again write a description of their moldy bread. At this point, ask if any student's bread has not begun a mold colony. There will always be at least one student who has been unable to grow mold. Suggest the four basic rules of mold growing that might stimulate growth and hasten the process: moisture, warmth, dark, and food (milk, eggs, yogurt).

On the last Friday, students bring their moldy bread into school for the contest. They write a final description of their mold and a conclusion about how the mold grew and the bread changed. Ask the science teacher at your school, a neighbor, or someone from a nearby university to don lab coat, mask, gloves, and other lab paraphernalia to judge the moldy breads. The vice-principal of my school showed up in a waitress costume to judge the contest. The principal donned a wig and his academic robe. Ask the judges to exaggerate their examinations of the moldy breads. I must warn you that your classroom will smell for days after the contest. Bring a large, plastic garbage bag to class on the day of the contest. You will want to dispose of the moldy bread as quickly as possible.

Give three prizes in each class, one for each category, and hand out appropriately stained ribbons and certificates to the winners. I found lovely ribbons at the local trophy shop. They even engraved them for me.

After the contest, students can spend some class time rewriting their four descriptions and their conclusion, revising them and combining them into a paper to be submitted for a final grade. The results can be wonderful and vividly disgusting.

This exercise in descriptive writing should work at almost any level. Gear the writing assignments to the ability of your students. While younger students may not be able to keep a log of the daily progress of their mold, they can write descriptive paragraphs using the mold as a subject.

Parents and tutors, since you lack the numbers of students to hold a contest, you may want to simply challenge your child to see how "gross" a mold he or she can grow. You could get a piece of bread of your own and hold a contest between you and your child to see whose bread becomes the most interesting. In order to model the daily note taking, you might want to keep a daily log yourself as to the progress of your mold. You and your child can share the contents of your logs. You can ask a neighbor to judge.

3. Journals

I always encourage students to keep a journal. These often become open dialogues with me over problems in my students' lives. I promise solemnly never to divulge the information I read in my students' journals, and I never have, even when this decision became awkward when facing a parent. I feel that if I reveal anything said to me in confidence that I am betraying the trust of my students. I now have a reputation, and students know from my previous classes that I will not reveal even the most damning information that I read. This encourages them to be honest.

For these journals to be successful, you must answer your students seriously, never passing judgement. This is sometimes very difficult. Keep your comments positive. You can sometimes make suggestions as to who or what agency might help solve a student's dilemma. If child abuse is involved, consult with the child first and then contact the authorities together. This covers you legally.

The only ironclad rule is the one against swearing. Students are instructed to be more inventive than using such trite invectives. This year's favorite evil wishes involve a cow with diarrhea and a flatulent, nasty-tempered camel with a flea problem.

Whether you require journals or suggest them is up to you. If you require them, set a minimum limit. Not all students enjoy writing a journal. Some find it excruciatingly painful to expose their inner feelings to anyone. It is a good idea to try to respect that. If you require journals, allow alternate exercises. Then, if you begin Ms. Atwell's writing workshop where the students decide what to write and journals are no longer mandatory, you will find that many students ask to continue their journals.

Journal writing can be addictive. As well as a place to vent problems and worries, journals provide a place to write a poem that a child has found and loves and wants to keep, a place to write a phrase that a child thinks of at an odd moment and wants to retain for use in his or her writing, a place to complain and to vent frustrations, to share a book that was enjoyed, or to have a very private conversation with an adult who neither passes judgement nor condemns. Other students write poetry, draw pictures, discuss books, movies, morals, and so on. One student discovered Nikki Giovanni and got very excited. She copied pages and pages of poems. She also wrote about how those poems affected her.

You will find that students write about neglect, abuse, drug use, even drug-selling, health problems, dire fears, rejection problems, etc. Many write about their "true loves." Boys often ask for advice in how to woo a girl. Feel honored by their confidences. We can provide the adult ear our children need. Attaching a lollipop to a journal which announces a birthday can add a special touch. Any student who writes a journal entry on his or her birthday deserves a reward.

Ms. Atwell describes the use of journals as a device to discuss books read in a reading workshop. While my students sometimes do discuss books they have enjoyed, this is not the thrust of the journals that I require during the time we are not having a writing workshop. I do not use Ms. Atwell's reading workshop since the reading teacher does that, but if you teach reading as well as writing, you might want to look into her book (*In the Middle*, 1987) and use both reading and writing workshops in your classroom.

Journals can be kept at any level of schooling. As with learning a foreign language, the earlier a child begins, the better. Writing can become a good, life-long habit, offering a creative, non-violent outlet for venting the frustrations of childhood and adolescence.

Parents can keep a two-way journal with their children. When your child writes in his or her journal, respond with at least a page of chit-chat and personal observations. It is important to share ourselves with our children. We expect the same from them. You may even want to keep your own journal and give it to your child for a written response. This way your child will feel that he or she is not the only one sharing. If you do this, you might want to talk a lot in your journal about the positive aspects of your child.

4. Poem Memorizing and Writing

(See also Mini-Lesson #13)

Maybe it is old-fashioned, but I always require my students to memorize at least three poems a year. The assignment stems from my own shyness as a child. Reciting poetry in front of an audience boosted my confidence. It helped my memorization skills. It certainly honed my study skills. Best of all, I still remember those poems after thirty years.

I combine poem memorizing with what I tell my students is "Kiester's Method to Study So You Don't Make a Fool of Yourself." I introduce the poem, discuss the poet, talk about the meaning of the poem, delve deeply into poetic devices used, and so on. Then, every day for a month or so the class choruses the poem. I also instruct my students to "give up an ad for English."

Since most of my students watch a lot of TV, I ask them to pick a commercial that they hate. They post the poem — or so they promise — by the television, and every time that commercial comes on, they repeat the poem to anyone who will listen — a dog, a parent, a sibling, the couch. Repeating the poem once a day in school as the mini-lesson and at least once a day at home for a month plants that poem so thoroughly in students' minds that they all fly through the torturous solo recitation before the class. Some shake more than others, but almost every student earns an "A." I even offer hand holding as extra reassurance during recitation. A few always take me up on it for the first poem. One student said that she hoped that the poem would flow through my hand to hers so that she wouldn't forget a line.

Even your shyest students will manage to recite the poem. They all feel so good about themselves afterwards, too! A big plus of this method is that the lowest and slowest students easily can memorize a poem with the daily repetitions and are able to shine before the class when they recite it perfectly. Some of my shy students, encouraged by success, have volunteered to recite a poem at a talent show or at their church!

The day of recital, I tell my students that I will add an extra two points to anyone who volunteers and gets up to the podium before the last person returns to his or her seat. In this fashion, we nip quickly through thirty-five recitals of the poem, and it is the students who decide when they feel ready to recite. This is important.

When the day of reckoning arrives, I am the first person to recite the poem. I explain the grading system to my students, and they grade me. While I always receive an "A," I don't always receive a perfect score. This lets my students know that I don't expect them to do anything I'm not willing to do as well.

Grading the recitation is easy. I count the number of words in the poem and then figure out how much each word is worth. If, for example, there are sixty-five words in a poem, each word is worth two points. I take off another two points for each long hesitation. If I supply a line (which isn't often needed), I subtract by counting each word missed and fine them double for the hesitation. As I said before, almost all of the students earn "A's." They have said the poem so often that they tell me they can say it anywhere, even in front of their peers.

The day before the solo recitations, I always hear the poem being recited in the lunchroom. One year my students had the whole lunchroom reciting Langston Hughes's poem, "I Dream a World," at the top of their voices. The dean complained.

Every year you will have one student who, initially, cannot recite in public. It is a good idea to allow that student to recite the first poem with only one or two other students present. You must, however, deduct fifteen points or so from that shy student's score in order to discourage other students who would rather recite the poem privately but are perfectly capable of reciting it before the entire class. By the second poem, these shy students usually can recite before the class. Knowing the poem backwards and forwards does a lot to booster courage.

Use any poem by a poet whom you like. I love Gwendolyn Brooks, Langston Hughes, Robert Frost, and Emily Dickinson. After the movie *Dead Poets Society* came out, the advanced eighth graders asked to memorize "Oh, Captain, My Captain" by Walt Whitman. I was delighted to oblige them. One year I happily assigned my eighth graders "The Road Not Taken" by Robert Frost and found out that most had already memorized it in the sixth grade. Gwendolyn Brooks's "The Bean Eaters" is, I think, the all-time favorite of my students. I even have a tape of Mrs. Brooks reading the poem. When I play this after all my students have recited the poem, it really excites them.

I don't know what it is about the memorization of poetry, but it really raises students' self-esteem. Poetry seems to lose its reputation for dullness. I notice that students approach it with a different, more positive attitude after successfully memorizing a poem. Once a poem is memorized, a student owns it. Classes often ask to study more poems by the same author, and they love to perform before guests. Parents tell me that my students look through poetry books at home and, when bored, recite poems in the car. If any assignment sparks students — especially middle school students — to pursue something on their own, I deem it a success.

Poetry memorizing and reciting engenders poetry writing. As a Christmas or Chanukah gift, I always require students to write a poem to an important adult in their lives. We practice using specific details in order to make each poem really personal. I can buy cheap frames for $1 each from the county warehouse, and students illustrate their poems, draw borders, and frame them to give as a present. Parents have stopped me in the supermarket to tell me how much they loved the poem that their child had written. I tell my students that the aim is to recall personal incidents in their lives that they shared with the recipient of the poem and include those incidents in the poem. The purpose is to reduce the recipient(s) to delighted tears. Often youngsters who are unable to express emotions orally can do so through poetry.

5. Pre-writing

Pre-writing, mapping, or clustering should precede any writing. This can be done in the form of an outline or a cluster where the larger topics are listed in the center and ideas are added as they are thought of, or a map using arrows and lines in which a student plans the path a paper will take.

Different techniques suit different students. Model all three techniques for your students on the blackboard or overhead and then let them choose which one is appropriate for their particular learning style. The process of pre-writing should be begun early in a child's school career. Teachers need to require pre-writing before any writing is begun.

Pre-writing helps organization of papers as well. I require my students to do a cluster, a map, or an outline and then put numbers (in colored pencil) by each main topic in the order in which he or she plans to use it in the paper. When the student sits down to actually write the paper, the order of paragraphs has already been planned.

6. Read Around Groups (RAGS)

Stephanie McGraw, a twelfth-grade teacher in our county, presented this at a workshop. She claims that she got the idea from Polly Nagle and Rosie Wysong in Lee County, Florida. Stephanie uses it during the third grading period of the year and does it once a week for a while. The idea as presented here has been modified and personalized by teachers of different grade levels.

First of all, each student needs to have a piece of writing, any writing. If a student does not have a piece of writing, that student must sit apart from the rest of the class and cannot participate. This practice ensures that the next time you use Read Around Groups, all students have a piece of writing to share.

Direct students into groups of four. Most teachers who use this divide by desk rows. Students remove their names from their papers and are assigned a number. Assign a group letter and an individual number (for example, "A - 4") to each student, who then writes it in the upper left-hand corner of the paper. Each group chooses a student to record the scores.

Instruct Group A to pass its papers to Group B who passes its papers to Group C and so on. Do this so that all students have one paper from a neighboring group. When each participating student has a paper in front of him or her, tell the class to begin reading. Allow 45 seconds to one minute for reading. Do not go over the time limit, even if students have not finished reading a paper. Keep track and call time. Tell the students to pass the papers on to the next person in their group and to begin reading again. Call time. Repeat the procedure until each student in each group has read all the papers of the neighboring group.

At this point, instruct students to discuss what they have read. Each group picks the paper that all members agree is the best. The group recorder notes the number of this paper. Then all the papers are passed to the next group.

The above procedures should be repeated until all participants in the class have read every paper. Papers are then returned to their authors. Allow a couple of minutes at this point to allow students within each group to read the papers of their own group. This time they do not choose a "best" one.

Ask the recorders to report their findings. Write on the board the numbers of the selected papers. If a number is chosen more than once, put a check by that number. When all the groups have reported the results, discuss the reasons why certain papers received more than one vote. Ask the author of each popular paper to identify himself/herself. Ask the authors to read their papers out loud. Discuss further what made these samples of writing stand out.

Cheryl Alexaitis, a seventh-grade teacher, uses Read Around Groups frequently. Her students beg her to do it even more often. She finds that introductions to papers have improved because of the limited reading time. She also tells me that the self-esteem of her students has risen considerably and insists that RAGS is a great motivator. My students also like RAGS. It motivates my below-level students in my skills class to complete their work so that they can participate!

Parents and tutors, obviously this idea is not for you. You need numbers of children for this to be successful. You can, however, have your child read a paper out loud to you. You can then discuss the positive aspects of the paper.

7. Response Sheets and Evaluation Sheets

I almost always require students to complete a response sheet for their peers. The response sheet is a guide that directs students to respond appropriately to a piece of writing by making comments and suggestions concerning the content. While it is a good idea to have a different response sheet for each assignment, a generic version has been included on the following page. You can modify it for different pieces of writing.

Similarly, I never attach a grade to any piece of writing without an evaluation sheet. Even short, one-page writing assignments usually warrant an evaluation sheet. This sheet (see example) clarifies for students exactly what comprises the grade for the paper. No more than twenty-five points are taken away for subjective judgement. This is only fair since we all have different tastes. If I do take off points for subjective reasons, I always list those reasons.

Please note that while I might use a generic response sheet, I usually make up a specific evaluation sheet for each piece of writing. The only exceptions to this are the SVP paragraphs (see next writing suggestion) and poetry. I don't use evaluation sheets for either of these. I don't grade poetry, and because my students know what I am looking for in the SVP paragraphs, I don't feel as if I need one there either.

It is important to digress here and make a note about the evaluation of poetry. It is not a good idea to assign a letter grade to poetry. How can anyone grade poetry? Instead, you can highlight the best lines with a highlighter pen. Even in the most trite poem, you can always manage to find at least one line to highlight. Poetry comes from the soul. Any rejection of something so personal can destroy a person's desire to write anything personal again. Poetry needs to be encouraged, not graded!

Because I use response and evaluation sheets, students tell me that they always know what I expect and that they feel as if they are being graded fairly. There is rarely a question in my students' minds as to the "why" of a grade. They never feel "put down," even when the grade is not good. This helps improve classroom morale.

Home-schooling parents should also use response sheets and evaluation sheets. Although you will be the responder as well as the evaluator, these sheets help children know what is expected of them. On a response sheet, you can make valuable suggestions for changes in context. The evaluation sheet lets your child know exactly what you are looking for in that particular paper.

Responder #1_____

Author _____

Responder #2_____

Generic Response Sheet

1. What do you like about this piece of writing? Please be specific.

#1 _____

_____

#2 _____

_____

2. Look at the beginning of the piece. Does the first sentence "grab" you? If it doesn't, can you suggest a good "grabber" sentence?

#1 _____

_____

#2 _____

_____

3. Is there any place where the author needs more detail? What kind of detail would you like to see there?

#1 _____

_____

#2 _____

_____

4. How many strong verbs can you find in the piece? Do you think that the author needs more of them?

#1 _____

#2 _____

5. Are there any questions you might have that the author needs to answer?

#1 _____

#2 _____

6. Please make a helpful, positive suggestion to help the author revise.

#1 _____

_____

#2 _____

_____

Grade_____ Class Period _____
Author _____

Sample Evaluation Sheet (Prose paper)

General requirements:

Mapping or cluster or pre-writing - (5)   _____

Sloppy copy—Context changes made - (10)   _____

Possible spelling errors circled in rough - (5)   _____

Verbs checked in at least one draft - (5)   _____

Final draft typed or in ink and neat - (5)   _____

Proofreader's signature on final draft - (5)   _____

Mechanics:

Frequent use of strong verbs - (5)   _____

Spelling errors in final - (5 each, up to 25 off)   _____

No inappropriate verb-tense shifts - (5)   _____

General grammar and mechanics - (up to 10)   _____

Content:

Specific use of detail - (10)   _____

Style and depth of thought— Author's voice - (10)   _____

Subjective - (20)   _____

(100 points total, unless lots of spelling errors)

Total off: _____

+5 if typed _____

Comments: _____

_____

_____

_____

_____

Total off: _____

8. Strong Verb Practice (SVP)

These artificially constructed paragraphs are based on Rebakah Caplan's idea of Showing Writing (*Showing Writing - A Training Program to Help Students*, 1980). Before you begin assigning these paragraphs to your students, however, you might want to do Mini-lesson #7 to prepare them and to teach them about strong verbs.

This year I began this activity at the end of September and have required that students write a weekly SVP paragraph. You can modify the idea to suit your students' needs.

To introduce the concept of strong verb usage, it is very effective if the teacher is dramatic. When I taught seventh-grade English, my seventh graders and I dressed in lugubrious clothes, made coffins with the "dead verbs" inside, and held a mock funeral. The "dead verbs" included be, been, am, are, is, was, were, have, has, had, and any verb ending in "ing." We solemnly walked to the edge of the campus, singing a sad rendition to the tune of "The Volga Boatman's Song" with the "dead verbs" as the words.

As we dug a hole and buried the coffins containing the "dead verbs," students delivered eulogies to the "dead verb" they felt that they used the most. We then made a bulletin board depicting a gravestone with the "dead verbs" listed so that we could use it for reference. From that point forward, "dead verbs" were to be avoided in student writing. I did this for years.

After several years passed, former students who visited told me that they still remembered the verbs to avoid. High school teachers have told me of students who hummed "The Volga Boatman's Song" when writing. Drama works! Other teachers in my school have taken up the shovel now that I have moved to teaching eighth-grade English. I miss it.

Since most of the eighth graders in my school have already buried the "dead verbs" in the sixth or seventh grade, it is a simple matter to put up a bulletin board that lists the "no-no" verbs. Even though we don't bury them, we chant and boogie the "dead verbs" to embed them even more firmly in our memory. The next step is to begin SVP paragraphs.

A Strong Verb Practice paragraph is composed of as many sentences as the grade level you teach — nine sentences for ninth graders, six sentences for sixth graders, three sentences for third graders, etc. Students think it is amusing to link the number of sentences to the grade level.

The teacher provides the first sentence, a telling sentence with a "dead verb." Popular "telling" sentences are "The students in the cafeteria were wild," or "My room is a mess," and "The party was fun." Students take the given sentence and use it as a topic sentence for their paragraphs. They then write the requisite number of sentences with "strong verbs" to support the topic sentence.

Strong verbs are action verbs which show what is going on — "Students *shouted* invectives at the top of their lungs." This substitutes for a sentence that tells what is going on, such as "Students were shouting invectives." The last sentence of the SVP paragraph is another "telling" sentence that serves as a conclusion to wrap up the paragraph. Ask students to rephrase the topic sentence if they can't think of any other concluding sentence. Students must supply their own title for the paragraph. Using the topic sentence is unacceptable. Students complete the exercise by underlining the main verb in each sentence.

Some examples have been provided on the following page to demonstrate what students can produce. You might want to read these to your students for clarification. A list of good "telling" topic sentences can be found in Rebakah Caplan's book.

Please note that these paragraphs are also good practice in keeping verbs in the same tense. If the given sentence is in the present tense, the rest of the paragraph has to be continued in the present tense, etc.

The Wild Westwood Cafeteria
(written by a class as a whole and dictated to me)

The students in the cafeteria **were** wild. Many **threw** food from table to table. Some **shouted** invectives at the top of their lungs. Soiled trays **littered** the floor where students had flung them. Students **stood** on the tables and **danced** to imaginary music. Others **burped** loudly to express their dislike of the school fare. One bold student even **yelled** at the dean, demanding that rock music be played during lunch. The dean **croaked** over the loud speaker in a vain attempt to quiet down the students. Food **splattered** on the walls. It **was** a typical eighth grade lunch in the Westwood cafeteria.

Or, more appropriate for a home-school situation . . .

The Messy Room
(written by another class as a whole and dictated to me)

My room **is** a mess. Clothes **litter** the floor. Sheets and blankets **hang** off the bed in great disarray. Half-empty Coke cans on their side **spill** their contents on the rug. Records **cover** my desk, burying last year's homework. A nasty smell of month-old pizza **wafts** from the overflowing trash can. Moldy school books **peek** out of my packed closet from underneath piles and piles of junk. Food stains from wild food fights **color** the walls. My room **is** a total disaster.

9. Summaries

The ability to summarize concisely and accurately is an important skill. Whatever level you teach, it is a good idea to require periodic summaries from your students. Students can summarize TV shows for lack of a better topic. Their descriptions are hilarious and are often much better than the original shows.

Students can also summarize books, the Caught'ya story, conversations overheard at lunch, fairy tales, newspaper clippings, each other's stories, the doing of chores, and the happenings during a class period. Give students a word limit. This drives them crazy, but they always rise to the occasion. They find that it is hard to be accurate and concise.

Elementary Level Suggestions

1. Conversations

Correctly punctuating and paragraphing conversations are skills that require much practice for mastery. This practice can begin at the elementary level. The following is a guaranteed child-pleaser that often produces rather amusing results.

You will have to precede this writing activity with some instruction about how to correctly punctuate and paragraph quotes. You can begin after a few conversations have occurred in the Caught'yas, and students are beginning to write them correctly.

Tell students about the story in which the wicked witch turned a handsome prince into a frog until he was rescued by a kiss from a beautiful princess. Elicit from your students what kinds of things the prince must have said to the witch to try to convince her not to turn him into an amphibian. Ask students what the response of the witch might have been. Ask them to come up with several ideas about why the witch wanted to turn the prince into a frog and list the answers on the board. Students are now ready to begin the writing assignment.

Students write an imaginary conversation between the witch and the prince just before she turns him into the toad. Require a minimum number of things that each character must say. When I taught fifth grade, I required that each person (or amphibian) say at least ten things to the other. If you teach lower grades, you may want to require only a few.

If the idea of a conversation between a witch and a prince / frog doesn't appeal to you, there are other situations that can stimulate lively conversations. How about the conversation that must have occurred between the tortoise and the hare at the beginning of the race or between one of the three little pigs and the wolf?

2. Descriptive Writing

The Moldy Bread Contest mentioned among the General Suggestions works very well with younger children. You must, however, keep the bread in the classroom. You might even want to link this to a science activity.

To engender good descriptive writing, you can also bring in an object — any object that is a bit different from the norm, like an oddly shaped rock, an unusual vase, a stuffed animal, etc. Place the object in front of the class first thing in the morning and say nothing. Let students wonder about it for a little, while they complete other activities. Then ask students to write as complete a description of the object as they can. Instruct them to describe it so that you can picture it as you read their papers.

Describing monsters is another appealing way for elementary-age children to practice descriptive writing. Students use crayons or markers to draw a monster or a robot. Remind them to keep their creation simple, using circles, lines, triangles, squares, rectangles, and other shapes they have learned in math.

After the pictures have been completed, ask students to write a verbal description of their monster or robot. Remind them not to show their pictures to any of their classmates. Pass out another piece of drawing paper to all students and instruct them to exchange their word descriptions of the monster or robot with a friend. The friend tries to draw the robot or monster according to the instructions. The results are often hilarious. After the friends' pictures have been completed, have students share the original drawings with each other. A discussion of the results can be very instructive. Some teachers like to repeat this activity every month or so using drawings of places, animals, etc., so that students can learn from their mistakes and see their improvement as the friends' drawings approach the original drawing.

It is also fun to ask students to write a description of how to make a peanut butter sandwich. As each child reads his or her paper, try to follow the directions. Some child always forgets to instruct you to open the jar of peanut butter. This can be a laughter-filled activity as students learn to be complete in their descriptions. This activity can be followed by writing descriptions of how to take out the garbage, feed the dog, and so on.

3. Interdisciplinary Writing

Since all elementary students are required to take science and social studies, studies in these areas can be springboards for interesting and thought-provoking writing activities. Any subject that the children are studying in science or social studies will do. Just narrow the subject down to the smallest denominator. For example, if your students are studying Colonial times in social studies, narrow that down to food or dress or customs of the period. If, in science, students are studying reptiles, pick one specific reptile.

Now that you have found a narrow topic, you can begin. With you at the board to record answers, elicit all that the students already know about the subject. When your board is almost full and students have run out of ideas, ask students to suggest categories. If, for example, you were talking about an animal, you might want to elicit the categories of habitat, food, traits, how they raise their young, and how they look.

After you have listed the categories on the board, assign a number to each category. Have them assign a category to each piece of information they have provided. Write the number of that category beside the item.

Now students are ready to write. Instruct them to write a page or so about the topic, making sure that they include something from each category. Fourth and fifth graders can write a paragraph about each category. Since all the information that children will need to write the paper is on the board, few students have difficulty writing. These papers are good practice for research papers that your students will be required to write in later grades.

4. Letter Writing

This is a popular activity with almost any age group. There is a booklet that is published each year called *Free Things for Kids to Write Away For* by Jack Aboff and published by Jetco Advertising in Livingston, New Jersey. This $2 booklet lists free things that children can obtain simply by writing for them. The items appeal especially to elementary-age children. Inspired by the assurance that they will receive something in return, children will willingly write business letter after business letter to the various companies who offer these trinkets. I like to order a class set of these booklets and drag them out every few months or so to practice letter writing.

Another, sometimes rewarding letter writing activity concerns writing to authors. This works best if you are also conducting a reading workshop to teach reading. About January, after the students have had time to read some books, ask each one to identify his or her favorite living author. Then each writes a fan letter. You can find the addresses of the publishers in any *Books in Print* in your library. They will forward the letters to the authors. Paula Danzinger, author of *The Cat Ate My Gymsuit* and many other popular books, makes certain that every letter from a child is answered. She claims that she is not the only popular children's author who answers fan mail. It certainly is worth a try.

5. Newspaper Activities

Elementary students love to be able to handle things. Perhaps that is why they love working with newspapers. Using newspapers can provide many "hands-on" activities to generate enthusiasm for writing. The Newspapers in Education program has published many booklets with ideas for using a newspaper in the classroom. Ask your local newspaper about the NIE program in your area.

Coming up with a newspaper activity to fit each English skill isn't difficult. The newspaper activity can involve cutting and pasting of some sort — an adverb collage, cutting out a news article and substituting odd nouns for each pronoun, rewriting a comic strip, copying a sports article minus punctuation and exchanging with another student to put the punctuation back in, etc. Newspaper offices often have pamphlets with all kinds of ideas in them. Many grammar books also have sections that suggest activities which involve newspapers.

Give your elementary-level students a choice of assignments to practice each writing skill. Offer a choice of several newspaper activities, or give a choice between a short writing assignment and a newspaper activity.

Many elementary school teachers still have to cope with mandatory meetings with each of several different reading groups and math groups. Newspaper activities, done individually or in groups, can constructively absorb the interest of students who are not meeting with the teacher.

Newspapers are ideal resources for home-schooling parents. You can engender all kinds of writing activities by reading the paper with your child. For example, after reading the sports page, a child can write an article about a favorite sports hero.

6. Pictures

Most young children like to draw. A popular writing activity among the younger set involves drawing a picture of anything the child chooses, exchanging the picture, and having a classmate write a story around the picture.

Younger students like writing a sentence about a picture they have produced. These are called Experience Stories.

7. Story Starters

There are a plethora of booklets and boxes that provide a list of story starters. Look in your local bookstore or teaching catalogue for them. They are often amusing, provide a wide variety of ideas from which to choose, and engender creative writing from those students who find it difficult to come up with their own topics.

A story starter is simply a title or the first sentence of a story. The children must develop the story. One great story starter that I used in the fifth grade years ago produced rather imaginative results. I asked the students to imagine that a skunk (one with its odor-producing sacs in full working order) sauntered into the classroom. Some students described the reactions of the other students. Others described in great detail just what the skunk did to another classmate. Still others catalogued the actions of the scared rodent as it searched for an exit. We shared the results.

Middle and High School Suggestions

1. Circle of Questions

This is an unusual way to complete the study of any piece of literature. It also has the advantage of making the students responsible for conducting the proceedings. I first used this method with Ursula Le Guinn's *A Wizard of Earthsea*.

I learned about the Circle of Questions from another teacher, Tillis Churchill, who learned it in a workshop as the "Circle of Knowledge." I have already personalized the idea to fit the needs of my students. You may need to modify it again to suit the needs of yours.

First, read the prescribed novel either silently as individuals or with the teacher reading it to the class. I often read novels in their entirety to my regular classes in which over half of the students read below level. They sit absolutely silently for several weeks as I read for thirty minutes a day. They love it! Many other teachers tell me that they, too, read books to their students. More advanced students, however, prefer to read silently as they can read faster that way.

If you read to your class, have students follow along in their books. I think there is something innate in all of us that makes us enjoy hearing a good story. This experience stimulates many of us to read on our own. Many students inform me that no one has ever read a whole book to them before. No wonder they don't read on grade level.

I often like to try to leave students "hanging" at the end of the day and assign the next few pages for home reading. While students complain that they don't like to be left hanging, they usually do read the required pages, if only out of frustration.

After the novel is finished, I divide the class into three groups. Each group elects a leader and chooses a name. Each group assembles fifty literal and analytical questions about the book. They can also ask the meaning of any word in the book! Everyone in the group must make a list of the questions and the answers to those questions. I then give the groups an extra day to study the answers to their own fifty questions. It is important that everyone in a particular group know the answers to that group's questions.

The day of the Circle of Questions game is an exciting one. I post the name of each group on a big card and place these cards on a table with three chairs behind the table. I pass out a photocopy of the class seating chart, one for each student. The leaders come up to the table with their questions and the seating chart. Everyone else must clear his or her desk except for a pencil and a copy of the class's seating chart. Only the leaders have the questions in front of them. Then the verbal mayhem begins.

Let's say the groups are named Group A, Group B, and Group C. Since students choose the names of their groups, they are usually more inventive. I silently choose a number between one and ten. The leader whose guess is closest to that number goes first. For clarity's sake, let's pretend that Group A guessed the number and goes first. The leader of Group A asks one of the group's fifty questions to someone in Group B. Everyone in the class puts a check by that student's name on the seating chart to indicate that someone asked that student a question. If the student correctly answers the question, Group B receives a point.

If, however, the student misses the question, the Group A leader calls on someone in Group C and asks the same question. Again, everyone in the class puts a check by that student's name. If that student correctly answers the question, Group C gets a point.

If that student misses the question, the leader of Group A poses the same question to a member of his or her own group. Again, everyone marks a check by that student's name on the seating chart. If the student in Group A can answer the question, Group A gets a point. If that student cannot answer the question, than Group A loses a point. This is why it is so important that everyone in a group knows the answers to the group's own questions.

The play continues. The leader in Group B then asks someone in Group C one of Group B's questions. Everyone in the class puts a check by that student's name. Often the competition gets hot and furious. The seating chart is kept so that no child is asked another question until all the students in his or her group have been asked a question. This keeps the weaker students from bearing the brunt of the questions. When everyone in a group has been asked a question, the leaders can begin again with anyone in that group until everyone has two checks by his or her name, and so on. I notice that leaders often make other marks on their charts, indicating who answered a question correctly and who did not.

After the first day of play, I always allow another class period to adjust or change any questions. Maybe the questions are too difficult or too easy and need to be changed, or maybe the group just needs to drill on the answers to its own questions.

The Circle of Questions game continues for at least three or four more days until all questions have been asked. Students always beg for another day to continue the game with some "neat" questions they looked up at home. One year we played for five straight days until I finally called a halt. Each day students came up with new questions that they wished to try out on their peers. Students remained attentive because questions could be repeated on succeeding days.

After playing the Circle of Questions game, students ace any quiz or test I can throw at them. They know the novel backwards and forwards. While I think that this activity was originally designed for below-level students, all of my students enjoy the Circle of Questions.

Of course, you can do this activity with fewer questions. Some groups of students can't handle fifty questions. Twenty, or even ten, questions will do the trick, and the unit won't take as long to complete.

Parents and tutors, please note that this is the only middle and secondary level suggestion that cannot be used in a home-school situation. All the other suggestions that follow need little or no revision in order to be taught to one child at home.

2. Field Notes - A Metaphor Paper

This is a paper which can result in incredibly beautiful writing from your students. I got the basic idea from a workshop given by Jean Stallings, but she said that she got the idea from Cindy Secor. Workshops are wonderful places to find ideas for writing. As always, I have personalized the idea for my classroom and my students' abilities and needs. This is a really unusual assignment, but I still give students options. They may write something else if they so choose.

Students work outside at the beginning of this project. Take your students to a nearby park or a favorite schoolyard tree. As an alternative, you can instruct students to bring in interesting natural items. In the park, students isolate themselves and pick an object of nature to observe. If a student prefers, he or she can bring an object from home, such as a shell or flower, and observe it outside with the rest of the class. One period is spent observing the object and filling out notes about that object on a sheet the teacher provides.

This sheet should include the following instructions:

Observation Guide 1

1. Name the object.

2. Describe the shape of the object. Be sure to include all sides of the object.

3. Describe the color of all sides of the object.

4. Describe the movements of the object, even if it is stationary. This means that you describe any movements that could have happened to the object before the time of observation. For example, a pine cone fell from the tree above.

5. Write how you feel about your object. Of what else does it make you think? Why do you feel the way you do?

6. Describe all the other elements that exist around your subject. For example, a sea shell begins its life with an animal living in it.

7. Explain, to the best of your knowledge, why the object is where it is.

8. Imagine the very beginning stages of the subject you have chosen. Describe just how you imagine your object came to be.

9. Look over your notes. Reread them. Look again at your object and add anything new that you see or feel about it.

10. Note the exact location you have chosen. Notice the sky, the street, whatever larger objects are near you. Describe these things in your notes.

11. Now, write at least three possible metaphors for your object.

The next day the class goes to the woods again. This time students have another observation guide. It should include the following:

Observation Guide 2

1. Go to the exact location you chose yesterday. If the object you observed previously is not there, look around for another just like it. If you brought your own object, try to place it in the exact spot you did yesterday.

2. Sit in the opposite direction from where you sat during the first observation.

3. Describe any new things you see about your object.

4. Describe how it would feel to actually be that object. Be very thorough, descriptive, and specific.

5. Explain how your object is necessary to the environment.

6. Explain why you chose this object over any other.

7. Discuss in a least three to five sentences the relationship this particular object bears to the rest of the world of nature.

8. Think of your own life. Write three ways your object is like you, your life, and/or life in general.

9. Explain why it is important that you, as a member of the human race, understand nature.

10. Thoreau once said, "I went to the woods because I wished to live deliberately, to front only the essential facts of life, to see if I could learn what it had to teach, and not, when I came to die, to discover that I had not lived. I did not wish to live what was not life, living is so dear . . ." After reading this quote, explain how nature teaches all people lessons we sometimes fail to recognize.

On day three of the observation, students choose a partner. Partners take turns reading each other's notes from the first two days of observation. Then each partner goes to the other person's object and studies it for a few minutes. Partners then add any new observations or thoughts to each other's notes.

The fourth day is spent in the library. Students make a bibliographical entry onto a third sheet of paper and note any factual information they can find about their object that might prove to be helpful or interesting. Sometimes I ask students to buy a small spiral notebook in which to note the first three days' observations as well as any information gleaned from library sources. This way they feel more like actual scientists recording data.

After the observations and the visit to the library, students are ready to write. I usually read several examples from previous years to give students ideas, but this assignment is so loose that I hate to bind it by suggesting anything other than the following broad parameters.

I always say this: "Consider what your object is like and what it is not like and, using your notes, focus on the metaphor ideas you noted on Day One. Using any or all of these metaphors, try to bring together in your paper both the observed data and the metaphor(s) to give a really in-depth look at your object. Let the metaphor you choose control the paper but be sure to include some of your observations. You may choose to use any information you found in the library, or you may choose not to use it at all."

Insist that students include a description of the object and its surroundings in the first half of the paper. This can also incorporate the one piece of information they found in the library. Students must then write a fulcrum sentence which links the object to the metaphor. The second half of the paper should contain a discussion of the chosen metaphor. In the concluding sentence, students need to bring back the original object and link it once again to the metaphor. You also might want to stress the use of "strong" verbs in the description of the object. I often make the use of strong verbs a requirement for an "A" paper.

This paper, necessarily, goes through several drafts. Students respond to each other's papers with a response sheet, share the problems of writing such a difficult paper, and really work on revisions.

The final draft must be accompanied by a bibliography and a visual aid which demonstrates the visual aspect of the two sides of the metaphor (the object and what it becomes in the student's mind).

This is not a simple paper to write and often takes great effort on the part of students. The end results, however, can be really beautiful and sophisticated. My students go into this apprehensively but are themselves surprised at and proud of the results.

I have included an example to show how a rather imaginative student handled this assignment. Please note the quality of the writing. When I chose the paper to include here, it was really difficult because almost all the papers I received were excellent. If you suggest this assignment to your students, you can read this paper to them as an example. I have retained the errors and typed the paper just as Lotta gave it to me. While she got carried away at the end, Lotta included the required description of her object, the fulcrum sentence, and a discussion of the metaphor. In her conclusion, she brought the object and her metaphor together. Please note the use of strong verbs in the first half of the paper.

Field Notes on a Suicidal Stinging Nettle
by Lotta Rao, age 14

These field notes are from a juice guzzling juvenility who happened to step upon a stinging nettle and realize it was something worth observing: A shaft of sunlight illuminates the purest of whites belonging to the flower of a fortress — the stinging nettle. Short, hairy thorns cover the leaves and the harmless, even tantalizing, white petals. (Who would think anybody had the courage to eat these thorny plants?) The nettle twists and turns, doing a slow dance as a glass lizard brushes its thorns with its tail, not seeming to notice the sting that is associated with the plant. The nettle towers above a brown carpet of pine needles, pine cones, and fallen leaves, a miniature giant in its field. Like the fragile enclosure around every person, the stinging nettle is only intimidating on the outside. It has built up an elaborate defense system designed to fend off the world.

One look at the stinging nettle, and I know what it feels like; only the outside is covered with thorns. Inside waits the softness and vulnerability of youth and a heart that is capable of being found, pierced, and broken. The one white flower sways and petals fall to the ground. This flower is the only clearly beautiful characteristic apparent to the human eye, and no one dares look any further.

The girl hangs her head. What use is one flower, one beauty? And even as these thoughts jumble and fill her head, another sight fills her eyes; one petal has lost its fast hold, one petal has touched the ground. One wrinkle has started to line her face. Who will seek her now, who will bother if they didn't bother before? All alone, she stands in the field, alone and desperate. She bows her head. Further and further as she has never dared go before. Yet this time no fear is felt until the puncture of skin gives away to one last thought, one last regret. Until she lies dead, killed by her own sting, dying at the point of her own thorn just as the nettle is yanked from the ground by any unwary being who has been impaled.

I, too, have built an elaborate defense system of thorns, yet, I, unlike the nettle, wish I could shed this skin and hold my head high by giving friendship a chance and risking having my heart die by someone else's hand rather than my own. ∎

3. "I Search" or "Career Search" Paper

This is what I use to satisfy the research paper requirement for eighth-grade English. The idea for this paper originated with Ken Macrorie. His book *The I-Search Paper* (1988) explains it more thoroughly with many examples. "I Search" papers can be written at any secondary level.

An "I Search" paper answers a question about which the student has always wondered. I tell the students the true story of my own "I Search." This sets their minds (and their eyes) rolling. Perhaps a high school teacher has to be more serious. We middle school teachers can be a bit crazy at times, just by the nature of the age of the delightful people we teach.

I tell students that once upon a time I had two big red Doberman Pinschers. My Dobermans had a very serious problem. After asking other Doberman owners, I soon discovered that this problem was not limited to my Dobermans alone. Indeed, it was a universal problem of Doberman owners. Simply stated, Dobermans are flatulent. This can become so offensive that serious research into the problem becomes necessary. The "I Search" problem that I investigated was "Why do Dobermans break wind?"

In truth, I investigated and questioned people about this problem for two odoriferous years until I found the answer —and a solution. The process I went through to find the answer is the same one I ask students to go through when they write their "I Search" papers.

While "I Search" papers can research the answers to similar ponderous questions, they can also be turned into "Career Search" papers if the student so chooses. In this way, a student can investigate a possible career choice. A "Career Search" paper can also be a part of an interdisciplinary unit on careers.

Essentially an "I Search" or a "Career Search" requires a minimum of five sources, including interviews. First the teacher instructs students to cluster all they already know about the subject. They then do the research and take notes. When the research has been completed, students cluster the information that they found that was new to them. At least one of the five required sources must be a book and at least one must be an interview.

At this point, students are ready to write a rough draft. I like to divide the paper into five parts although I do let my students vary this form if they wish and if they can give me a good reason. (I accept almost any well thought-out reason.) In part one, the students write all that they already knew about the subject before doing the research. In the second part, they describe the process of ferreting out the answer to the question — where they looked, whom they asked, what each source contributed or didn't contribute, questions still left unanswered.

The third part of the paper is the biggest part. Here students report in their own words what they found and give a full explanation of their question. In the conclusion, students briefly summarize the results of their research and critique the assignment itself. What did they like and dislike about it? How can the teacher change the assignment for future students?

Since I usually assign this paper at the end of the year, I limit the length to three or four typed pages. Nothing beyond these pages gets read. This helps prevent "paper padding," commonly known among my eighth graders as "cow manure." Since it is the end of the year, after students have been involved in months of writing workshops, I do allow students to continue writing on their own if they have any unfinished piece that they wish to complete. This gives students a choice. Enough of the students (about eighty percent) choose to do the research paper to satisfy my county's requirement. Since we work on bibliographies all year (see Mini-Lesson #15), and students do research in their social studies class, I am not worried about my students learning how to write a good research paper.

By the way, the solution to the Doberman's social problem was chicken-based dog food. Dobermans and related breeds, such as Rottweilers and Weimaraners, cannot assimilate meat very well.

4. Modeling Poems

After reading, studying, and perhaps memorizing a poem, students can write a model of it, changing subject, style, or anything the student wants to change. In general, students stick to the format of the poem. Don't set any parameters other than the requirement that students credit the author of the original poem. I don't even like to read examples of models to my students. This forces originality. Some students abandon the original poem entirely and write one of their own. This, too, is just fine. Students younger than seventh graders have difficulty handling this assignment.

5. Persona of Another Character

Suggest this paper after your students have read any book that is written in the first person singular, such as *The Diary of Anne Frank*. Ask students to retell a chapter or a section of the book from another character's point of view. Students are supposed to assume the persona of this character. Each year that I suggest this paper, some student always takes the point of view of Mouschi, Peter's cat. The idea for this paper and the poetry paper that follows this originated with Sally Larson. I'd like to be in her class. She does such neat things!

6. Poetry Paper

Most of the research in this "research" paper is done inside the writers' minds. It is also a good mechanism to introduce poetry to students. Each year I am astounded with the results. Precede this paper with several pre-writing assignments designed to spark the students' interest in poetry and get them thinking.

Begin the unit by reading a poem a day for about a week. Choose poems that you personally adore. Spend about five to ten minutes a day after the Caught'ya. After you read each poem, talk about it. Tell your students why you like it, discuss the rhyme scheme, and go over the meaning (See Mini-Lesson #13 in Chapter 4.).

After about five poems, begin the poetry unit. Cull all the poetry books your school library has to offer. I also cart in all my personal poetry books and raid the public library. Display all the poetry books you can find on a cart in your classroom.

For the second pre-writing assignment, I instruct students to work in their response groups, heterogeneous writing groups which frequently work together to respond to writing. Students elect leaders, and leaders choose response groups, splitting up friends, etc. Each response group peruses the poetry books to find one poem that everyone in the group likes. If you do not use response groups in your classroom, you can arbitrarily divide your students into groups of three or four.

To begin the lesson dramatically, grab up five or six books from the poetry cart and plunk them down in the middle of a group. Since a class usually contains at least seven groups, you will need about fifty poetry books for this exercise. You may be pleasantly surprised at how many books of poetry your school library has on hand; I certainly was.

The students in each group pour over the books, argue, read, and eventually come up with a poem they all like. At this point, instruct students to find out all that they can about the poem, using all they have learned about poetry in all their years of school. They prepare to deliver an informal presentation of their poem.

After the presentations, which can be very interesting and often amusing, students are ready to begin the paper. Tell your students that they have one week to find three to five poems that they really like (I assign three for regular classes and five for advanced.) These poems must have different authors and must be out of different books. At least one of the poems has to be by a well-known poet.

Students should study the poems and take notes on them. It's a good idea to provide a study guide. This guide can be in the form of a ditto which leaves space to write down things about each poem. I simply have four headings at the top of the paper and a space under each heading for each poem. The headings are the following: 1) Why did you choose and like this poem? 2) Meaning? 3) How is this poem different from the others? 4) How is this poem similar to the others (beyond the required common factor)? I make my guide look like a chart that, when completed, serves as notes for the major part of the paper.

A trip to the library is in order next, to look up information about one of the authors they used or one of the poems they chose. This information does not have to be used in the paper, but it might prove helpful for background knowledge. This also forces students to have a bibliography of at least one source. It also really helps students if you can supply them with a list of poetic devices. Review these devices orally before the actual writing begins. See the facing page for a sample of the one I use with eighth graders. Teachers of higher grades may want to add more to this list.

Students then are ready to begin the first draft of the paper, which includes four parts plus a bibliography. In the first part, students describe how the poems are related and talk about the selection process (honestly). In the second and longest part, students think about and discuss each poem they have selected. This is where the notes on that chart come in handy.

The third part of the paper contains comparisons and contrasts among the poems that the students chose. They can use the chart.

The final part of the paper is a reaction to the project and the paper. Students usually report that they find the paper extremely difficult. They also say that it is one of the few papers they have ever had to write where they really had to think hard. They also like the fact that all the research came from within themselves rather than from outside sources.

After the first draft has been completed, students exchange papers. They use a Response Sheet like the one on page 98 to comment on the content of each other's papers. Using peer comments as a guide, students then make changes and write a second draft of the paper. This draft is changed yet again, checked for grammar, mechanics, and usage errors, and proofread by the author as well as a parent or fellow student. A final draft is made. All drafts and notes are turned in to the teacher for grading.

Suggested Steps in Analyzing a Poem

1. How does this poem look? (shape, length, etc.)

2. Does the title seem to have any significance to the meaning of the poem?

3. How many stanzas are in the poem?

4. What are the length of the lines? The rhythm (beat)? The number of syllables?

5. Does the punctuation, or lack of it, seem important?

6. Is the rhythm (beat) significant to the poem?

7. What is the poem trying to say? What is it trying to make you feel?

8. Analyze the poem for the following:

> A) rhyme and rhyme scheme
>
> B) repetition of words, sounds, phrases, or lines
>
> C) alliteration
>
> D) personification
>
> E) metaphors
>
> F) similes
>
> G) imagery evoked when it is read

(Teachers, leave space between each question.)

Author _____

Responder _____

Response Sheet — Poetry Paper

Please comment on whether the author has answered all the questions or discussed all that needs to be discussed. To help the author, please be specific and circle any question that the author did not fully cover.

Number of poems copied _____

Paragraph #1 — Did the author discuss how the poems related in a general way and why he/she selected those poems? Did he/she name the poems?

Paragraph #2 - 6 — Did the author discuss each poem for content, style, why he/she liked it, meaning, voice, imagery, rhyme scheme, and poetic devices such as alliteration, personification, imagery, metaphors, and similes?

Paragraph 7 — Did the author compare and contrast all five poems to each other, pointing out major differences and likenesses?

Final Paragraph — Did the author discuss fully his/her reaction to the project, supporting answers and giving reasons?

Helpful Comments ??

7. Question Paper

Years ago Gwen Barnett, an eighth grade teacher, introduced this idea at a workshop at the University of Florida. Like the Circle of Questions, the Question Paper is designed to be assigned after completion of a novel, a play, or a poem. Since my eighth graders read St. Exupery's *The Little Prince* as a part of the curriculum, I like to use this thought-provoking book as a starter for this paper.

Each student thinks of a question that the book leaves unanswered. The paper begins by asking that question. The student then converses with himself or herself about possible answers. The student should come up with at least three possible answers for the question and must support each answer with information from the book or with outside information. Usually one of the answers generates another question which requires at least three more possible answers, and so on. A Question Paper need not be long — two to three typed pages at most.

Of course, a high school teacher can require more sophistication for this paper. My eighth graders complain that it makes them have to think, but they do like doing it. There are no right or wrong answers as long as all answers are supported. What students like about this exercise is that they are doing research from within.

Give students a few weeks of class time to write the rough draft. Allow another two days for response. Use a response sheet — see "General Suggestion" #7 in this chapter for an example. Still another few days should be spent making contextual changes to turn the rough draft into what I call a "sloppy copy" (for obvious reasons), editing, proofreading, and making a final draft. Collect all drafts.

It is important to note here that, as usual, you should give students a choice of assignments. Ask students who simply cannot face the Joycean quality of the Question Paper to write a chapter to add to *The Little Prince.*

After completing one teacher-directed Question Paper, some students like the format and continue to use it when writing on their own in a writing workshop. Children are, by nature, curious. The Question Paper models a way to come up with answers. It also gives a new twist to traditional research papers.

Included below is a sample of a Question Paper written by an eighth grader. This paper was written after reading *The Little Prince*. It appears as Laura gave it to me in her final draft, errors, repetitions, and all. You might want to read it to your students to give them an example of the format.

Why Did the Little Prince Die in the End of the Story?
by Laura Gamm, age 13

This question doesn't sound very inquisitive, but I can't figure out why the Little Prince had to lose his life. I liked this little figure because of his charm and his wisdom. Through his adventure, the Little Prince showed me the values of life. The author kind of let me down by having the Little Prince die in the end of the story. While thinking about this question, I could only come up with four possible answers.

Maybe the author was trying to make the Little Prince more human. The author could have thought that by killing the Little Prince he (the author) wouldn't make the Little Prince sound like such a fairy tale character. Some people find it easier to relate to a real person than an extraordinary super hero. Sometimes super heroes can make you feel like such a low life!

The author may have been adding another meaning of life to the book. Maybe he was trying to say that death comes with life just as love, hate, and friendship do. All through the book the Little Prince experienced life. Each stage was a new stage. In the book, every chapter taught you something about life. Maybe this was the Little Prince's last stage of life. The Little Prince learned enough about life, and then it was time for him to go. Death may be dreaded, but it's a fact of life that each of us will experience.

But wait! I have another possible answer! The author could have been trying to end the story. In some books, if the main character lives, the story leaves the reader hanging on to what could have happened after the book ends. Maybe the author didn't want another sequel like Star Wars 5 and 6. He may have just wanted to end the story. I mean, the Little Prince could have returned to his planet alive and explored more about life, but maybe that wasn't what the author wanted. What the author wanted was an ending. KABOOM!! Story over! No sequels!

The theory that I like best is that the author wanted to be different. He didn't want a fairy tale ending. The author may have wanted an ending that people would remember, an ending that was different. He made the Little Prince die to show that life, even though it is special, has to end. Life even has to end for fairy tale figures like the Little Prince. By having the Little Prince die at the end of the book, the author was trying to be different. Even though I like happily-ever-after endings, this one will stick out in my mind because of the death of a respected character.

All through this book I loved watching the Little Prince learn about life. I will probably never be able to guess why the author killed such a lovable character. You may come up with some good answers, but ask Antoine de Saint-Exupery for the real answer! ∎

8. Publishing

The suggestions for teacher-directed writing assignments in this chapter are only a few among many ideas floating around out there. I'm sure you have your own favorites. We teachers are each other's best resources. We also need to listen to what our students want to write.

Students, like anyone else who writes, yearn to see their work published. There are many magazines like *Merlyn's Pen* which encourage submissions by students. Lists can be found in your school library. Other places to publish can be your local newspaper; writing contests sponsored by publishers (they usually send fliers announcing such contests); a book that is self-composed, self-bound, and given to someone; or a poem, paper or article that is posted on a bulletin board.

English teachers in my county think that publishing is so important that we sponsor a yearly story contest as well as a yearly poetry contest. Each of us contributes five dollars to the prize money for the prose contest and our local newspaper donates the rest. The newspaper also publishes some of the winners of the story contest. The winners of the poetry contest are published in a book produced by the county.

We English teachers judge both contests, middle school teachers judging the high school papers and vice-versa. For the prose contest, each teacher is allowed five entries total. This keeps the entries down to a workable number. The title pages are removed and numbers are put on each paper so they are judged anonymously. Each judge is given a paper with the numbers written on it. Two judges read all the papers for a grade level and, independently of each other and without discussion, grade each paper holistically and assign a number to each paper. We use numbers from one to six, six being a paper that knocks the reader's socks off. After all the papers for a grade level have been read twice, the scores are compared. If there is s split of two numbers or if there are several papers which received the same total, a third teacher reads those papers. There are two winners for each grade from six through twelve. Winners are honored at a big reception where they read their stories to the assembled English teachers, parents, and administrators. They also publicly receive their monetary prize. It is a fine moment for young writers.

The poetry contest is run a bit differently. Each teacher is allowed to submit twenty poems. Students are asked to put their names and their school and their teacher's name on the back of the paper. Judges do not look at the names so these, too, are graded anonymously. Again two teachers read all the poems for a grade level, but this time there is discussion. Together, the teachers pick five winners for that grade level. We do not break winners down into first, second, third, and so on. Winners of our poetry contest are published in a rather professional-looking booklet, published by the county, and placed in all the school libraries. Winners receive two copies of the booklet.

It is important to students that they receive some acknowledgement and some commendable, special "finish" for writing that they carry through many drafts and bring to completion. If you can't find any other source for overt "publication" of students' achievements, you can provide it yourself by "publishing" literary magazines (the Xerox machine is a wonderful invention) or by using those little blank books for students to produce their own works. Maybe you can organize your fellow English teachers to initiate contests like ours. Since you run the contests, you can set them up any way you wish. Most counties have a local Teachers of English organization. Our contests are organized through our local branch.

Six More Story Ideas

(Plus Ninety Sentences of "Adolescent Transmuted Karate Otters")

Introduction

Caught'ya! Grammar with a Giggle provided six story ideas for those teachers who felt uncomfortable coming up with their own story line but who wanted to write their own sentences. This chapter gives you six more story ideas that you can modify, twist, or improve. Only the bare bones are provided here. Change these stories to suit the interests of your students or your home-schooled children.

While none of these stories is brilliant nor worthy of any applause, they are funny (I hope), and the humor is designed to appeal to children. They also all contain a moral: niceness pays, working together solves problems, good grades are desirable, never give up fighting for what is right, moderation and thinking before you act is important, one should not judge people by appearances, and so on. I figure that we need to reinforce these good ideals in our classrooms. In addition, the mother in me just couldn't resist.

103

There are two plots each for elementary, middle, and high school levels. Obviously, you can ignore the grade-level suggestions and use whichever story idea you like. Unlike the stories in Chapter 5 of *Caught'ya! Grammar with a Giggle,* only two have been tested in my classroom. The third is currently being used in two elementary school classrooms — one in a public school, the other in a multi-grade-level classroom in a church school. The feedback so far has been positive. In formulating these plots, however, I have made sure to include the child-pleasing elements mentioned in Chapter 3.

Three of the story lines were used to write the sentences in Chapters 7, 8, and 9. In these chapters, there are one hundred Caught'ya sentences for each story. Again, you can use one of the stories in this chapter as a springboard for your own sentences. Just keep flexible so that your sentences can be changed if your students need more practice in a particular skill.

At the very end of this chapter is a delightful story suggestion along with 90 Caught'ya sentences that came from the fertile minds of two middle-school teachers in Jacksonville, Florida. They sent me a letter with their Caught'ya story (the board sentences) enclosed. They are delighted to share their creation with the rest of us.

Elementary School Story Ideas

"The Meanest Teacher in the World"

Use the one hundred Caught'ya sentences for this story already written in Chapter 7 or use the plot to write your sentences that fit the needs of your students.

This story centers on an elementary school class (any grade will do) which comes to school the first day only to find the ugliest, nastiest, most bizarrely-dressed teacher they have ever seen. This apparition of horror is appropriately named Mrs. Obnoxious. The first day of school, she reduces several children to tears. Within the first week of school, Mrs. Obnoxious manages to insult each student in the class. She has no pity and seems to hate children. She never cracks a smile.

In a state of panic, the students in Mrs. Obnoxious's class meet at lunch and try to work out a strategy to deal with this teacher. At first they decide to wait a few days. In class, however, Mrs. Obnoxious continues her insults, reducing most of her students to quivering heaps of jelly. (When you write these sentences, use each of your student's name at least once.) After a few days, the students meet again. They decide to complain to every adult who will listen. Several students seem certain that their influential parents will come to their rescue.

No adult listens to the pleas of the children. The principal and the parents maintain that the teacher has the best of reputations, and they even hint that maybe it is the students who are causing the problem, not Mrs. Obnoxious. One desperate student even looks up the word "obnoxious" in the dictionary.

The children meet again, after school this time. After a long debate, they decide to try to be meaner than the teacher. (Put lots of conversation here.) Every time Mrs. Obnoxious is obnoxious, the students plan to be even more obstreperous.

They try this strategy for a few weeks. It only makes Mrs. Obnoxious worse. They — politely, of course, — insult her choice of clothes, point out that her pointing finger is rude, chide her for making students cry, etc. In other words, they combat meanness with meanness.

When this strategy makes matters worse, the students meet again. One really nice girl who frequently has been reduced to tears by Mrs. Obnoxious comes up with the idea to try to "out-nice" the teacher. In other words, every time Mrs. Obnoxious is mean, students must counter that with kindness, or a nice compliment. Reluctantly, the rest of the class agrees to try this new idea.

The onslaught begins the next day. Students bring apples and flowers to their teacher. They try to be as perfect as they can. The messy student tries to be neat. Students help the poor reader to read more fluently. The talkers never open their mouths unless called upon by Mrs. Obnoxious. Students greet their teacher at the door in the morning, compliment her on her clothes, ask her to join them for lunch, etc.

One day, Mrs. Obnoxious is absent. Her students bake cookies for her and bring them to her. They make get-well cards. They draw her pictures. They write her short notes, telling her how much they miss her. (Practice letter writing here.) When Mrs. Obnoxious returns, students hold her hands on the way to lunch, line up at the end of the day to hug and kiss her before they leave for the day. They even make sure that *every* student has his or her homework completed each day.

Slowly, day by day, week by week, the students see improvements in their teacher — a smile here, a hug there, a word of encouragement to a student. Mrs. Obnoxious is changing!

By the end of the year, the class and Mrs. Obnoxious are very close. The students think that their teacher is the best in the world, and Mrs. Obnoxious tells each of her students how wonderful the class is. The last day of school is flooded with tears by all. The story ends with Mrs. Obnoxious practicing her ugly grimace before the mirror in preparation for the next year's students. . . . ■

"The Teacher's Pet"

In this story I use a Florida panther as the animal. You can substitute a large animal on the Endangered Species List indigenous to your area. Whatever endangered animal you choose, make it big enough to be a problem and big enough so that people are afraid of it. I have not written the sentences for this story. Although it has not been tried out on students, it does have the elements that would appeal to younger children.

This story takes place in a normal classroom. Pattern the classroom, the students, and the teacher after your classroom. Home-school parents, this one might be perfect for you as it is easily adaptable to a home situation. Just substitute your home, your children, yourself, and your neighbors for the setting and the characters.

One day some boys are walking to school as usual. They always pass a forest. Now, this forest scares them, but they don't usually let their peers know how they feel. On this day, while passing the forest, the boys hear a strange mewling noise. A brave child goes past the palmettos to the source of this sound. He spies, under a clump of wild azalea bushes, a small tawny creature that looks like a cat with a funny face. It is about the size of the child's arm.

The brave child calls his friends over to the animal. One bright lad identifies the creature as a Florida panther. Having been well trained by their teacher and parents, they know not to touch a baby animal. They note the spot so that they can report this baby to the authorities and quickly leave. A few blocks down the road, the boys hear the mewling sound again. This time it is coming from behind them.

They turn around and find the baby panther following them. Not wanting to scare it, but knowing that it must return to the woods so that its mother can find it, the boys try to shoo it away. The panther ignores them and continues to "dog" their heels all the way to school.

The panther boldly follows the boys into the school and into their classroom. (At this point, you can have individual students react to the animal. This is a good place for a conversation and for an introduction to the children in the story. It is always a good idea to use the names and personalities of your students. They love this.)

The teacher (who resembles you), takes advantage of the situation and launches into a lesson on endangered species, specifically the Florida panther. The panther curls up under a desk and sleeps through the proceedings. At lunch, it follows the children to the lunchroom and refuses to leave them. Knowing it isn't good for the animal but knowing it is a baby and is hungry, they feed it their lunches — milk and meat from sandwiches.

The panther follows the children back to their classroom and crawls into a little girl's lap for a nap. That afternoon, when school ends, the panther follows a child home, eats dinner, and sleeps on that child's bed. (You can continue this narration through a few school days, making the panther follow a different student home each night. You can include the reactions —negative, positive, and funny — of the various parents to the animal. Have the parents not know what kind of animal it is. Students can inform their parents about the animal.)

After a few days of this, the principal sees the panther and calls the Game and Fish Commission. The teacher and her students have not done so yet because they are in the middle of writing a letter to the authorities and are enjoying studying the panther up close. Besides, the panther seems attached to the entire class. It likes to sleep on a different lap each day and on a different bed each night. At recess it even follows the students down the slide.

The authorities come. The panther hisses, spits, growls, and scratches the animal catchers. It does not want to leave its friends. Finally, the children cooperate and help the officials put the panther in a cage. They take it away, the panther protesting all the while and the children crying. Since the mother panther has been found to have been killed by a car, the authorities decide to raise the baby in captivity.

As usual with news about a Florida panther, the newspapers write about the progress of the cub. (Be sure to give your endangered animal a name early in the story. Poll your students for the name. This gets them involved.) The children all become avid newspaper readers since the panther has been taken to a place far away from their school.

They read that the cub is pining away, not eating its food, and is rapidly losing weight. When the newspapers report that the cub might die and the adults can't figure out why it won't eat, the children and their teacher begin a massive letter campaign to the state officials. They even write to the governor. (At this point you can insert a letter writing unit and have your students write the letters.) The letters all beg the government to return their beloved panther to the class. They insist that all it needs is love.

The government agency writes letters back to the children, explaining that they can't give the animal to a private citizens, but they might bring the cub for a visit to see what happens. The students prepare for the visit by finding all they can about the Florida panther, its habits and its needs. The day of the visit arrives. The students are prepared with the proper food. When the cub arrives, it screams to be let out of its cage. When let out, it rushes to the children, licks them all over, gobbles up the food, and promptly crawls up into the teacher's lap and falls asleep.

When the time comes to return the panther to the zoo, the animal protests again. Once again, the poor baby does not do well with the government officials, loses weight, and pines. Finally, after reading the impassioned letters of the students, the Governor of Florida steps in. He makes an exception and gives the panther to the class to raise.

Reunited with the children, the panther baby thrives. No one accuses the teacher that year of having a teacher's pet who is not a panther! ■

Middle-School Story Ideas

"Tales of a Four-Eyed Weirdo"

This story is the basis for the one hundred Caught'ya sentences in Chapter 8. It has proven to be very popular with both seventh and eighth graders in several schools. Students like Harold and empathize with the characters. They enjoy the fight and love Harold's heroism with the fire. This is the story that is outlined in Chapter 3 after the dialogue.

Harold Weird (using this last name all year really seems to help students with the spelling of "ie" and "ei" words) is a bespectacled, portly, black, short student with zits all over his face, a mother who thinks that any grade less than an "A" is very bad, a father who is too involved in his work to pay any attention to him, and a brother in college whom Harold is expected to emulate. Harold is not adept at any sport he attempts. He has to deal with his parents' recent divorce and his mother's overprotection. Most of all, he has to deal with being an adolescent who has been uprooted from his friends and transferred to a school in another town.

Harold, glasses and all, arrives at school. (Use the name of your school.) The other students call him a "four-eyed weirdo," trip him, tease him, and ignore him at lunch. He feels alone and unhappy.

This is the point at which you have to introduce the rest of the characters. In middle-school stories you need to really describe the protagonists well. Give the teachers your worst traits — you know, the ones that drive your students wild. Give them names that vaguely resemble your name and the names of your colleagues — Mrs. Keck (which means to gag), Mrs. Hassle, Mr. Haggle, Ms. Hard, Mr. Nag-a-Lot, etc., to give you a few ideas.

The main villain is Conan, a "cool" dude with lots of gold chains, an "F" average, and a bad attitude. Conan has a lot of sycophants who are equally obnoxious, earn equally bad grades, and also wear a plethora of fake gold chains. Belinda Beautiful is vapid and queen of the snobs. She is always surrounded by other "beauty" queens whose noses are stuck permanently in the air. Gnarly Nerd is the Caucasian version of Harold. Like Harold, he is an "A" student, is chubby, and has a problem fitting in because of his looks and his grades. Gnarly quickly becomes Harold's best friend. Finally, Classy Cassandra is the most beautiful girl in the school. With big dark eyes, dark honey-colored skin, long, luxurious black hair, a shy demeanor, a straight "A" grade point average, and niceness of personality as well, Cassandra is the dream of every young man in the school.

Now that the scene has been set, the action (such as it is) can begin. Belinda gives a party and invites everyone. Harold and Gnarly are invited in order to be the butt of much ridicule. After much discussion, Harold and Gnarly decide to go. (This is a good place for conversation practice.)

At the party they encounter Conan and his cohorts, lounging against the wall, smoking cigarettes. Harold spies Cassandra sitting on a couch and debates whether to talk with her. Conan and his friends, angered by Cassandra's indifference to them, insult the beautiful Cassandra and throw a punch at Harold. Not wanting to appear to be a wimp in front of Cassandra, Harold fights Conan. He is hopelessly outmatched. From under Conan's armpit and from under the pounding that he is receiving, Harold spies the trash can which is on fire from the dropped remains of Conan's cigarette. He calls a halt to the fight just as the flames begin to lick up the curtains.

Harold grabs some baking soda, throws it on the fire, and saves the day. When Belinda's irate parents arrive home, Harold shoulders the blame for the fight and the fire. He does this in order to save Cassandra from possibly being blamed. Everyone is stunned.

The next day in school everyone, even Conan, sends Harold a note. (This is a good spot to review the friendly letter format.) The students are beginning to soften towards Harold and Gnarly.

Then one day every student's nightmare of a substitute shows up in English class. (Use your imagination here.) The sub corners Conan because he doesn't have his homework, as usual, and is busy combing his hair in class. Before the sub can send Conan to the Dean, Harold slips him his homework.

The next day Harold and Gnarly organize a trick to confound the substitute. (You can use any trick that your students love to try on poor, unsuspecting substitutes, but I always like the book dropping routine at a given signal. Thirty books clattering to the floor at the same time is enough to make even the most seasoned teacher jump. While this has never happened to me, students tell me that this trick is a sure-fire "substitute unnerver.") The trick works, and the substitute is unnerved.

Harold and Gnarly gain new respect for their trick. Students also are impressed at how these two "nerds" get all the students to work together. Conan, threatened with flunking the grade, realizes that maybe Harold and Gnarly are right to study and get good grades. He asks Harold for help. You see, Conan really is intelligent, but he always thought it was "cool" to get bad grades.

Conan changes and turns out to really be a nice guy after all. Harold becomes a happy camper. His dad realizes his worth. Pleased with all Harold's good grades, Harold's mom gets off his back about grades. His big brother praises him. Harold even gets contact lenses. Belinda and her crew take Harold and Gnarly under their wings to help them lose weight. Wonder of wonders, Cassandra falls in love with Harold. The finale is held at a party at Harold's house with everybody having a good, safe time. Harold's zits disappear, and everything ends happily ever after! P.S. The mean substitute never comes back either. ∎

"The Oak Tree Heroes and Heroines"

This story probably would do especially well in big city schools where trees are often at a premium. I think it would probably fall flat with my students whose school borders a park and who live in a smallish city of 100,000 once dubbed "Tree City." My husband disagrees. He says that all boys love big, climbing trees. I also would suspect that this story would work better with fourth through seventh graders than with older students. It would be ideal for home-schooled children. Instead of a tree near a school, have a tree near your home. Instead of the variety of children, use your child's friends, thinly disguised.

Again, you have to set the scene (your school) and the protagonists. As in the story about Harold Weird and his friends, you can have the teachers resemble the most annoying parts of you and your colleagues. The names of the students, like those of the elementary school stories, probably should reflect the names of your students. You should also thinly disguise the personalities of your students as well, stressing the good points. Once your Caught'ya sentences have set the scene and established your characters, the story can begin.

Right near the grounds of a school is a huge oak tree. Students have passed by it for years without giving it a thought. Old kites still sit in the branches. No birds nest in the tree due to its proximity to so many noisy children. Carved names and hearts scar the bark. A few boards from an abandoned, summer tree fort jut out from a high branch. In short, it is a large, normal oak tree without anything to make it special except that there are not many other trees that size anywhere near it.

Students casually interact with the tree. They lounge in the shade, meet friends under it, use it as a reference, and carve names into it. (Use the name of a student who has shown a propensity to write on desks for this one.) Boys even climb up into the upper branches as a show of bravado.

One day, during a current events session in social studies, someone reads an article that tells of the impending cutting of the tree to make way for the nearby road to be widened. The rumors spread around the school. Normally apathetic students are horrified. Fights even break out between those concerned with doing something and those who maintain that as children they are powerless to change anything. (Although I personally abhor violence of any kind, students love reading about it. My fights are always mild and contain much humor. I always imply the futility of the exercise.)

One group of concerned students holds a meeting. (This is a good place for practice with the punctuation and paragraphing in conversations.) The leader of the group is one of the most popular boys in the school. He organizes the students to ask their English teachers to help them write letters. The usually "mean" teachers are delighted to oblige their students in a frenzy of business letter writing to their local planning board, city commission, mayor, and government agency officials. One unpopular girl even drafts a letter to the governor of the state. (Describe her as a girl with whatever traits are the norm for a "nerd" in your school. This part of the story, of course, can be accompanied by a unit on the writing of business letters. You can put the format of some of the letters in the Caught'yas.)

Students meet again and vote to erect a fence around the tree. They go to the library in search of articles about the desirability of preserving trees in general. To keep the tree, they get a petition signed by every student and teacher in the school. They send this petition to the mayor. Students clean up the tree, remove kites, boards, etc. No one carves names into the bark any more. The student who previously defaced the tree is now the chief protector. The students in the shop class build a lovely fence to surround the tree.

At this point, the threatening surveyors arrive. Students elicit the cooperation of parents and teachers, and they man a twenty-four hour vigil by the tree. A romance flourishes between the popular guy and the shy girl who wrote the letter to the governor.

Just as the bulldozer is scheduled to knock out the tree, the governor arrives in response to the shy girl's letter. He declares that the tree belongs to the students of the nearby school as long as they take care of it. He promises to mandate that the road shall be designed to go around the tree. All is saved. Students triumph. Teachers rejoice. Our hero and heroine are happy. ■

I need to inject a note here. Since humor is a major ingredient of these stories, you have to insert it in this story via the antics of the students and teachers since it is not, by its nature, a funny story.

High School Story Ideas

"Charlie Excess Does It Again!"

This story forms the basis of the one hundred Caught'ya sentences in Chapter 9 of this book. As in the previous story, give your student protagonists the exaggerated personalities of your students and have the teachers resemble you and your colleagues. This is another story that can easily be adapted for home-schooled children. Charlie can still pursue grades, sports, and parties to excess, but he can do it at home. Instead of seeing the guidance counselor, he can ask his grandmother.

Charlie Excess is the hero. Please notice that almost all of my heros are male. I do this deliberately since the male students are often more difficult to interest in schoolwork than the female students. If I can get a couple of boys interested in the story, the rest of the class, including my most recalcitrant students, usually follows suit.

The hero of this story is Charlie Excess, an exaggeration of your typical "nerd." He seems to have no friends except his books. He works all the time, never having any fun. His parents put unbelievable pressure on him to earn a 4.0 average. Charlie's equally studious companions are Suzie Meretricious and Howard Matriculating. They, too, study all the time and do not interact because of competition.

According to the students, the teachers at Horribly Hard High School seem to take a certain malicious pleasure in piling on the work. Students are certain that their teachers work together to plan big assignments that are due on the same day. They collect papers only to lose them in their cars — or so the students think. They also put pressure on Charlie to earn that 4.0 grade point average.

Charlie's parents, like typical parents of teenagers from the teen's point of view, show no mercy. They are on his back for everything. If he doesn't study at least three hours a night, they chastise him. They make it quite clear that to bring home a grade of a "B" or below is the kiss of death — not to mention severe punishment. Charlie is unhappy.

One day Charlie wakes up and decides that his life of study, study, study and nothing else is no fun. He realizes that he has grown ten inches in the past year and is beginning to fill out. He also realizes that there are girls out there besides Suzie, whose nose is always buried in a book anyway.

Something snaps, and Charlie decides that he has had enough. He goes out for basketball and makes the team! He buys Karim Abdul Jabbar protection goggles for his thick glasses. He practices every afternoon for three hours on his jump and lay-up shots. He runs ten miles a day. He abandons his studies entirely. He fools his parents by reading books at night about basketball stars and strategies. His parents, naturally, assume he is studying.

Charlie gets so good at basketball that he can make a basket from thirty feet out. He becomes the best forward Horribly Hard High School has ever had. Near the end of one game, a giraffe-like player from the other team is moving the ball toward the basket. Charlie is able to reach in and knock the ball out of the wraith-like arms of his opponent. He grabs the bouncing spheroid, runs down the court, and dashes in for a lay-up shot. This maneuver wins the game for the Horribly Hard High School Hurricanes. Overnight, Charlie becomes a sports hero. (This action scene is included, courtesy of my husband, for those of you who are sports cretins like me.)

Suddenly, Charlie wakes up and discovers that concentrating on nothing but sports is dull, even with the applause and the accolades. He is not really having any fun. Where are the girls?

Sure, lots hang onto him after the games, but he has no special girl. He is lonely, even in the limelight. He decides to make another change.

Parties become his *raison d'etre*. He becomes a hedonist. Girls occupy his every thought. Now he doesn't even make a pretense of studying. His parents are on to him for everything anyway, he rationalizes. Charlie becomes belligerent. Adults no longer like him. He sneaks out almost every night and parties his bespectacled eyeballs out. He begins to drink. He tries cigarettes to look cool.

Since Charlie is hung over and his lungs hurt from smoke most days, he can no longer run quickly. His playing drops off. He doesn't show up for practice several times. Finally, when report cards come out, Charlie gets kicked off the basketball team because he doesn't even make the mandatory 2.0 grade-point average necessary to participate in sports.

Charlie's parents hit the proverbial roof. He is campused within an inch of his life. His parents watch his every move. His kid sister, Melinda, teases Charlie for his bad grades. Charlie suddenly finds himself with no friends. It seems that the kids who hung around Charlie because he was a sports hero or a "party animal" were all the fair-weather type. Suddenly, Charlie realizes that unless he does something to bring up his grades, he won't have the choice of entering college when he graduates. He doesn't like being alienated from everyone. He likes his parents, strict as they are, and his teachers, hard as they are.

Charlie can't leave the house except to go to school. His mom even embarrasses him by coming to school several days to make sure he is working hard. Parties and the like are a definite "no-no." Charlie decides that that's okay; he isn't happy with the hedonistic kind of life either. All the people at the parties seem to say the same vapid things over and over. He doesn't really have friends. He realizes that getting drunk only makes him feel bad and that he hates the feeling of weight on his chest that comes from smoking. Charlie is fed up with the party life.

Poor Charlie is in a real bind. His old study buddy, Suzie, lifts her nose up from her books long enough to advise him to talk to the guidance counselor. Since he is so low anyway, one more "degradation" can't hurt. Charlie goes to the counselor. The lady is kind, understanding, and gives him practical advice—moderation. She even brings in Charlie's parents to help them realize that they also need to practice moderation.

Charlie begins to study again although this time he does not hound himself to get only high "A's." He makes time for sports and, at the end of the grading period when his grade-point average has risen to a 3.5, he goes out for cross-country. He takes another look at Suzie and begins to date her. He even convinces her that moderation is the key to happiness.

Charlie and Suzie organize study groups and pool their resources to help each other study efficiently. He and Suzie even have study dates where they study in between kisses in the library. Charlie and Suzie give "paper parties" where all the kids get together and write their papers for their classes, commiserating over the hard work. Charlie's parents, now aware that "B's" and "A's" denote considerable achievement, realize Charlie's maturity and lay off pressuring him. All ends well. ■

"The Mystery Music"

I love this story. Although it has not been classroom tested, I think that it will appeal to tenth, eleventh, and twelfth graders because of the music and because of its novelty. I don't think that names matter in this story. You can use any names that you wish. I'll supply a few, but if you use this story, build the characters on the

good traits of your students. Please note, those of you who do not
speak French, that Mr. Hautbois's name means "Mr. Oboe"
in English.

One day a bunch of students at the high school stay after school
for detention. It seems that they had unwisely but successfully
terrorized a substitute. After detention, a few of these students
wander the now-empty halls of the school. For one or two seconds,
their chatter grinds to a halt, and in the silence Chris thinks he hears
music. Intrigued, the students tune their ears to the strange sound,
trying to track it down.

They wander up and down the echoing corridors following the
music, trying to ascertain its origin. (You can write lovely, strong verb
descriptions of your school in this part as the students search for the
music.) This music is nothing they have ever heard before. It haunts them.
It seems to float on the air. Although it is one note at a time, not chords, it
is clear and almost bell-like in its precision. The melodies seem to waft in
and out of the kids' bodies. The kids cannot seem to find the source.

Suddenly, a custodian appears and orders the kids out of the
building. Chris and his friends go home, but they can't forget the music.
It really haunts them. The sound of the music goes round and round in
their heads.

The next few days the kids stay after school voluntarily, helping
teachers and custodians. This amazes all the adults because this group of
students, although not usually a problem, aren't habitually into helping
out others — especially if the others happen to be teachers. Chris and his
friends just want the excuse to stay after school in order to have more
time to trace the source of that music.

Somehow they manage to volunteer for something every day
for a while. They clean up the band room. They help teachers carry
their loads of papers to their cars. They wash the boards. They make
elaborate bulletin boards. They even join a group of students
decorating the gym for a dance. Every day that Chris and his friends
stay late, they hear the music. They become almost obsessed by it.

The music is not jazz. It is not rock. It is not spiritual although
it certainly moves them deeply. It is something new and haunting. (At

this point you can build the mystery by having Chris and his friends search everywhere. They can have conversations.)

Finally, after volunteering for everything they can think of, Chris and one of his friends find themselves at school late in the evening. Again the halls are deserted. Again they hear the sound of the mysterious instrument. Chris thinks he hears the music a bit louder in the hallway near the boys' bathroom. He tiptoes towards the sound. A door to a book room is only a few feet away from the bathroom. Chris carefully puts his ear to the door and hears the music. It is loud, clear, and beautiful.

He slowly opens the door of the book room. There, on an old wooden chair sits an old, gray-haired, dark-complexioned custodian whose name Chris can't remember even though the man has been at the high school since Chris's parents attended it. There, in that musty book closet, filled with unused, outdated dictionaries, sits the custodian playing an instrument. (Describe an oboe here.) His head is bent in concentration. His mouth is pursed, and the most beautiful sound fills that tiny room.

The custodian stops playing and greets the students. They talk about the music and about the oboe. (You can devote many Caught'ya sentences to this conversation to practice the correct punctuation of quotes.) The custodian, Raymond Hautbois, plays for Chris and his friend. For over an hour they sit on the floor, spellbound, watching that gray head move up and down with the music.

They ask Mr. Hautbois if they can come back the next day and bring a few friends. Mr. Hautbois agrees, but only if the children "merit" staying late by helping someone at the end of the school day. The next afternoon a half-dozen boys and girls volunteer to help teachers after school. Then they, too, hear Mr. Hautbois play. They, too, are fascinated with the sound.

Suddenly there is a growing revolution of teacher help! Students volunteer right and left to help teachers, custodians, secretaries, each other, etc. The school gets written up in the newspapers. It becomes a local mystery for the adults. More and more students stay after school to be able to stand at the bookroom door for an hour just to listen to Mr. Hautbois play. He plays almost every classical oboe piece ever written. Mr. Hautbois also plays his own compositions. The students are spellbound. Never have they heard such an instrument play such music.

Finally, one smart English teacher, Mrs. Longpapers, questions Chris about this revolution in after-school help. The next day, after receiving Mr. Hautbois's permission, Chris tells her the story of Mr. Hautbois. She wants to believe Chris, but she doesn't. The one day that Chris persuades Mrs. Longpapers to stay after to listen to Mr. Hautbois play, no music comes from the book room; Mr. Hautbois is at home, ill.

After Mr. Hautbois's return to work, the number of students staying after school gets to be too many to fit around the book room. Mr. Hautbois invites the kids to his house to hear him play on a Saturday. Band and orchestra members beg to be able to bring their instruments to play with him. Mr. Hautbois is delighted. The Saturday music time becomes a regular thing. Students still help after school and go to the bookroom, but they also go to Mr. Hautbois's house every Saturday afternoon. There, they behave like angels. There is a renewed interest in oboes. The oboe player in the school orchestra suddenly becomes popular.

One day Chris asks Mr. Hautbois if he can bring his tape recorder. Mr. Hautbois agrees. Chris tapes Mr. Hautbois for hours. Mr. Hautbois is so modest about his rare talent that he is pleased and surprised that the kids enjoy his music.

Chris takes the tapes to Mrs. Longpapers. Meanwhile, other students are telling their favorite teachers about Mr. Hautbois. Mrs. Longpapers now feels ashamed about having doubted Chris. Impressed with the quality of Mr. Hautbois's oboe playing, Mrs. Longpapers borrows Chris's tape and shares it with the other teachers.

The next Saturday, most of the high school, teachers and all, show up at Mr. Hautbois's house to hear him play. Mrs. Longpapers begs Mr. Hautbois to give a concert for her English classes. Mr. Hautbois agrees. The principal, Ms. Strict, shows up during fifth period. She is amazed at the way in which the students are totally wrapped-up in Mr. Hautbois's music. She has never seen them so polite and so engrossed in something — and classical music at that!

Ms. Strict writes a letter, inviting Mr. Hautbois to give a concert for the whole school. Mr. Hautbois writes back and agrees to give the concert since he loves the children who listen to him. (This is a good spot for some letter-writing practice.) A local reporter gets wind of the story and has Chris write it up for a feature in the town newspaper.

Because of Chris's very articulate article, an agent comes to Mr. Hautbois's concert. (This could engender a writing assignment.) Mr. Hautbois becomes famous but, being the nice person he is, he still maintains contact with his friends and gives a free concert at least twice a year at the local high school. ∎

Extra Because I Can't Resist

"The Adolescent Transmuted Karate Otters"

This story was written by two creative teachers, Laura Strickland and Gail Hubbard. Laura teaches seventh grade at Mayport Junior High in Jacksonville, Florida, and Gail teaches eighth grade at J. E. B. Stuart Junior High in the same city. I received their letter and couldn't resist including their story in this book. I knew that other teachers also would appreciate their wit. While Laura and Gail wrote this story for their own middle-school students, I see no reason why it can't be used for any level — simplified for elementary and made more difficult for high school. It is perfect for home-schooled children. Have the otters cavort around your home instead of a school.

Laura says that her students love the story and become quite excited about it. She has decorated a bulletin board with pictures of the protagonists. Her students even want to make up a theme song for them.

Laura and Gail sent me the board sentences of their story. (See the sentences labeled "B" in Chapters 7, 8, and 9.) I will give them to you in their corrected form so that you can program in the errors you think are appropriate for the level of child that you teach. I can envision the younger set going crazy over this story. I love the bookworm!

This year I am trying this hilarious story on my below-level English skills class. I already changed some of the actual Caught'yas that Laura and Gail wrote and simplified them to adapt to the particular needs of a skills class. You can combine sentences if I have rendered these too simple for your students. So far, my students like the story very much.

The vocabulary words are in bold print. There are 90 sentences in this story and lots of places where more sentences easily can be added. The sentence has an asterisk if a paragraph is needed. I thought that it would be easier for you if I numbered the Caught'ya sentences the way Laura and Gail did rather than write the story in paragraph form.

One more note. This clever story leaves lots of room to add other skills. As the year progresses I probably will change the sentences even more in order to include more practice in plurals and plural possessives, verb-tense shift problems, the comma rules, titles of poems and books (one otter can read a book), letter writing, antecedents and their corresponding pronouns and verbs, and lots more practice with irregular verbs like "lie" and "lay."

When I wrote the Caught'ya sentences in Chapters 7, 8, and 9 of both books, I kept in front of me a long list of grammar points, mechanics, and usage skills. I made sure to include most of them at least once in each story. I compiled this list from several standard grammar books designed for diverse levels of students as well as from a list my fellow teachers and I once made. It was a long and tedious process, but then I knew (hoped) that my sentences would be used by thousands of teachers.

Gail and Laura, on the other hand, wrote the "Karate Otter" sentences only for their own students, reflecting their students' skill needs. These sentences, therefore, do not contain all the grammar points and mechanics and usage rules that you might want to teach during a year. You can insert them yourself when you feel the need.

The story involves five, large, adolescent, talking otters who like to play in water and eat whenever the opportunity presents itself. They worry about their Nintendo sets and about food. These otters live in a school or home — your school or your home — and hide out in vacant closets, store rooms, bathroom sinks, and air-conditioning ducts. The following is only one story in the lives of our five intrepid heroes.

By the way, Laura and Gail have cleverly named the five otters after five American authors — Langston Hughes, John Steinbeck, James Fenimore Cooper, Mark Twain, and Ernest Hemingway. This gives teachers a perfect excuse to acquaint students with the writings of these authors . . .

(*Note:* *An asterisk denotes the start of a new paragraph.)

The Adolescent Transmuted Karate Otters

1. *Not so long ago, in a school much like ours, five large **adolescent** otters happily **scampered** in a vacant storage room.

2. It was in this **vacant** room that they met Wiley Worm.

3. Wiley was much older than the otters, and he became their **mentor**.

4. *Wiley Worm was skilled in **martial arts.**

5. He had learned his Karate skills from the writings of the **Masters**.

6. Wiley read **incessantly** which was why he was often called a **bookworm**. (This sentence would be a great one to switch the tense of the verb.)

7. *The five otters were very social, and they liked to **frolic** in water whenever they could find any.

8. The otters grew older and more **judicious** from Wiley's teachings.

9. Wiley named the otters after five **distinguished** American authors.

10. Their names were **Twain, Steinbeck, Hughes, Fenimore,** and **Hemingway**.

11. Not only did the five otters like to **cavort** in water, they also were always hungry.

12. The otters knew that they were destined to **fumigate** the school in order to **exterminate** crime and bad attitudes.

13. *One day, during their daily search for water in which to play, the otters noticed a trail of **rubbish**.

14. *"Hey, Sliders, check this out," Steinbeck called to the others, using their affectionate name for the group.

15. *"What's up, Steiny?" asked Fenimore.

16. *"Wow, garbage, Sliders, **remarked** Twain.

17. *"Pheeew! That's **repugnant**," said Fenimore.

18. *Hemingway pointed to the **offal**.

19. "This is a job for the fabulous adolescent transmuted Karate otters," he **pontificated**.

20. *"Yeah!" **bellowed** the other four otters in unison.

21. *Hughes suggested that they follow the garbage trail to see if it led to the **culprit**.

22. The other otters, after grumbling about their empty stomachs, **unanimously** agreed to his suggestion, and they began their investigation.

23. *"This is an **abomination**, Sliders," cried Twain.

24. *"I hope we catch this **refuse rogue**," added Fenimore.

25. *"I'm **famished**," cried Hemingway.

26. *The sun **ascended**. A lot of students were arriving at the school.

27. The otters returned to their hideout and **donned** their disguises.

28. Wiley reminded them to be discreet as they once again set out after the **litter** monster.

29. *The otters **commenced** their investigation of the crime.

30. Hughes, who was disguised as a teacher, noticed that the **litter** trail seemed to **junction** with a lot more trash.

31. Before long, all five of the otters each were following a **separate, distinct** trash trail.

32. They **reunited** in a deserted classroom where there was a **veritable** mountain of trash.

33. *Fenimore **peered** around the corner and said, "Radical, Sliders, I think it's a sculpture out of garbage!"

34. *"You're right, Fenimore," Steinbeck **concurred**.

35. "I think I **recognize** who it is supposed to be."

36. *Hughes, Fenimore, and Twain **simultaneously** asked, "Who?"

37. *Steinbeck reminded them of a **villain** Wiley had once **encountered**.

37. This **criminal** was half-man and half-snail. His name was Shellback.

38. *"You see, Wiley and his third cousin, Seymour Snail, were once **abducted** by an evil, mad scientist," he explained.

39. The **moniker** of this evil, mad scientist was Dr. I. M. Kraized," he continued.

40. "Kraized **concocted** a chromosome transporting machine," Steinbeck finished.

41. *"This sounds **preposterous**," retorted Twain.

43. *"Don't be so **skeptical**," said Hughes.

44. *"Do you remember the movie **The Fly**?" **inquired** Fenimore.

45. *"Right!" said Steinbeck and Hemingway in **unison**.

46. *"Kraized planned to break into Fort Knox through **cellular metamorphosis,** just like in that movie, " Steinbeck continued.

47. "That experiment of **cellular metamorphosis** went **awry**," Steinbeck added.

48. "When he couldn't find Wiley, Dr. Kraized became impatient, and instead of using the two cousins as **guinea pigs,** he entered the **chamber** himself with Seymour."

49. Steinbeck **concluded**, "Seymour had already been captured and placed in the **metamorphosis** chamber of Kraized's machine."

50. *"So, you're telling us that Shellback was really only half-Kraized and half-Seymour," **interjected** Fenimore.

51. *"Sliders, this is **incredulous!**" threw in Hughes.

52. *"Wow, guys! Who would believe this?" **queried** Twain.

53. *"Sliders, this is a **bizarre** case of a really split person." **exclaimed** Fenimore.

54. *Hemingway and Twain laughed **uproariously** at Fenimore's puny attempt at a joke.

55. *"You guessed it!" Steinbeck **proclaimed**.

56. "Shellback has spent a lot of **eons** sliming and trashing this school," he continued.

57. *"He must **cease** this immediately," **insisted** Hughes.

58. *Suddenly and **enigmatically,** the classroom door closed and locked behind the otters.

59. The **intercom** system **crackled** into activity.

60. *"I've captured my **nemesis**," it spluttered.

61. The **raspy** voice continued, "You **mammalian** crime fighters, I have you just where I want you."

(*Note*: The following two sentences need to go together on the board because they are spoken by the same person and are a part of the same paragraph. Thus, there are no end or beginning quotation marks.

62. The voice did not stop. "The only thing left for you to do is to **wallow** in my garbage instead of in the sinks in the boys' bathroom!

63. Now I'm going to **rout** out Wiley, and I'm going to rule this school," the voice concluded.
*"Who was that?" asked Hemingway.
*"Dr. Kraized, you **cretin**," said Hughes.

64.* Rather than being concerned about Wiley's **welfare**, Fenimore **fretted** about his unprotected Nintendo set being slimed by the **unscrupulous**, half-crazed Shellback.

65. *Twain, too **oafish** and too hungry to be **cognizant** of the danger, asked, "When is lunch?"

66. Steinbeck, however, took control of the **perilous** situation.

67. "Here are the **tactics**, Sliders," he said.

68. "Escape is **imminent**. This room has only one door which is locked."

69. He continued, "Our **egress** is through the air-conditioning shaft."

70. *"Radical! We can **scamper** up the garbage sculpture and swing from the chandeliers, just like at our last party," said Hemingway as he **scaled** the **debris** with Fenimore close at his heels.

71. *The **hassling** voice of Shellback was heard echoing through the air conditioning shaft.

(*Note*: This one would be great for discussing active and passive voice.)

72. *Steinbeck **pondered** the **predicament** and **devised** a fool-proof plan.

73. He must rid the school of this **pernicious** villain, save Wiley, and **transfigure** Shellback into Seymour and Dr. Kraized.

74. Steinbeck, the intellectual among the five otters, explained his plan to his **cohorts** in a series of notes.

75. He used a written form of communication rather than a **verbal** one because he was afraid that Shellback could hear him **via** the intercom.

(*Note*: This is where I intend to insert some friendly letters.)

76. *The other four otters agreed to try Steinbeck's **scheme**.

77. Being **lithe** and quick, the otters **camouflaged** themselves to resemble the surroundings in the storeroom.

78. Then they descended and gained **ingress**.

79. Upon the signal word from Steinbeck, "Conestoga," the five Karate otters **pounced** on Shellback.

80. They **restrained** him by using a famous Karate headlock.

81. *Wiley **blazed** the path to Dr. Kraized's **notorious** laboratory where the **intrepid** five mammals and their mentor found the **chromosome transporter**.

82. Wiley and the otters were **perplexed** about how to operate the complicated machine.

83. Shellback **spurned** all requests for instructions.

84. *As Twain, the "chow hound" of the otters, **scoured** the laboratory for something to eat, he **espied** Dr. Kraized's diary.

85. Wiley **deciphered** Dr. Kraized's **hieroglyphics** and **manipulated** the complex control panel.

86. Sparks began to fly and the machine **executed** its **bizarre** transformation.

87. *When the smoke cleared, Seymour and Dr. Kraized had been **re-animated** as their natural selves.

88. To **vindicate** himself and to prevent **incarceration,** Dr. Kraized volunteered for gum scraping and cafeteria duty for the next twenty-thousand years.

89. Seymour and his cousin Wiley were **reunited**.

90. The **intrepid quintet** rested to prepare themselves for their next, thrilling adventure. ■

(*Note*: You will need to add more sentences of another adventure with the daring Karate otters if you wish to use Caught'yas all year. I'm already working on mine. I think Dr. Kraized will put a virus into the school's computers . . .)

Chapter 7

100 Caught'ya Sentences

for Grades 2 – 5

"The Meanest Teacher in the World"

Important Notes

In almost every Caught'ya, students are required to capitalize the first letter of each sentence, capitalize proper nouns, and supply end punctuation. These, therefore, are not listed each time in the skills. Note, too, that there are blanks in the sentences. Use these to fill in the names of the students and the information about them. Younger children love to have personalized Caught'ya stories in which they are the protagonists.

Only one-hundred Caught'ya sentences are given here. If you do three a week, these one-hundred sentences are all that you will need. If you do one Caught'ya a day, you'll need eighty more of them. Having to come up with some of your own gives you the flexibility to add sentences anywhere you wish. You easily can give more detail to the basic story line for more practice in the skills you determine that your students need. (See the Appendix for an annotated list of these skills.)

The story is fairly simple, and there are plenty of places where more detail can be added. Sentences requiring new paragraphs are indented.

Older students who use this story may need more practice in punctuating the quotations. You can make up a number of Caught'yas that prolong the conversations in this story. Younger students may need more practice with the comma rules. In fact, in order for mastery to be achieved, younger children may need more repetition of all of the skills you want to teach.

Those of you who teach the younger grades will need to simplify the sentences, shorten them (especially in cases where there are two sentences in one Caught'ya), or include only a few of the errors in the sentence you put on the board. For example, you may wish to provide the required quotation marks and have the students supply only the commas. Only you know how much your students can handle.

Play with the sentences to make them fit your students' needs. Fifth or sixth grade students may need longer sentences. You can elaborate on the efforts of the children to render their teacher palatable and use more complicated sentence structure in the additions.

You will notice that some of the vocabulary words used in the elementary-school story are found, too, in the middle- and high-school stories. A fourth grader can have just as much fun rolling a twenty-dollar word around on his tongue as a seventh grader or an eleventh grader. The only difference is that older students can use the word in their writing as well.

All of the skills referred to at the left of each Caught'ya sentence are listed, annotated, and explained with examples in the Appendix. This supplement will be helpful to those of you who did not major in English in college and may not be aware of all of the technical reasons why things are written as they are. Many of these explanations are for you and not for your students. You do not have to teach all of these things. In fact, at this level, you probably want to include only about half of them.

Since you explain the "why" of all the corrections when you go over the Caught'ya, you don't want to go beyond what your students can learn at this level. For example, for grades two through seven you probably do not want to teach about subordinate clauses, and yet there are subordinate clauses in the sentences. If the clause comes at the beginning of the sentence, you can explain the comma without using the term "subordinate clause." Keep your explanations understandable. I would not ask elementary-age children to supply hyphens, semicolons, or colons, but when they appear, you can discuss them if you wish.

You also need to keep in mind that the end result is not to learn the terms but to write correctly. If a third grader can write a clear paragraph of simple sentences with very few errors, you have accomplished a lot! At this point, it isn't how complex the writing is that counts, it's how well it is written. Indeed, authors like Hemingway illustrate that simple writing works just fine and can be quite beautiful.

Those of you who are home-schooling or tutoring only a few children can still use this story even though it revolves around a class of thirty-two youngsters. You can change the sentences so that the teacher (Mrs. Obnoxious) does all these things to only one or two children. All the conversations among the children can be reduced to conversations between two children. Instead of featuring a classroom, you can describe the room in which you and your children work. By changing a few words here and there, you should be able to modify the story.

Use these sentences to forge a partnership with your students, a partnership that will result in improved writing, increased vocabulary, and lots of shared laughs. A summary of this story can be found in Chapter 6.

100 Caught'ya Sentences: The Meanest Teacher in the World	**B** – Sentence for the board. **C** – Corrected version of the sentence.
1. bizarre Paragraph (beginning of story) Ordinal numbers Comma (between city, state) Proper nouns (Capitalize names of schools, cities, states.)	B - the first day of school a bizarre new teacher appeared in the _____ grade at _____ (your school or address here) in _____ (your city and state) C - The first day of school a bizarre new teacher appeared in the _____ grade at _____ in _____ , _____ .
2. chartreuse No paragraph (continuing description) Comma (compound sentence)	B - she was dressed all in chartreuse from her hair ribbon to her pointed shoes and she was very ugly C - She was dressed all in chartreuse from her hair ribbon to her pointed shoes, and she was very ugly.
3. plain (as in "not pretty") No paragraph (continuing description) Apostrophes (2 singular possessives) Strong verbs (stuck, pointed) Comma (compound sentence) Simile (like a witch's chin)	B - this bizarre teachers nose stuck way out on her plain face and her chin pointed at the floor like a witchs chin C - This bizarre teacher's nose stuck way out on her plain face, and her chin pointed at the floor like a witch's chin.
4. limply, hunched No paragraph (continuing description) Strong verb (hung) Comma (compound sentence)	B - her white hair hung limply down to her hunched shoulders and it looked greasy C - Her white hair hung limply down to her hunched shoulders, and it looked greasy.

100 Caught'ya Sentences: The Meanest Teacher in the World	**B** – Sentence for the board. **C** – Corrected version of the sentence.
5. spindly No paragraph (continuing description) Apostrophe (singular possessive) Simile (like a live stick)	B - the teachers spindly arms and legs were so skinny that she looked like a live walking stick with her long nose as the handle C - The teacher's spindly arms and legs were so skinny that she looked like a live walking stick with her long nose as the handle.
6. beheld No paragraph (still describing) Commas (interrupter) Comparative adjectives (ugly/uglier/ugliest)	B - she was in fact the ugliest teacher the students had ever beheld C - She was, in fact, the ugliest teacher the students had ever beheld.
7. homely, repulsive, obnoxious No paragraph (still about description) Comma (2 adjectives before a noun) Apostrophe (singular possessive) Abbreviation (Mrs.)	B - this homely repulsive teachers name was mrs obnoxious C - This homely, repulsive teacher's name was Mrs. Obnoxious. **NOTE:** *At this point, if you are doing four or five Caught'yas a week, you can add another paragraph of description. Let your students help you come up with a vivid picture of this horrible teacher. Since we have been working on singular possessives, you might want to make sure to include these in your sentences.*

100 Caught'ya Sentences: The Meanest Teacher in the World	B – Sentence for the board. C – Corrected version of the sentence.
8. utter Paragraph (talking about class now) Ordinal numbers (Write them out.) Proper nouns (school name and city, state,) Commas (subordinate clause at beginning; city, state,)	B - when the _____ grade class at _____ (your school name) in _____ , _____ (your city and state) took a look at this teacher, they all groaned in utter despair C - When the _____ grade class at _____ in _____ , _____ , took a look at this teacher, they all groaned in utter despair.
9. visage Paragraph (person speaking) Quotation marks (quote) Comma (2 adjectives) Question Confused spellings (quiet/quit/quite)	B - how are we going to look at that ugly disgusting visage all year without throwing up? asked _____ (use a male student's name) in a quiet voice C - "How are we going to look at that ugly, disgusting visage all year without throwing up?" asked _____ in a quiet voice.
10. remorseless Paragraph (new person speaking) Quotation marks (quote) Comma (interjection, quote, too) Apostrophes (2 contractions) Homophones (to/too/two)	B - well ill bet shes mean too _____ whispered back (name of another male student). she looks remorseless. C - "Well, I'll bet she's mean, too," _____ whispered back. "She looks remorseless."
11. rasping Paragraph (new person speaking) Abbreviation (Mrs.) Commas (appositive, direct address, quote) Homophones (two/to/too) No compound sentence (no subject, compound predicate) Quotation marks (quote) Exclamation marks (discuss use of)	B - mrs obnoxious the new teacher stared at the two boys with an evil look and said in a rasping voice shut up you nasty boys! C - Mrs. Obnoxious, the new teacher, stared at the two boys with an evil look and said in a rasping voice, "Shut up, you nasty boys!"

100 Caught'ya Sentences: The Meanest Teacher in the World	**B** – Sentence for the board. **C** – Corrected version of the sentence.
12. boorish No paragraph (same speaker) Quotation marks (quote) Commas (quote, too) Homophones (you're/your and to/too/two)	B - she continued maliciously your horrible and boorish too C - She continued maliciously, "You're horrible and boorish, too."
13. alacrity Paragraph (something new happening) Conjunction (Do not begin a sentence with one.) Comma (compound sentence) Strong verb (rang)	B - and the bell rang and the students left the classroom with alacrity C - The bell rang, and the students left the classroom with alacrity.
14. hapless Paragraph (new speaker) Quotation marks (quote) Placement of question mark within quotation marks Comma (appositive)	B - what are we going to do? asked _____ (use name of a female student) a girl in the hapless class C - "What are we going to do?" asked _____ , a girl in the hapless class.
15. proffered Paragraph (new speaker) Quotation marks (quote) Homophone (we're/were) Comma (appositive, quote) Strong verb (proffered)	B - were going to change her proffered _____ (use name of a female student) another girl C - "We're going to change her," proffered _____ , another girl.

100 Caught'ya Sentences: The Meanest Teacher in the World	B – Sentence for the board. C – Corrected version of the sentence.
16. queried Paragraph (new speaker) Quotation marks (quote) Placement of question mark within quote	B - how queried everyone C - "How?" queried everyone.
17. bide time Paragraph (new speaker) Punctuation after "wait" (Discuss possibilities—comma or exclamation.) Quotation marks (quote) Contraction (let's) Article ("a" before consonant; "an" before vowel) Comparison (good/better/best)	B - wait! suggested _____. (insert a male student's name) lets bide our time for a few days. maybe things will get better C - "Wait!" suggested _____. "Let's bide our time for a few days. Maybe things will get better."
18. apprehensively Paragraph (time lapse) Comma (introductory adverb phrase, verb series) Verb tense shift (story in past tense) Homophones (their/there/they're)	B - the next day all the students arrived in class early took their seats and wait apprehensively for their teacher to arrive C - The next day, all the students arrived in class early, took their seats, and waited apprehensively for their teacher to arrive. **NOTE:** *After this point I may misspell the common homophones in the sentence on the board so that the children will have to think about them. I shall not be consistent. You already have discussed their/there/they're, to/too/two, quit/quite/quiet, your/you're, and were/we're. From now on, whenever you include one of these words in a Caught'ya, remind your students to examine it closely because it could be misspelled.*

100 Caught'ya Sentences: The Meanest Teacher in the World	**B** – Sentence for the board. **C** – Corrected version of the sentence.
19. malevolently No paragraph (same topic) Comma (subordinate clause at beginning) Cardinal numbers (Write them out.)	B - when the teacher arrived in the classroom she glared malevolently at her _____ (put number in the class here in digits) students C - When the teacher arrived in the classroom, she glared malevolently at her _____ (put the number of students in your class here in words) students.
20. singled No paragraph (same topic) Comma (predicate series) Agreement between subject and pronoun (each one or him/her)	B - she singled out each student called him or her by name and said something rude to them C - She singled out each student, called him or her by name, and said something rude to each one. **NOTE:** *In the following blanks (I have thirty-two of them for you) fill in the names of all of your students so that each one is mentioned at least once. Parents who teach only one or two children can use the names of their children over and over with appropriate insults that will induce giggles. Change these sentences to fit your individual circumstances.*
21. mannerly Paragraph (new speaker) Quotation marks (quote) Commas (noun series, direct address, quote) Simile (like mannerly children)	B - _____ _____ _____ sit up straight like mannerly children she said C - "_____ , _____ , _____ , sit up straight like mannerly children," she said.

100 Caught'ya Sentences: The Meanest Teacher in the World	**B** – Sentence for the board. **C** – Corrected version of the sentence.
22. agape No paragraph (same speaker, same subject) Quotation marks (quote) Cardinal numbers (Write out.) Homophones (there/their/they're, your/you're) Commas (direct address) Apostrophe (contraction) No apostrophe (none in "mothers" since it is plural, not possessive) Placement of question mark inside quote	B- you 2 over their by the window _____ and _____ didn't your mother's ever tell you not to let your mouths hang agape? she continued C - "You two over there by the window, _____ and _____ , didn't your mothers ever tell you not to let your mouths hang agape?" she continued.
23. rail No paragraph (same speaker, same subject) Commas (2 adjectives, noun series, direct address) Punctuation (quote) Homophone (your/you're) Placement of question mark in quote	B - the nasty ugly teacher continued to rail at the class. _____ _____ and _____ did you comb your hair today C - The nasty, ugly teacher continued to rail at the class. "_____ , _____ , and _____ , did you comb your hair today?"
24. remonstrated No paragraph (same speaker, same subject) Quotation marks (quote) Capitalization of the word "I" Numbers (Write them out.) Homophones (there/their/they're) Apostrophe (contraction) Commas (compound sentence, quote)	B - i see 3 boys over there who dont look ready to work she remonstrated. i bet they never do there homework and there names are _____ _____ and _____ C - "I see three boys over there who don't look ready to work," she remonstrated. "I bet they never do their homework, and their names are _____ , _____ , and _____ .

100 Caught'ya Sentences: The Meanest Teacher in the World	**B** – Sentence for the board. **C** – Corrected version of the sentence.
25. vermillion Paragraph (She changed place.) Abbreviation (Mrs.) Run-on (4 sentences) Commas (appositive, direct address) Hyphen (Discuss if you teach fifth or sixth grade.) Article ("a" before consonant; "an" before vowel)	B - mrs obnoxious the obnoxious teacher sat down at her desk and her eyes dared anyone to move and she pointed her vermillion-painted fingernail at an timid girl _____ and she frowned evilly C - Mrs. Obnoxious, the obnoxious teacher, sat down at her desk. Her eyes dared anyone to move. She pointed her vermillion-painted fingernail at a timid girl, _____ . She frowned evilly. NOTE: *There are other ways to write this run-on sentence correctly. You do not have to stick to simple sentences.*
26. inanely No paragraph (she's addressing the girl referred to) Quotation marks (quote) No commas (Use "and" instead of commas in the series.) Comma (quote)	B - you and _____ and _____ and _____ were giggling inanely in the hall this morning she said meanly C - "You and _____ and _____ and _____ were giggling inanely in the hall this morning," she said meanly.
27. blurted Paragraph (new speaker) Quotation marks (quote) Apostrophe (contraction) Question mark inside quote	B - whats wrong with that blurted out _____ and _____ together C - "What's wrong with that?" blurted out _____ and _____ together.

100 Caught'ya Sentences: The Meanest Teacher in the World	**B** – Sentence for the board. **C** – Corrected version of the sentence.
28. screeched Paragraph (new speaker) Quotation marks (quote) Numbers (Write them out.) Homophones (your/you're and to/two/too) Commas (appositive, noun series) Exclamation mark within quote Comparatives (good/better/best) Hyphen (big-mouthed friends)	B - you 2 and your 3 big-mouthed friends _____ _____ and _____ need to learn better manners! the teacher screeched C - "You two and your three big-mouthed friends, _____ , _____ , and _____ , need to learn better manners!" the teacher screeched.
29. cringed Paragraph (new description) Conjunction (Do not begin a sentence with one.) Numbers (Write them out.) Comma (participial phrase)	B - and the 5 students cringed in their seats trying to be invisible C - The five students cringed in their seats, trying to be invisible.
30. beleaguered Paragraph (new action) Comma (2 adjectives)	B - the teacher continued to attack every member of the poor beleaguered class C - The teacher continued to attack every member of the poor, beleaguered class.
31. gossiped No paragraph (same topic) Strong verb (told) Commas (noun series) Indirect quote Homophone (too/two/to)	B - she told _____ _____ _____ and _____ that they gossiped to much C - She told _____ , _____ , _____ , and _____ that they gossiped too much.

100 Caught'ya Sentences: The Meanest Teacher in the World	**B** – Sentence for the board. **C** – Corrected version of the sentence.
32. bellowed No paragraph (same topic) Strong verb (bellowed) Commas (noun series) Plural of lady (spelling rule) No comma before "and" (not a compound sentence—it is a compound predicate) Homophones (wear/ware, to/two/too) Indirect quote	B - she bellowed at _____ _____ _____ and _____ to inform them that they were young ladys and should wear skirts and not shorts to school C - She bellowed at _____ , _____ , _____ , and _____ to inform them that they were young ladies and should wear skirts and not shorts to school.
33. ruthless No paragraph (same topic) Strong verb (growled) Commas (noun series, quote) Verb tense shift (story in past tense) Quotation marks (quote)	B - then this ruthless teacher growls at _____ _____ _____ and _____ go to the board C - Then this ruthless teacher growled at _____ , _____ , _____ , and _____ , "Go to the board."
34. shuffled No paragraph (same topic) Apostrophe (contraction) Comma (subordinate clause) Homophone (their/there/they're)	B - when they didnt move fast enough for her and shuffled there feet as well she yelled even more C - When they didn't move fast enough for her and shuffled their feet as well, she yelled even more.

100 Caught'ya Sentences: The Meanest Teacher in the World	B – Sentence for the board. C – Corrected version of the sentence.
35. gripe, miserable Paragraph (now talking about day, topic change) Run-on (4 sentences) Apostrophe (contraction) Strong verbs (continued, shrieked, cringed, could not wait) Homophone (their/there/they're, to/two/too)	B - the day continued to be miserable and the teacher shrieked and the kids cringed and they couldnt wait to get home to gripe to their parents C -　　The day continued to be miserable. The teacher shrieked. The kids cringed. They couldn't wait to get home to gripe to their parents. **NOTE:** *There are other ways to correct this run-on sentence. You do not have to stick to simple sentences.*
36. sympathetic Paragraph (topic change) Apostrophe (plural possessive of plural not ending in "s") Commas (interrupter) Negatives	B - none of the childrens parents however were sympathetic. C -　　None of the children's parents, however, were sympathetic.
37. reputation No paragraph (same topic) Homophone (their/there/they're) No comma before "and" (not a compound sentence—it is a compound direct object) Indirect quote Spelling (a lot) Parallel construction (Sixth grade teachers can discuss "that/that.")	B - they told their children that this teacher had a good reputation and that they would learn alot C - They told their children that this teacher had a good reputation and that they would learn a lot.

100 Caught'ya Sentences: The Meanest Teacher in the World	**B** – Sentence for the board. **C** – Corrected version of the sentence.
38. desperate Paragraph (topic change) Irregular plurals (You can discuss irregular plurals like "children.")	B - the children became desperate C - The children became desperate.
39. rank, dingy No paragraph (idea continues) Commas (2 introductory adverb phrases, 2 adjectives) Article ("a" before consonant; "an" before vowel)	B - one day after school they held a secret meeting in the rank dingy basement of the school C - One day after school, they held a secret meeting in the rank, dingy basement of the school.
40. solution No paragraph (same topic) No comma (not a compound sentence—it is a compound predicate) Use of negatives Article ("a" before consonant; "an" before vowel)	B - they discussed the problem for a long time but did not find an solution C - They discussed the problem for a long time but did not find a solution. NOTE: *From now on, articles will not be pointed out. If your students still have difficulty distinguishing between "a" and "an," have a discussion every time one of them appears in a Caught'ya.*
41. shrewd No paragraph (same topic) Commas (introductory adverb, appositive) Indirect quote	B - finally _____ a very shrewd student suggested that the class become as mean as the teacher C - Finally, _____ , a very shrewd student, suggested that the class become as mean as the teacher.

100 Caught'ya Sentences: The Meanest Teacher in the World	**B** – Sentence for the board. **C** – Corrected version of the sentence.
42. vindictive Paragraph (new speaker) Quotation marks (2 quotes, same speaker) Commas (interjection, appositive, quote)	B - well maybe that will change her said _____ not normally a vindictive person. we can get even C - "Well, maybe that will change her," said _____ , not normally a vindictive person. "We can get even."
43. sneers Paragraph (new speaker) Quotation marks (2 quotes, same person) Abbreviation (O.K. or Okay) Comma (interjection, quote) Apostrophe (contraction) Homophone (their/there/they're)	B - ok lets try it agreed the rest of the class with sneers on they're faces. lets give the old bat a taste of her own medicine C - "Okay, let's try it," agreed the rest of the class with sneers on their faces. "Let's give the old bat a taste of her own medicine."
44. eagerly Paragraph (new day) Strong verb (arrived) Optional comma (to make sense) Homophone (their/there/they're) Use of adverbs (Fourth, fifth, and sixth grade teachers may want to introduce adverbs since there are two in this sentence: "the next day" and "eagerly.")	B - the next day the children eagerly arrived at school ready to try out their plan C - The next day the children eagerly arrived at school (,) ready to try out their plan.
45. strutted No paragraph (same topic) Abbreviation (Mrs.) Strong verb (began)	B - _____ (put a male student's name here) began the day by speaking out the minute mrs obnoxious strutted in the door C - _____ began the day by speaking out the minute Mrs. Obnoxious strutted in the door.

100 Caught'ya Sentences: The Meanest Teacher in the World	**B** – Sentence for the board. **C** – Corrected version of the sentence.
46. subdued, chartreuse Paragraph (new speaker) Quotation marks (2 quotes, same person) Homophone (you're/your, it/it's) Capitalization of "I" Apostrophe (contraction) Commas (compound sentence, quote)	B - i see your wearing chartreuse again today he said bravely. i think its not subdued enough for a teacher and it distracts us from our work C - "I see you're wearing chartreuse again today," he said bravely. "I think it's not subdued enough for a teacher, and it distracts us from our work."
47. glared, offending Paragraph (about different person) No comma (not a compound sentence — it's a compound predicate) Participle (Fifth and sixth grades can talk about a verb that acts as an adjective: "offending.")	B - the teacher glared at the offending student and sent him to stand in a corner for the rest of the morning C - The teacher glared at the offending student and sent him to stand in a corner for the rest of the morning.
48. hovered Paragraph (time change) Book title (underline and capitalize) Comma (introductory adverb, subordinate clause at beginning) No comma in appositive since the title is necessary as there are many language books (restrictive modifier) Strong verb (hovered) Apostrophe (contraction)	B - then after the language arts book Boring language had been passed out the teacher hovered over her students to make sure that they didnt cheat C - Then, after the language arts book *Boring Language* had been passed out, the teacher hovered over her students to make sure that they didn't cheat.

100 Caught'ya Sentences: The Meanest Teacher in the World	**B** – Sentence for the board. **C** – Corrected version of the sentence.
49. tremor Paragraph (new speaker) Verb tense shift (story in past tense) Strong verb (spoke) Quotation marks (quote) Apostrophe (contraction) Homophone (they're/their/there) No comma (subordinate clause at end)	B - _____ speaks up with a tremor in her voice. it isnt polite to hang over people when there working C - _____ spoke up with a tremor in her voice. "It isn't polite to hang over people when they're working."
50. blasted Paragraph (about new person) Strong verb (blasted) No comma (not a compound sentence—it's a compound predicate) Apostrophe (singular possessive) Homophone (principal/principle)	B - the teacher blasted _____ with her tongue and sent her to the principals office C - The teacher blasted _____ with her tongue and sent her to the principal's office.
51. chastened No paragraph (debatable—you could argue a time change) Strong verbs (continued, spoke, chastened) Verb tense shift (story in past tense) Use of dashes Comma (compound sentence)	B. the rest of the day continues about the same—students spoke up to complain and the teacher chastened them C - The rest of the day continued about the same—students spoke up to complain, and the teacher chastened them.

100 Caught'ya Sentences: The Meanest Teacher in the World	**B** – Sentence for the board. **C** – Corrected version of the sentence.
52. pupil No paragraph (same topic) Strong verbs (called, sent, filled) Commas (introductory adverb phrase, verb series) Numbers (Write them out.) Apostrophe (singular possessive)	B - all in all she called 20 parents that day sent 5 kids to the principals office and filled every corner of her room with a pupil C - All in all, she called twenty parents that day, sent five kids to the principal's office, and filled every corner of her room with a pupil.
53. onslaught Paragraph (now about students, new topic) Comma (2 adjectives) No comma (subordinate clause at end and no compound sentence—it's a compound predicate) Homophone (their/there/they're) Parallel construction (were/were) Inversion to avoid splitting verb	B - the desperate brave students continued they're onslaught for a few more days until all of them were not only miserable at school but were grounded at home C - The desperate, brave students continued their onslaught for a few more days until all of them not only were miserable at school but were grounded at home.
54. strategy No paragraph (debatable—you could argue a place change) Strong verb (met) Two prepositional phrases (in the basement, of the school) Use of infinitive (to try)	B - they met again in the rank basement of the school to try a new strategy C - They met again in the rank basement of the school to try a new strategy.
55. capable, effect No paragraph (same topic) Commas (appositive) Difference between "affect" and "effect" Abbreviation (Mrs.)	B - this time _____ another capable student came up with a brilliant idea that might effect a change in mrs obnoxious C - This time _____ , another capable student, came up with a brilliant idea that might effect a change in Mrs. Obnoxious.

100 Caught'ya Sentences: The Meanest Teacher in the World	**B** – Sentence for the board. **C** – Corrected version of the sentence.
56. in kind Paragraph (new speaker) Quotation marks (2 quotes, same speaker) Apostrophes (3 contractions) Abbreviation (Mrs.) Comma (quote)	B - lets kill mrs obnoxious with kindness she suggested. maybe shell respond in kind C - "Let's kill Mrs. Obnoxious with kindness," she suggested. "Maybe she'll respond in kind."
57. fiendish Paragraph (new speaker) Quotation marks (continued quote) Comma (interjection - "naaaaaah," quote) No comma with "because" (subordinate clause at end of sentence) Apostrophes (2 contractions)	B - naaaaaah said everybody at once, shell just be fiendish right back in our faces because shes just mean C - "Naaaaaah," said everybody at once, "she'll be fiendish right back in our faces because she's just mean."
58. unmerciful Paragraph (new speaker) Quotation marks (2 quotes, same speaker) Commas ("no" at beginning of sentence, subordinate clause at beginning) Apostrophe (contraction) Capitalization of the word "I" Agreement of subject and pronoun (one "unmerciful person" so you can't use "they," which refers to more than one person)	B - no she wont argued _____ . i read somewhere that if you are always kind to an unmerciful person like our teacher they might change NOTE: *Those of you who teach younger grades should write—* "*. . . teacher, that person might change.*" C - "No, she won't," argued _____ . "I read somewhere that if you are always kind to an unmerciful person like our teacher, that person might change."

100 Caught'ya Sentences: The Meanest Teacher in the World	**B** – Sentence for the board. **C** – Corrected version of the sentence.
59. attempt Paragraph (new speaker) Quotation marks (2 quotes) Homophone (it/it's) Apostrophe (contraction) Comparatives (good/better/best) Difference between the words "further" and "farther" Placement of question mark within quote	B - its worth an attempt said _____. does anyone have a better solution before we go any further C - "It's worth an attempt," said _____ . "Does anyone have a better solution before we go any further?"
60. hag Paragraph (new person speaks) Quotation marks (quote) Comma ("no" at beginning) Apostrophe (contraction) Use of "well" (adverb) and "good" (adjective)	B - no our other solution only made the old hag meaner. it didnt work so good put in _____ C - "No, our other solution only made the old hag meaner. It didn't work so well," put in _____ .
61. except Paragraph (new speaker) Quotation marks (quote) Apostrophe (contraction) Difference between "except" and "accept" Use of negatives Commas (to make sense—optional, quote)	B - it didnt work except that we all got to say something nasty back to her added _____ C - "It didn't work (,) except that we all got to say something nasty back to her," added _____ .

100 Caught'ya Sentences: The Meanest Teacher in the World	**B** – Sentence for the board. **C** – Corrected version of the sentence.
62. malevolent, backfired Paragraph (new speaker) Quotation marks (quote) Apostrophe (contraction) Commas ("yes" at the beginning, quote) No comma before "since" (subordinate clause at end) Abbreviation (Mrs.) Comparatives (nasty/nastier/ nastiest and malevolent/more malevolent/most malevolent)	B - yes id say it backfired since mrs obnoxious is nastier and more malevolent than ever said _____ C - "Yes, I'd say it backfired since Mrs. Obnoxious is nastier and more malevolent than ever," said _____ .
63. dislodge Paragraph (new speaker) Quotation marks (quote, noun used as adjective) Comma (appositive) Difference between "who" and "whom"	B - we have to dislodge from our minds all mean thoughts about her said _____ the pupil who had come up with the "kindness" idea C - "We have to dislodge from our minds all mean thoughts about her," said _____ , the pupil who had come up with the "kindness" idea.
64. amiable Paragraph (different topic) Verb tense shift (story in past tense) Comma (participial phrase) Abbreviation (Mrs.) Comparisons (amiable/more amiable/most amiable)	B - the students go home trying to think only the most amiable thoughts about mrs obnoxious C - The students went home, trying to think only the most amiable thoughts about Mrs. Obnoxious.

100 Caught'ya Sentences: The Meanest Teacher in the World	**B** – Sentence for the board. **C** – Corrected version of the sentence.
65. misguided No paragraph (same topic) Homophone (their/there/they're) Comma (2 adjectives)	B - they dreamed about all the nice things they would try on their poor misguided teacher C - They dreamed about all the nice things they would try on their poor, misguided teacher.
66. banished No paragraph (same topic) Strong verb (banished) Two prepositional phrases (about her, from their minds) Homophone (their/there/they're)	B - they banished all nasty thoughts about her from their minds C - They banished all nasty thoughts about her from their minds.
67. gorgeous Paragraph (time change) Strong verbs (arrived, carried) Homophone (their/there/they're) Sentence combining (When you put this on the board, tell kids to make into one sentence.)	B - the next day all the students arrived at school with smiles on there faces. they also carried gorgeous flowers in there hands C - The next day all the students arrived at school with smiles on their faces and gorgeous flowers in their hands.
68. propped No paragraph (same topic) Commas (subordinate clause at beginning, predicate series, appositive—they only have one language book) Difference between "sit" and "set" Apostrophe (singular possessive) Abbreviation (Mrs.) Strong verbs (put, sat, propped, and began) Title of book (underline and capitalize)	B - before the bell rang they put the flowers in a vase on mrs obnoxious desk sat in their seats propped up their language books Boring language and began to work C - Before the bell rang, they put the flowers in a vase on Mrs. Obnoxious's desk, sat in their seats, propped up their language books, *Boring Language*, and began to work.

100 Caught'ya Sentences: The Meanest Teacher in the World	**B** – Sentence for the board. **C** – Corrected version of the sentence.
69. chorused Paragraph (new speaker) Quotation marks (quote) Commas (direct address, quote) Abbreviation (Mrs.) Strong verb (chorused) No comma (subordinate clause at end)	B - good morning mrs obnoxious they chorused as the teacher came into the room C - "Good morning, Mrs. Obnoxious," they chorused as the teacher came into the room.
70. gruffly Paragraph (new topic) Abbreviation (Mrs.) Commas (subordinate clause, appositive) Collective noun/verb agreement (everyone was) Verb tense shift (story in past tense)	B - when mrs obnoxious gruffly asked for homework everyone even _____ and _____ is prepared C - When Mrs. Obnoxious gruffly asked for homework, everyone, even _____ and _____ , was prepared.
71. noxious No paragraph (debatable—you could argue a time change) Abbreviation (Mrs.) Comma (compound sentence) Plurals (Discuss plurals with words that end in "o.")	B - the rest of the day mrs obnoxious was her usual noxious self but the students acted as if they wore halos C - The rest of the day Mrs. Obnoxious was her usual noxious self, but the students acted as if they wore halos.
72. trilling No paragraph (same topic) Quotation marks (something referred to—Note comma inside quote mark.) Comma (compound sentence) Confused spelling (quiet/quit/quite) Capitalization of "M" in "Ma'am" (title given to person)	B - they called her "Ma'am" and they were so quiet that they could hear the birds trilling outside C - They called her "Ma'am," and they were so quiet that they could hear the birds trilling outside.

100 Caught'ya Sentences: The Meanest Teacher in the World	**B** – Sentence for the board. **C** – Corrected version of the sentence.
73. yawped No paragraph (same topic) Abbreviation (Mrs.) Comma (subordinate clause at beginning) Strong verbs (smiled, thanked)	B - whenever mrs obnoxious yawped at someone that person smiled very sweetly and thanked her for her comment C -Whenever Mrs. Obnoxious yawped at someone, that person smiled very sweetly and thanked her for her comment.
74. delectable Paragraph (time passed) Abbreviation (Mrs.) No comma (not a compound sentence—compound predicate within a subordinate clause)	B - at lunch _____ and _____ gave mrs obnoxious a pretty lunch bag that was decorated with flowers and filled with delectable goodies C - At lunch _____ and _____ gave Mrs. Obnoxious a pretty lunch bag that was decorated with flowers and filled with delectable goodies.
75. suspiciously No paragraph (same topic) Abbreviation (Mrs.) Comma (compound sentence)	B - mrs obnoxious took the lunch suspiciously but she did eat it C - Mrs. Obnoxious took the lunch suspiciously, but she did eat it.
76. anxious Paragraph (time lapse) Use of "who" (subject) and "whom" (object) Optional commas (adjective clause with who—commas determine meaning: commas = all students; no commas = only some students) Abbreviation (Mrs.) Apostrophe (plural possessive)	B - the students who were anxious to see if their teacher had liked the lunch waited for mrs obnoxious outside the teachers lunchroom C - The students (,) who were anxious to see if their teacher had liked the lunch (,) waited for Mrs. Obnoxious outside the teachers' lunchroom.

100 Caught'ya Sentences: The Meanest Teacher in the World	**B** – Sentence for the board. **C** – Corrected version of the sentence.
77. solemnly, escorted No paragraph (same topic) Strong verb (escorted) Optional comma (After lunch,—introductory adverb phrase) Homophone (their/there/they're)	B - after lunch they solemnly and silently escorted their teacher back to the classroom C - After lunch (,) they solemnly and silently escorted their teacher back to the classroom.
78. buss Paragraph (time lapse) Comma (subordinate clause at beginning followed by adverb phrase) Abbreviation (Mrs.) Hyphen (tip-toe)	B - when the bell rang at the end of the day each of the children stayed to tip-toe up and give mrs obnoxious a buss on her cheek C -　　When the bell rang at the end of the day, each of the children stayed to tip-toe up and give Mrs. Obnoxious a buss on her cheek.
79. devious Paragraph (change to general—topic change) Numbers (Write them out.) Homophone (whole/hole)	B - the devious children kept all this up for 3 whole weeks C -　　The devious children kept all this up for three whole weeks.
80. clasp No paragraph (same topic for topic sentence above) Comma (introductory adverb phrase of time—debatable comma)	B - after one week the teacher let _____ and _____ clasp her hands on the way back from lunch C - After one week, the teacher let _____ and _____ clasp her hands on the way back from lunch.

100 Caught'ya Sentences: The Meanest Teacher in the World	**B** – Sentence for the board. **C** – Corrected version of the sentence.
81. actually No paragraph (same topic) Abbreviation (Mrs.) Optional comma (introductory adverb of time) Homophone (their/there/they're)	B - next mrs obnoxious actually thanked the children for they're daily flowers C - Next (,) Mrs. Obnoxious actually thanked the children for their daily flowers.
82. cracked No paragraph (same topic) Comma (long introductory adverb phrases about time) Strong verb (cracked) Use of dash	B - by the end of the second week she cracked a smile—just for a second C - By the end of the second week, she cracked a smile—just for a second.
83. beatific No paragraph (same topic) Collective noun (all) Strong verb (gave)	B - all the students gave her a beatific smile C - All the students gave her a beatific smile.
84. good-humored Paragraph (new day) Abbreviation Mrs.) Hyphen (good-humored) Comma (subordinate clause at beginning) Subject/pronoun agreement (each - he or she—With younger kids, write correctly.) Optional comma after "day" (introductory adverb phrase in subordinate clause)	B - one day when mrs obnoxious was ill each student wrote her a good-humored letter telling her how they missed her C - One day (,) when Mrs. Obnoxious was ill, each student wrote her a good-humored letter telling her how he or she missed her.

100 Caught'ya Sentences: The Meanest Teacher in the World	**B** – Sentence for the board. **C** – Corrected version of the sentence.

NOTE: *At this point, since there are none included in the story, you might want to teach a lesson on the form of a friendly letter (See Appendix for the form.). On the board, you could model a letter from a student in Mrs. Obnoxious's class. Then you could practice writing the letter of another student in her class, with your students telling you what to write. Finally, you could instruct your students to write a letter to Mrs. Obnoxious on their own.)*

85. blithely Paragraph (new idea)	B - the children blithely planned more nice things they could do C - The children blithely planned more nice things they could do.
86. merrily Paragraph (new speaker) Quotation marks (quote) Subject pronoun in correct order No comma (appositive is restrictive and thus necessary— she has many friends) Comma (quote) Spelling of friend (can go over "i" before "e" rules)	B - me and my friend _____ will clean her desk for her said _____ merrily C - "My friend _____ and I will clean her desk for her," said _____ merrily.
87. portal, offered Paragraph (new speaker) Conjunction "and" (Do not begin a sentence with one.) Quotation marks (continued quote) Subject pronoun in correct order Spelling (friend)	B - and me and my freind are going to greet her at the portal of the school tomorrow morning offered _____ and give her a hug C - "My friend and I are going to greet her at the portal of the school tomorrow morning," offered _____ , "and give her a hug." **NOTE:** *The redundancy of "my friend and I" can be avoided by the use of "we." I left it as it is in order to provide practice with the subject/pronoun order.*

100 Caught'ya Sentences: The Meanest Teacher in the World	**B** – Sentence for the board. **C** – Corrected version of the sentence.
88. magnanimously Paragraph (new speaker) Quotation marks (quote) Subject pronoun in correct order Numbers (Write them out.) Difference between "sit" and "set" Spelling (friend)	B - me and my 2 friends will ask her to sit with us at lunch said _____ magnanimously C - "My two friends and I will ask her to sit with us at lunch," said _____ magnanimously.
89. except Paragraph (time change) Difference between "except" and "accept" Run on (2 sentences) Comma ("except that" is used like "but" for a compound sentence)	B - the next day the teacher was better she was the same person except that she looked different C - The next day the teacher was better. She was the same person, except that she looked different.
90. outmoded, radiant No paragraph (same time, same topic) Commas (2 compound sentences, subject/verb series)	B - she still wore outmoded clothes in bizarre colors but her nose seemed not so pointed. her smile was radiant and she hugged the children back when they greeted her C - She still wore outmoded clothes in bizarre colors, but her nose seemed not so pointed. Her smile was radiant, and she hugged the children back when they greeted her.
91. simultaneously Paragraph (new speaker) Quotation marks (quote) Comma (interjection—Discuss possible use of "!" instead. "Wow! We've . . .") Apostrophe (contraction) Exclamation mark	B - wow weve really changed her! thought all the children simultaneously C - "Wow, we've really changed her!" thought all the children simultaneously.

100 Caught'ya Sentences: The Meanest Teacher in the World	**B** – Sentence for the board. **C** – Corrected version of the sentence.
92. certainly No paragraph (same topic) Conjunction "and" (Do not begin a sentence with one.)	B - and they certainly had C - They certainly had.
93. congenial Paragraph (new topic) Comma (introductory prepositional phrase of time—debatable) Abbreviation (Mrs.)	B - from that day on mrs obnoxious was the most congenial teacher in the school C -　　From that day on, Mrs. Obnoxious was the most congenial teacher in the school.
94. mused Paragraph (new speaker) Quotation marks (quote) Subject pronoun in correct order Comparatives (good/better/best)	B - me and my classmates have the best teacher ever mused ＿＿＿ several months later C -　　"My classmates and I have the best teacher ever," mused ＿＿＿ several months later.
95. beamed Paragraph (new topic) Difference between "well" (adverb) and "good" (adjective) Use of semicolon in a compound sentence Spelling (a lot)	B - all the students did good in school that year; they learned alot and beamed a lot at their teacher C　　All the students did well in school that year; they learned a lot and beamed a lot at their teacher.

100 Caught'ya Sentences: The Meanest Teacher in the World	**B** – Sentence for the board. **C** – Corrected version of the sentence.
96. detested No paragraph (same topic) Abbreviation (Mrs.) Use of "who" (subject) and "whom" (object) Commas (appositive)	B - mrs obnoxious the teacher who everyone had detested had become the teacher everyone wanted to hug C - Mrs. Obnoxious, the teacher whom everyone had detested, had become the teacher everyone wanted to hug.
97. droll No paragraph (same topic) Commas (predicate series) Homophone (their/there/they're)	B - she joined her class for lunch every day baked them cookies and made there lessons droll instead of boring C - She joined her class for lunch every day, baked them cookies, and made their lessons droll instead of boring.
98. sniveled Paragraph (time lapse) Commas (long introductory prepositional phrase of time, appositive) Use of semicolon in compound sentence Homophone (their/there/they're)	B - at the end of the year everyone cried and sniveled; they would miss their favorite teacher mrs obnoxious C - At the end of the year, everyone cried and sniveled; they would miss their favorite teacher, Mrs. Obnoxious.
99. caterwauled No paragraph (same topic) Abbreviation (Mrs.) Homophone (too, two, to—Write correctly on board for clarity, but discuss.) Commas (interrupter, compound sentence) Split infinitive (to *all* visit)	B - mrs obnoxious too wept and caterwauled the last day of school and she made the children promise to all visit her over the summer C - Mrs. Obnoxious, too, wept and caterwauled the last day of school, and she made the children all promise to visit her over the summer.

100 Caught'ya Sentences: The Meanest Teacher in the World	**B** – Sentence for the board. **C** – Corrected version of the sentence.
100. wailed, beloved Paragraph (new speaker) Quotation marks (quote) Apostrophe (contraction) Capitalization of the word "I" Comma (quote) No comma before "as" (subordinate clause at end)	B - this is the best class ive ever had she wailed as she waved farewell to her beloved students. C - "This is the best class I've ever had," she wailed as she waved farewell to her beloved students.
P.S. dismay Paragraph (new people) Ordinal numbers (Write them out.) Homophone (their/there/they're) Commas (appositive—This one is debatable; do you need to identify the teacher? There is only one new teacher.)	B - the next august the new group of _____ graders greeted there new teacher mrs obnoxious with dismay. she looked and acted so mean . . . C - The next August the new group of _____ graders greeted their new teacher, Mrs. Obnoxious, with dismay. She looked and acted so mean . . .

CAUGHT'YA TEST   Name _____
Elementary School   Date _____

DIRECTIONS: Look this paper over very carefully. There are many mistakes in it, just as in your Caught'yas. Find and correct all the errors right on this paper. If a word is spelled wrong, cross it out and spell it correctly. All the periods and paragraphs are there for you. Good luck! Just pretend that this is one big Caught'ya.

the meanest teacher in the world

at the end of the year the students in mrs obnoxious class in the city and state of _____   _____ debated what it was that had made there teacher change. the girls thought that it was the hugs the kisses and the smiles. the boys thought that it was the letter they had written to mrs obnoxious when she was ill. they argued and talked alot but they could not agree on anything. they disagreed to much.

well i think that it was the flowers said one girl.

no it was the fact that we asked her to sit with us at lunch. argued one of the boys.

i think your both wrong said another student.

lets ask mrs obnoxious suggested a sweet capable girl.

yes shell know what changed her said a bright handsome boy.

when they all were gathered around mrs obnoxious they asked her what it was that had finally changed her. they are surprised at the answer but they were not disappointed. mrs obnoxious told them that it was their kindness that had changed her. she then kissed them all hugged them tight and told them that she loved them. wow what a wonderful teacher she was!. the students hearts were glad.

CAUGHT'YA TEST KEY
Elementary School

NOTE: *If you wish, you can tell your students how many errors can be found in each line. I don't like to do this, but sometimes it helps students feel more secure. It doesn't really make much difference in the grades. If you have been working on the parts of speech, you might want to ask them to identify the parts of speech in a simple sentence as part of the test.*

The Meanest Teacher in the World

At the end of the year, the students in Mrs. Obnoxious's class in the city and state of _____ , _____ , debated what it was that had made their teacher change. The girls thought that it was the hugs, the kisses, and the smiles. The boys thought that it was the letter they had written to Mrs. Obnoxious when she was ill. They argued and talked a lot, but they could not agree on anything. They disagreed too much.

"Well, I think that it was the flowers," said one girl.

"No, it was the fact that we asked her to sit with us at lunch," argued one of the boys.

"I think you're both wrong," said another student.

"Let's ask Mrs. Obnoxious," suggested a sweet, capable girl.

"Yes, she'll know what changed her," said a bright, handsome boy.

When they all were gathered around Mrs. Obnoxious, they asked her what it was that had finally changed her. They were surprised at the answer, but they were not disappointed. Mrs. Obnoxious told them that it was their kindess that had changed her. She then kissed them all, hugged them tight, and told them that she loved them. Wow, what a wonderful teacher she was! The students' hearts were glad. (Or: Wow! What a wonderful teacher she was.)

Chapter 8

100 Caught'ya Sentences

for Grades 6 – 8

Important Notes

In almost every Caught'ya, students are required to capitalize the first letter of each sentence, capitalize proper nouns, and supply end punctuation. Therefore, these skills are not listed each time to the left of the sentences.

In almost twenty years of teaching middle school, I have observed that children eleven to fourteen love to read about peers who started out unpopular and became one of the "in" crowd. The girls enjoy a love element, and the boys relish a fight or an exciting adventure in which the protagonists barely escape capture. These elements have been included in this story.

One-hundred Caught'ya sentences are given, enough for three a week for an entire year. If you plan to do a Caught'ya more often, you'll need more sentences.

It is relatively easy to add more sentences at certain spots in the story, a few of which have been pointed out. In this way, a teacher or a parent can flesh out the basic story line in order to give students more practice in the skills they need (see the Appendix for an annotated list of these skills). Consult the writing of your students to determine which skills need more repetition for mastery to occur.

Sixth-grade teachers and parents may wish to simplify some of these sentences or retain only a few of the errors in the board sentences. For example, unless you have a really precocious group of sixth graders, they probably can't handle collective nouns, misplaced modifiers, or subordinate clauses. Write that part of the sentence correctly when you initially write it on the board. When you go over the sentence at the board after your students have attempted to write it correctly, point out the possible error(s). This will appeal to a few really bright students who can pick up on it.

Those of you who teach very astute eighth graders or average ninth graders can make the sentences more difficult by adding errors to the board sentence. For example, last year my eighth graders needed much more practice with antecedent/pronoun agreement and correctly placing modifiers. Their writing revealed that they occasionally continued to make inappropriate shifts in the tenses of verbs. To correct this, I simply switched the tense of the verb in the sentence, added a misplaced modifier for them to remove, or added an antecedent/pronoun problem in another clause tacked onto the original sentence.

Toward the end of the year, you might want to begin adding punctuation marks (correct and incorrect!) to the board sentence. This will give students practice in editing *out* errors as well as putting in appropriate punctuation. After all, students put in extraneous punctuation in their writing. They need practice removing it.

Remember that the idea behind these Caught'yas is to provide students with practice in the specific skills that they lack. This should be used as prescriptive grammar and editing. Revise these sentences to fit the needs of your students.

You may notice that some of the vocabulary words are repeated from stories in other levels. As I said in Chapter 7, a fourth grader can have just as much fun rolling a twenty-dollar word around on his tongue as a seventh grader or an eleventh grader. The only difference is that older students can use the word in their writing. A few of the words are repeated in subsequent sentences. This is deliberate. See whether your students recognize them.

All the skills referred to at the left of each Caught'ya sentence are listed, annotated, and explained with examples in the Appendix. That supplement will be helpful to those of you who did not major in English in college and who may not be aware of all of the technical reasons for correct English. Many of these explanations are for you and not for your students. You do not have to teach all of the grammar. In fact, please don't. Teach only as much as you think your students can handle.

Some of the mechanics rules are debatable. I, for example, always put the comma before the "and" in a series. Others do not. Do not spend an anguished moment if you disagree with me. You can almost always find a source that agrees with your position. Even the experts disagree. A well-known author of over fifty popular books wrote to inform me that every word in English can be every part of speech, depending on how it is used. While this is a slight exaggeration (try using "and" as a verb), it is a valid point.

Another debatable point is the use of conjunctions to begin sentences. Technically this is not allowed, but all modern authors begin sentences with "and," "but," and "yet." I tell my students not to do so since they are learners and, therefore, are not yet ready to play around. Since a number of my students begin every sentence with "and" or "but," my goal is to stop this practice. At a later date, if a student becomes a proficient writer, I allow the judicious use of conjunctions to begin a sentence.

Since you explain the "why" of all the corrections when you go over the Caught'ya, you don't want to go beyond what your students can learn. You also need to keep in mind that the end result is not to learn the terms, but to write correctly. Who cares if sometime in the future your students can recognize and label subordinate clauses? Future employers do care, however, that their employees can punctuate them correctly in their writing.

By using the eight parts of speech (terms you do want to teach to your students), you easily can explain all the essential grammar and usage without using the more technical terms. For example, you can explain a participial phrase by identifying it as a phrase that has a verb in it and is used as an adjective. Follow that up with examples to illustrate the use of commas to set off the phrase. Only English teachers need to know how to recognize participial phrases by name. For further suggestions, you might want to read the "Introductory Notes" to the Appendix.

Those of you who are home-schooling or tutoring only a few children can still use this story even though it is set in a public school. Use the story as is, or modify it to center around your child's neighborhood.

The story is generic enough to appeal to a mixed-grade level classroom. Eighth graders really enjoy it, but I can also see it generally appealing to students in any grade from five through nine.

I teach in a bi-modal school, a school with very few students in the middle-ability range. I have used this story with advanced eighth graders, who test and perform way above grade level, as well as with regular eighth graders, the majority of whom read and write slightly below grade level. Both groups of children enjoyed the story and achieved success in finding the errors.

Use these sentences to forge a partnership with your students, a partnership that will result in improved writing, increased vocabulary, and lots of shared laughs. Please note that a summary of this story has been included in Chapter 6.

100 Caught'ya Sentences: Tales of a Four-eyed Weirdo	**B** – Sentence for the board. **C** – Corrected version of the sentence.
1. volition Paragraph (beginning of story) Homophone (there/their/they're) Hyphen (four-eyed) Difference in use of "who" (subject) and "whom" (object) Spelling (Go over "'i' before 'e' except after 'c' and 'neighbor' and 'weigh' are weird" rule.) Spelling (weird) Commas (introductory adverb—optional; city, state,)	B - once there was a four eyed weirdo from baltimore maryland who moved to _____ _____(put your town and state here) against his volition C - Once (,) there was a four-eyed weirdo from Baltimore, Maryland, who moved to _____ , _____ , against his volition.
2. hapless, chubby No paragraph (still describing Harold — same topic) Commas (appositive; noun series to go with preposition; city,state; 2 adjectives where second is not color or size) Hyphen (horn-rimmed) Capitalization (name of school) Spelling rule ("i" before "e" except after "c") Spelling (weird) Homophone (to/too/two)	B - hapless harold weird a chubby kid with horn rimmed glasses fat tummy chocolate brown skin and zits on his cute round face was assigned to _____ (put your school's name here) in _____ _____ (your town and state) C - Hapless Harold Weird, a chubby kid with horn-rimmed glasses, fat tummy, chocolate brown skin, and zits on his cute, round face, was assigned to _____ in _____ , _____ .
3. inept No paragraph (same topic) Commas (2 adjectives, interrupter) Verb tense shift (story in past tense) Numbers (Write them out.)	B - poor hapless harold however is inept at every sport he had tried so far in his 13 years of life C - Poor, hapless Harold, however, was inept at every sport he had tried so far in his thirteen years of life.

100 Caught'ya Sentences: Tales of a Four-eyed Weirdo	**B** – Sentence for the board. **C** – Corrected version of the sentence.
4. pachyderm No paragraph (still describing) Commas (2 adjectives, compound sentence) Quotation marks (something that is not a word) Apostrophes (to form plural of single letters) No comma ("pachyderm meat" is like "jet plane" and treated as one word)	B - unfortunate hapless harold also had to get all A's and B's on every report card or he would be diseased pachyderm meat at home C - Unfortunate, hapless Harold also had to get all "A's" and "B's" on every report card, or he would be diseased pachyderm meat at home.
5. cringed, peers Paragraph (new subject—school) Commas (interjection, long introductory adverb phrase) Ordinal numbers (Write them out.) Spelling (weird) Strong verb (cringed)	B - well the 1st day of school hapless harold wierd cringed at the cool treatment he got from his peers C - Well, the first day of school, hapless Harold Weird cringed at the cool treatment he got from his peers.
6. porky, disdain Paragraph (change of character) Commas (appositive, adjective series) Parallel construction (Discuss it with the adjective series.) Quotation marks (slang use of "cool") Hyphens (four-eyed, non-athletic)	B - conan a really "cool" dude looked at nonathletic porky four eyed harold with disdain as if he were lower than the belly of a rat C - Conan, a really "cool" dude, looked at non-athletic, porky, four-eyed harold with disdain as if he were lower than the belly of a rat.

100 Caught'ya Sentences: Tales of a Four-eyed Weirdo	**B** – Sentence for the board. **C** – Corrected version of the sentence.
7. virility (use manliness to define) No paragraph (same topic—Conan) Commas (appositive) Verb tense shift (story in past tense) Vocabulary review (peers) Quotation marks (something that is not a word) Apostrophe (to form plural of single letter) Period (positioned inside quotation mark)	B - conan an otherwise intelligent dude is so busy impressing his peers with his virility that his grades dropped to F's C - Conan, an otherwise intelligent dude, was so busy impressing his peers with his virility that his grades dropped to "F's."
8. sycophants No paragraph (same topic) Commas (appositive, 2 adjectives) Spelling (a lot) Pronouns (correct use and order—"he and his sycophants") No comma (2 adjectives where second one is color) Run-on (2 sentences) Strong verbs (led, wore)	B - conan the flunking macho dude led alot of the hip dudes at school and him and his sycophants all wore alot of fake gold chains C - Conan, the flunking, macho dude, led a lot of the hip dudes at school. He and his sycophants all wore a lot of fake gold chains. **NOTE:** *There are other correct ways to correct this run-on sentence and others that follow.*
9. pondered Paragraph (new speaker) Commas (2 adjectives, interjection, quote) Quotation marks (quote) Strong verb (pondered) Interjection "wow" (Discuss different punctuation after it - "Wow! Those . . .")	B - poor chainless harold pondered wow those dudes are awesome C - Poor, chainless Harold pondered, "Wow, those dudes are awesome!" (OR: "Wow! Those dudes are awesome."

100 Caught'ya Sentences: Tales of a Four-eyed Weirdo	B – Sentence for the board. C – Corrected version of the sentence.
10. appalling No paragraph (same topic) Apostrophes (contraction, singular and plural possessives) Homophone (know/no) Spelling (friends)	B - harold didnt know about conans and his freinds appalling grades C - Harold didn't know about Conan's and his friends' appalling grades. **NOTE:** *If you have students who persist in throwing extraneous capital letters into their writing, you might want to do the same with the Caught'ya sentences in order to discuss again and again why they should be eliminated. Just add them as you wish.*
11. audacious, exterior No paragraph (same topic) Overuse of pronouns (use of "he" unclear — need noun) Commas (2 adjectives, compound sentence) Coordinating conjunctions (and, or, nor, for, so, but, yet) Apostrophe (singular possessive) Homophone (to/too/two)	B - all he could see was conans cool audacious exterior and he wanted to be like him C - All Harold could see was Conan's cool, audacious exterior, and he wanted to be like him. **NOTE:** *It is a good idea to have your students memorize the conjunctions (coordinating and subordinating) and the prepositions. (See the Mini-Lesson suggestions #4, #5, and #6 in Chapter 4.) Every time you hit a compound sentence, you can go over the conjunctions. When your students are comfortable with these, you might want to start reciting the prepositions on a daily basis. A list of forty or so of the common prepositions is listed in the Appendix. My students and I make up hand motions and a beat to ensure that the daily repetition is fun and memorable.*

100 Caught'ya Sentences: Tales of a Four-eyed Weirdo	**B** – Sentence for the board. **C** – Corrected version of the sentence.
12. clutches Paragraph (new topic) Homophones (there/their/they're, to/too,two) Collective noun (clutches) Apostrophe (contraction, singular possessive) Plural rules (Discuss nouns that form plurals with "es.") Comma (compound sentence) Hyphen (four-eyed) Spelling review (weirdo)	B - there were other clutches of kids in harolds classes but they didnt want to have anything to do with a four eyed wierdo either C - There were other clutches of kids in Harold's classes, but they didn't want to have anything to do with a four-eyed weirdo either. **NOTE:** *From this point on I shall misspell the common homophones about half of the time. The students always will have to think every time they see one. Make sure that you discuss the correct spelling and use of each homophone, even if you spell it correctly in the board sentence.*
13. pulchritudinous No paragraph (same topic) Homophone (there/their/they're) Commas (appositive) Article ("a" before consonant; "an" before vowel) Use of "who" (subject) and "whom" (object) Parallel construction (who—who) No comma (2 adjectives where second is color)	B - their was belinda beautiful a pulchritudinous babe with long blond hair and designer clothes who was queen of the snobs C - There was Belinda Beautiful, a pulchritudinous babe with long blond hair and designer clothes, who was queen of the snobs. **NOTE:** *I always use the "who" form of that relative pronoun in the sentence on the board. This makes the children have to think whether to use "who" or "whom" every time. You might want to point this out to your students. Make them think.*

100 Caught'ya Sentences: Tales of a Four-eyed Weirdo	**B** – Sentence for the board. **C** – Corrected version of the sentence.
14. cohorts, gnarly No paragraph (same topic) Apostrophe (singular possessive) Plural rules (Discuss plurals of words ending in "s" such as "glasses.") Commas (noun series, compound sentence) No comma (2 adjectives where second is color) Parallel construction (Discuss in relation to noun series.) Collective noun (crew) No comma (appositive—Gnarly Nerd—is a restrictive modifier and thus necessary) Strong verbs (took, dismissed)	B - belinda and her cohorts took one look at harolds ugly brown glasses round face and serious expression and the whole crew dismissed him as worse than the kid gnarly nerd C - Belinda and her cohorts took one look at Harold's ugly brown glasses, round face, and serious expression, and the whole crew dismissed him as worse than the kid Gnarly Nerd.
15. jabbed No paragraph (same topic) Pronouns (correct use) Apostrophe (contraction) Quotation marks and capital letter (what is said aloud) Strong verb (jabbed) No comma (not a compound sentence—compound predicate) Commas (around quote)	B - her and her friends jabbed their noses in the air and didnt even say hello to harold C - She and her friends (OR Her friends and she) jabbed their noses in the air and didn't even say, "Hello," to Harold.

100 Caught'ya Sentences: Tales of a Four-eyed Weirdo	**B** – Sentence for the board. **C** – Corrected version of the sentence.
16. perambulating Paragraph (change of subject) Comma (participial phrase—discuss verbs as adjectives and the difference between a phrase and a clause) Misplaced modifier (hands didn't perambulate)	B - perambulating to the only vacant desk harold's hands began to shake C - Perambulating to the only vacant desk, Harold felt his hands begin to shake. **NOTE:** *Other variants are possible as long as the word "Harold" follows soon after the word "desk." Now that you have introduced the difference between a phrase and a clause, you can elicit that difference from your students every time you encounter a phrase or a clause.*
17. corpulent No paragraph (still describing Harold's reaction) Comma (compound sentence) Plural rule (words that add "es" in the plural) Comparatives (big/bigger/biggest) Strong verb (knocked)	B - his corpulent knees knocked together in shock and his eyes grew bigger under his glasses C - His corpulent knees knocked together in shock, and his eyes grew bigger under his glasses.

100 Caught'ya Sentences: Tales of a Four-eyed Weirdo	**B** – Sentence for the board. **C** – Corrected version of the sentence.
18. apparition No paragraph (same topic) Homophone (there/their/they're) Difference between "affect" and "effect" Commas (participial phrase) Title of book (underline and capitalize) Article ("a" before consonant; "an" before vowel) No comma (appositive is restrictive and thus necessary—lots of books) Use of "who" when referring to a person, not "that" Use of "who" (subject) and "whom" (object)	B - sitting there at the desk in front of him reading the book war and peace was a apparition of beauty that affected his ability to move C - Sitting there at the desk in front of him, reading the book _War and Peace_, was an apparition of beauty who affected his ability to move.
19. manifested No paragraph (same topic) Run-on (2 sentences and a series) Commas (adjective series, 2 adjectives, compound sentence) Article ("a" before consonant) Alliteration (lovely lips)	B - she was beautiful and she was classy and she was wonderful and she had long curly black hair and a ghost of a smile manifested itself on her lovely lips C - She was beautiful, classy, and wonderful. She had long, curly black hair, and a ghost of a smile manifested itself on her lovely lips. **NOTE:** _There are other good ways to correct this run-on sentence. Accept any correct answer students give._

100 Caught'ya Sentences: Tales of a Four-eyed Weirdo	B – Sentence for the board. C – Corrected version of the sentence.
20. mesmerized, smitten No paragraph (same topic) Comma (participial phrase in middle) Strong verb (stared) Article ("a" before consonant) Semicolon (compound sentence)	B - harold mesmerized by the sight stared at classy cassandra for a full minute before he sat down; he was smitten. C - Harold, mesmerized by the sight, stared at classy Cassandra for a full minute before he sat down; he was smitten.
21. stunning Paragraph (new speaker) Difference between "effect" and "affect" Comma (subordinate clause, quote) Pronoun (unclear in new paragraph—use noun) Apostrophe (singular possessive, contraction) Quotation marks (quote) Homophone (too/to/two) Strong verb (shouted)	B - as the effects of her stunning beauty wore off harold heard conan shouting at him she thinks shes too good for us NOTE: *Here's a good place to insert a misplaced modifier.* C - As the effects of Cassandra's stunning beauty wore off, Harold heard Conan shouting at him, "She thinks she's too good for us." NOTE: *It is a good idea to familiarize your students with the subordinating conjunctions each time you run across a subordinate clause. The most common ones are listed in the Appendix, and an activity with them is suggested in Mini-Lesson #6 in Chapter 4. If your students become familiar with the conjunctions that always begin a subordinate clause, they will be able to recognize the clauses themselves and learn the proper use of commas with them. (If at beginning—comma; if at end—no comma.)*

100 Caught'ya Sentences: Tales of a Four-eyed Weirdo	**B** – Sentence for the board. **C** – Corrected version of the sentence.
22. obese Paragraph (new speaker) Article ("an" before a vowel) Commas (2 adjectives, quote) Hyphen (pimply-faced) Quotation marks (quote) Apostrophes (contractions) Incorrect double negative (don't . . . no) Homophone (to/too/two) Verb tense shift (story is in past tense)	B - a obese pimply faced kid in the next desk leans over to harold dont pay no attention to conan he whispered. hes not as tough as he looks C - An obese, pimply-faced kid in the next desk leaned over to Harold. "Don't pay any attention to Conan," he whispered. "He's not as tough as he looks."
23. elucidated, gnarled Paragraph (topic change) Commas (appositive, quote) Article ("a" before consonant) Quotation marks (something that is not a word) Quotation marks (quote) Conjunction (Don't begin a sentence with one.) Homophone (too/to/two)	B - gnarly nerd a straight A student continued to inform harold. and classy cassandra is to good a student to be interested in conan he elucidated C - Gnarly Nerd, a straight "A" student, continued to inform Harold. "Classy Cassandra is too good a student to be interested in Conan," he elucidated.
24. comely No paragraph (same topic) Apostrophe (contraction) Run-on (2 sentences) Commas (adjective series, 2 compound sentences) Parallel construction (Discuss in relation to adjective series.) Single quotation marks ("cool" is sarcastic and inside quote) Verb tense shift (story in past tense)	B - shes shy and shes nice and shes comely and she gets good grades and all the cool dudes are after her but she ignores them gnarly concludes C- "She's shy, nice, and comely, and she gets good grades. All the 'cool' dudes are after her, but she ignores them," Gnarly concluded.

100 Caught'ya Sentences: Tales of a Four-eyed Weirdo	**B** – Sentence for the board. **C** – Corrected version of the sentence.
25. sauntered, bizarre, loathsome Paragraph (introduce new character) Commas (subordinate clause, appositive, 2 adjectives) Hyphen (middle-aged) No commas (adjectives of age and color before noun) Article ("a" before consonant; "an" before vowel) Strong verb (sauntered)	B - as gnarly concluded his sentence the teacher a short bizarre middle aged lady dressed in tennis shoes and an loathsome purple dress sauntered in the door C - As Gnarly concluded his sentence, the teacher, a short, bizarre middle-aged lady dressed in tennis shoes and a loathsome purple dress, sauntered in the door. NOTE: *After this point, articles will no longer be pointed out. If your students are still having difficulty distinguishing between "a" and "an," you can have a discussion whenever an article appears in a Caught'ya.*
26. keck (to make gagging sounds) Paragraph (new speaker) Quotation marks (continued quote) Ordinal numbers (Write them out.) Run-on (make 2 sentences) Commas (compound sentence, interrupter, quote) Homophone (you're, your) Abbreviation (Mr., Mrs., Ms.)	B - this may be the 1st day of school she said but you have homework tonight my name in case your interested is mrs keck NOTE: *You can insert your "bad" trait here for the name and make it the vocabulary word. "Keck" is an obscure word.* C - "This may be the first day of school," she said, "but you have homework tonight. My name, in case you're interested, is Mrs. Keck."

100 Caught'ya Sentences: Tales of a Four-eyed Weirdo	**B** – Sentence for the board. **C** – Corrected version of the sentence.
27. aside Paragraph (new speaker) Quotation marks (quote) Commas (interjection, verb series) Parallel construction (Discuss in relation to verb series.) Exclamation (emphatic exclamation—"Oh no, not Mrs. Keck!") Abbreviation (Mrs.) Capitalization of the word "I" Homophone (hear/here) Strong verbs (groaned, gives, calls, makes)	B - oh no not mrs keck groaned gnarly in an aside to harold. i hear she gives tons of homework calls parents and makes students write and write C - "Oh no, not Mrs. Keck!" groaned Gnarly in an aside to Harold. "I hear she gives tons of homework, calls parents, and makes students write and write."
28. transcribed Paragraph (new topic) Antecedent/pronoun agreement (indefinite pronoun "everyone" is singular) Strong verb (transcribed) Use of "who"(subject) and "whom" (object of preposition) Comma (adjective clause)	B - everyone transcribed the assignment into their notebook except conan from who nobody ever expected any homework C - Everyone transcribed the assignment into his or her notebook except Conan, from whom nobody ever expected any homework.

100 Caught'ya Sentences: Tales of a Four-eyed Weirdo	**B** – Sentence for the board. **C** – Corrected version of the sentence.
29. sallied forth Paragraph (new location) Comma (subordinate clause) Run-on (2 sentences) Spelling (friend) Comparatives (good/better/best) Strong verb (sallied forth)	B - when the bell rang harold sallied forth from the classroom with gnarly he had found a best freind C - When the bell rang, Harold sallied forth from the classroom with Gnarly. He had found a best friend.
30. dilemmas Paragraph (time change) Conjunction (Do not begin a sentence with one.) Optional comma (short introductory adverb phrase) Verb tense shift (story in past) Strong verb (told)	B - and after school harold tells gnarly all about himself and his dilemmas C - After school (,) Harold told Gnarly all about himself and his dilemmas.
31. lament No paragraph (quote follows the introduction in previous sentence) Quotation marks (quote) Commas (interjection, direct address, quote) No comma (not a compound sentence—compound predicate) Comma rules	B - well gnarly my mom and dad are getting divorced and are fighting over me he said with a lament C - "Well, Gnarly, my mom and dad are getting divorced and are fighting over me," he said with a lament. **NOTE:** *This is a good place to introduce the comma rules if some of your students tried to insert a comma after "divorced" in this sentence. You can Xerox that part of the Appendix to give to your students as a reference.*

100 Caught'ya Sentences: Tales of a Four-eyed Weirdo	**B** – Sentence for the board. **C** – Corrected version of the sentence.
32. dapper No paragraph (Harold still speaking) Quotation marks (quote) Commas (2 adjectives, adjective clause in middle, quote) Use of "who" and "whom" (This is tricky here as "who" is subject of "is.") Collective noun ("family" is singular and needs a singular verb) Apostrophe (singular possessive) Capitalization (God) Verb tense shift (story in past tense) Strong verb (nags)	B - my big dapper brother in college who my family thinks is gods gift to parents nags me about my grades he continues C - "My big, dapper brother in college, who my family thinks is God's gift to parents, nags me about my grades," he continued.
33. sibling Paragraph (new speaker) Quotation marks (quote) Commas (interjection, direct address, quote) Exclamation mark (comment emphatically meant) Run-on Capitalization of the word "I" Homophone (know/no) Use of "who" (subject) and "whom" (object)	B - oh poor you said gnarly. i know what you mean i have a sibling just like that who drives me crazy C - "Oh, poor you!" said Gnarly. "I know what you mean. I have a sibling just like that who drives me crazy."

100 Caught'ya Sentences: Tales of a Four-eyed Weirdo	**B** – Sentence for the board. **C** – Corrected version of the sentence.
34. shrew Paragraph (new speaker) Quotation marks (quote and continued quote) Commas (compound sentence, "too" meaning "also," quote, compound sentence) Apostrophes (contractions) Homophone (too/to/two) Use of "good" (adjective) and "well" (adverb)	B - my dad is busy with his own new life and my mom thinks that im an infant. shes a real shrew about good grades too harold moaned and i always do good C -. "My dad is busy with his own new life, and my mom thinks that I'm an infant. She's a real shrew about good grades, too," Harold moaned, "and I always do well."
35. interjected Paragraph (new speaker) Quotation marks (quote) Capitalization of the word "I" Homophone (know/no) Commas (subordinate clause, adjective clause, quote) Use of "well" (adverb) and "good" (adjective) Use of "whom" as the object of a preposition (with whom) Spelling (a lot)	B - i no what you mean gnarly interjected. even if i do good i can never do good enough to suit my mom with who I argue alot C - "I know what you mean," Gnarly interjected. "Even if I do well, I can never do well enough to suit my mom, with whom I argue a lot."
36. adjusted, harridans Paragraph (time change) Comma (subordinate clause, 2 adjectives) Antecedent/pronoun agreement ("a school" is singular) Verb tense shift (story in past tense) Strong verb (adjusted)	B - as the weeks wore on harold adjusted to _____ (put your school name here) and their terrible nagging harridans who are called teachers C - As the weeks wore on, Harold adjusted to _____ and its (OR the) terrible, nagging harridans who were called teachers.

100 Caught'ya Sentences: Tales of a Four-eyed Weirdo	**B** – Sentence for the board. **C** – Corrected version of the sentence.
37. aloof No paragraph (continuation of narrative) Quotation marks (slang use of "hip") No comma (subordinate clause at end) Spelling (friends) Strong verb (made)	B - conan and his "hip" crowd made occasional fun of harold and gnarly while classy cassandra and her friends remained aloof C -Conan and his "hip" crowd made occasional fun of Harold and Gnarly while classy Cassandra and her friends remained aloof.
38. circulated Paragraph (time change) Optional comma after "day" (short introductory adverb) Abbreviation (Mrs.) Apostrophes (singular possessive, contraction) Comma (compound sentence) Antecedent/pronoun agreement (indefinite pronoun "everyone" is singular) Strong verb (circulated) Avoidance of preposition at the end of a sentence	B -one day a rumor circulated around mrs kecks classroom and everyone couldnt wait for their class to be over C - One day(,) a rumor circulated around Mrs. Keck's classroom, and everyone couldn't wait for the class to end. **NOTE:** *Since collective nouns and pronouns have been used several times by now, it might be a good idea to go over the common ones. Agreement of pronouns with indefinite pronoun antecedents and agreement of verbs with indefinite pronoun or collective noun subjects prove very difficult for students to understand. From now on, whenever a collective noun or indefinite pronoun appears in a sentence, it would be a good idea to go over several of them. See lists of the most common ones in the Appendix. While most of your middle school age students probably are not sophisticated enough to transfer this skill to their writing, you are setting them up for eventual success in high school.*

100 Caught'ya Sentences: Tales of a Four-eyed Weirdo	**B** – Sentence for the board. **C** – Corrected version of the sentence.
39. converged Paragraph (time change) Verb tense shift (story in past tense) Comma (subordinate clause) Strong verb (converged)	B - when class is finally over the popular students converged in the hallway C - When the class was finally over, the popular students converged in the hallway.
40. incredible, expounded Paragraph (new speaker) Quotation marks (interrupted quote) Use of exclamation with interjection "Awesome" (Discuss alternative comma.) Plural rule (nouns that end in "y") Comma (quote)	B - awesome said conan belinda is going to throw one of her incredible partys he expounded C - "Awesome!" said Conan. "Belinda is going to throw one of her incredible parties," he expounded.
41. bespectacled No paragraph (same speaker—Conan) Quotation marks (quote) Commas (adjective phrase in middle, 2 adjectives, compound sentence, quote) Subject/verb agreement (indefinite pronoun) Spelling (weirdo, friend) Pronouns (correct use and order—"my friends and I)	B - everyone even gnarly and that bespectacled weirdo friend of his are invited and me and all my friends are going conan added C -"Everyone, even Gnarly and that bespectacled, weirdo friend of his, is invited, and all my friends and I are going." Conan added. **NOTE:** *If you are doing more than three Caught'yas a week, and your students need more practice with the punctuation of quotations, you can have Conan and his friends chatter some more about the party.*

100 Caught'ya Sentences: Tales of a Four-eyed Weirdo	**B** – Sentence for the board. **C** – Corrected version of the sentence.
42. queried Paragraph (new speaker) Quotation marks (quote with question) Commas (interjection, direct address) No comma (subordinate clause at end) Homophone (to/too/two)	B - hey gnarly are you going too go? queried harold when he heard the news C - "Hey, Gnarly, are you going to go?" queried Harold when he heard the news.
43. supplicating Paragraph (new speaker) Quotation marks (quote) Commas ("yes" at beginning of sentence, interjection, direct address) Question mark (note placement inside quotation marks) Run-on	B - yes i think i will well how about you harold asked gnarly in a supplicating voice C - "Yes, I think I will. Well, how about you, Harold?" asked Gnarly in a supplicating voice.
44. stoutness, reiterated 2 paragraphs (new speaker) Quotation marks (quote) Commas ("no" at beginning of sentence, quote) Apostrophes (contractions) Capitalization of the word "I" Plural rule (plurals of nouns ending in "s")	B - no im afraid theyll make fun of my stoutness and my glasses said harold. they always do reiterated gnarly C - "No, I'm afraid they'll make fun of my stoutness and my glasses," said Harold. "They always do," reiterated Gnarly.

100 Caught'ya Sentences: Tales of a Four-eyed Weirdo	**B** – Sentence for the board. **C** – Corrected version of the sentence.
45. beseeched, piranhas Paragraph (new speaker) Quotation marks (quote) Metaphor (pool of piranhas) Commas (interjection, direct address, quote, compound sentence) Capitalization of the word "I" Apostrophe (contraction)	B - aw come on harold beseeched gnarly i dont want to go alone into that pool of piranhas but i do want to go C - "Aw, come on, Harold," beseeched Gnarly. "I don't want to go alone into that pool of piranhas, but I do want to go."
46. capitulated, corpulent Paragraph (new speaker) Quotation marks (quote) Abbreviation (O.K. or okay) Commas (interjection, direct address, quote, 2 adjectives) Capitalization of the word "I" Strong verb (capitulated)	B - ok ill go gnarly capitulated hapless corpulent harold C - "O.K., (Okay,) I'll go, Gnarly," capitulated hapless, corpulent Harold.
47. apprehension Paragraph (time change) Capitalization (day of the week) Verb tense shift (story in past tense) Commas (interrupter) Plural rule (nouns ending in "y") No comma before "as" (subordinate clause at end)	B - the next saturday however gnarly and harold are filled with apprehension as they get dressed for the party C - The next Saturday, however, Gnarly and Harold were filled with apprehension as they got dressed for the party.

100 Caught'ya Sentences: Tales of a Four-eyed Weirdo	B – Sentence for the board. C – Corrected version of the sentence.
48. stylish, qualms, quivered No paragraph (same topic) Commas (participial phrase, compound sentence) Misplaced modifier (show how to avoid—his body did not pull up pants) Homophone (whole/hole)	B - attempting to pull up his only stylish pair of pants his hole body quivered and harold felt qualms about his decision to attend the party C - Attempting to pull up his only stylish pair of pants, Harold felt qualms about his decision to attend the party, and his whole body quivered. **NOTE:** *There are other possible answers. Just make sure that "Harold" follows "pants."*
49. jaunty Paragraph (place change) Commas (adjective phrase in middle, subordinate clause) Verb tense shift (story in past tense) Apostrophes (singular and plural possessives)	B - when harold jaunty in his good slacks and chubby gnarly arrived at belindas parents house the party is already in full swing C - When Harold, jaunty in his good slacks, and chubby Gnarly arrived at Belinda's parents' house, the party was already in full swing. **NOTE:** *At this point, those of you who need more sentences might want to elaborate on the description of the party. You could consult your students for advice and descriptive details. You also might want to assign your students to write a descriptive paragraph about the party. This is always a popular assignment for those whose imaginations run wild.*

100 Caught'ya Sentences: Tales of a Four-eyed Weirdo	**B** – Sentence for the board. **C** – Corrected version of the sentence.
50. attire No paragraph (same topic) Antecedent/pronoun agreement (indefinite pronoun "everyone" is singular) Use of "who" (subject) and "whom" (object) Difference between "except" and "accept" Homophones (whole/hole, there, and holy/holey/wholly) Plural rules (nouns ending in "f" or"fe") Difference between "effect" and "affect" Commas (2 adjectives, to make sense after "attire"—optional)	B - everyone was their in their best attire except conan who wore his best holey jeans which had been cut with knifes for effect C - Everyone was there in his or her best attire, except Conan who wore his best, holey jeans which had been cut with knives for effect.
51. lounged No paragraph (same topic) Difference between "among" (more than 2) and "between" (exactly 2) Quotation marks ("cool" is mocking) Commas (participial phrase in middle) Misplaced modifier (wall is not smoking cigarettes) Strong verb (lounged)	B - conan lounged between all his cool friends against a wall smoking a cigarette to look cool C - Conan, smoking cigarettes to look cool, lounged among all his "cool" friends against a wall. **NOTE:** *There are other possibilities but make sure that it is Conan who is smoking the cigarette and not the wall.* *Example: Lounging against a wall, Conan smoked cigarettes to look cool among all his "cool" friends.*

100 Caught'ya Sentences: Tales of a Four-eyed Weirdo	**B** – Sentence for the board. **C** – Corrected version of the sentence.
52. rasped Paragraph (new speaker) Quotation marks (quote) Comma (interjection, quote) Apostrophes (contraction, singular possessive) Difference between "further" and "farther" (distance only) Strong verb (rasped)	B - hey lets get out of here before we go any further harold rasped in gnarlys left ear C - "Hey, let's get out of here before we go any farther," Harold rasped in Gnarly's left ear.
53. reiterated Paragraph (new speaker) Quotation marks (quote) Collective noun/verb agreement ("group" is singular and needs a singular verb) Confused spelling (were/we're) Homophones (whole/hole, to/too/two) Commas ("no" at beginning, compound sentence, quote)	B - no the whole group are here and were going too stick it out reiterated gnarly C - "No, the whole group is here, and we're going to stick it out," reiterated Gnarly.
54. sneered Paragraph (new speaker) Quotation marks (quote) Comma (interjection) Apostrophes (contractions) Difference between "who's" (who is) and "whose" (possession) Exclamation mark (Conan is talking emphatically) Spelling (friend, weird) Homophone (it's/its—Students have a lot of trouble with this one.) Run-on (2 sentences) Hyphen (four-eyed)	B - well look whose here sneered conan to his friends its the obese creep and the four eyed wierdo C - "Well, look who's here!" sneered Conan to his friends. "It's the obese creep and the four-eyed weirdo."

100 Caught'ya Sentences: Tales of a Four-eyed Weirdo	**B** – Sentence for the board. **C** – Corrected version of the sentence.
55. spied, chattering Paragraph (change of person) Use of "sit" (no object) and "set" (always takes object) Comma (participial phrase) Use of "who" (subject) and "whom" (object)	B - just then harold spied cassandra who was setting on the couch chattering to another classy girl C - Just then Harold spied Cassandra who was sitting on the couch, chattering to another classy girl.
56. mortified, wimp No paragraph (same topic) Commas (participial phrase in middle) Verb tense shift (story in past tense) Strong verb (stood up) Simile ("like a warrior")	B - harold mortified that the lovely cassandra might think that he is a wimp stood up to conan like a true warrior C - Harold, mortified that the lovely Cassandra might think that he was a wimp, stood up to Conan like a true warrior.
57. taxed, atrocious Paragraph (new speaker) Quotation marks (quote) Commas (interjection, quote, direct address) Apostrophe (contraction) Single quotation marks (sarcasm within quote) Homophone (your/you're) Question mark within quote	B - well if it isnt the cool dude with the fake chains and the atrocious grades he said. hello conan have you taxed your brain lately C - "Well, if it isn't the 'cool' dude with the fake chains and the atrocious grades," he said. "Hello, Conan, have you taxed your brain lately?"

100 Caught'ya Sentences: Tales of a Four-eyed Weirdo	**B** – Sentence for the board. **C** – Corrected version of the sentence.
58. flatulent No paragraph (same speaker) Quotation marks (quote) Homophone (you're, your) Proper noun of dog breed (Note the clue.) Comma (quote)	B - your lower than the belly of a flatulent basset Hound he added C - "You're lower than the belly of a flatulent Basset Hound," he added.
59. gaping, aperture Paragraph (new action) Run-on Hyphen (ham-sized) Apostrophes (singular possessives) Comma (compound sentence or participial phrase) Strong verbs (leapt, aimed, ducked, slammed, fell)	B - conan leapt at harold and he aimed his ham sized fist for harolds face and harold ducked and conans fist slammed into the wall and his cigarette fell from the now gaping aperture of his mouth C - Conan leapt at Harold. He aimed his ham-sized fist for Harold's face. Harold ducked. Conan's fist slammed into the wall, and his cigarette fell from the now gaping aperture of his mouth. (Or . . . wall, his cigarette falling from the now . . .)
60. ensued No paragraph (same topic) Verb tense shift (story in past tense) Commas (compound sentence, 2 adjectives, adjective series, participial phrase) Apostrophe (possessive) Use of "good" (adjective) and "well" (adverb) Hyphens (four-eyed, brown-eyed) Spelling (straight/strait) Quotation marks (something that is not a word)	B - the fight that ensued is not a pretty sight but harold fueled by cassandras lovely brown eyed gaze did good for a chubby four eyed strait A student C - The fight that ensued was not a pretty sight, but Harold, fueled by Cassandra's lovely, brown-eyed gaze, did well for a chubby, four-eyed, straight "A" student.

100 Caught'ya Sentences: Tales of a Four-eyed Weirdo	**B** – Sentence for the board. **C** – Corrected version of the sentence.
61. blubber, egregious No paragraph (same topic) Apostrophes (singular possessives) Comma (compound sentence) Plural rule (nouns ending in "s" and irregular plurals like "feet") Quotation marks (slang expression—"bit the dust") Use of "lie/lay" (no object) and "lay/laid" (always takes object) Strong verbs (protected, bit)	B - harolds blubber protected him from any egregious harm but his glasses bit the dust as they laid under conans feet C - Harold's blubber protected him from any egregious harm, but his glasses "bit the dust" as they lay under Conan's feet.
62. shriek, unison Paragraph (subject change) Quotation marks (quote) Homophone (heard/herd) Spelling (Discuss the "i" before "e" except after "c" rule for "shriek.") Apostrophe (contraction) Commas (introductory adverb phrase—optional, direct address)	B - in the distance harold heard gnarly and cassandra shriek in unison harold the trash cans on fire C - In the distance (,) Harold heard Gnarly and Cassandra shriek in unison. "Harold, the trash can's on fire!"
63. alerted Paragraph (now about Harold) Comma (introductory adverb clause) Homophone (heard/herd) Misplaced modifier (voices not receiving the pounding, Harold is) Apostrophe (plural possessive)	B - from under the pounding that conan was delivering his friends voices alerted harold to the danger C - From under the pounding that Conan was delivering, Harold heard his friends' voices alert him to the danger. **NOTE:** *Other variations are possible as long as the word "Harold" follows "delivering."*

100 Caught'ya Sentences: Tales of a Four-eyed Weirdo	**B** – Sentence for the board. **C** – Corrected version of the sentence.
64. espied, licked No paragraph (same topic) Comma (long introductory adverb phrase) Apostrophe (singular possessive)	B - from beneath conans armpit harold espied flames that licked up the curtains C - From beneath Conan's armpit, Harold espied flames that licked up the curtains.
65. engulfed No paragraph (same topic) Homophone (to/too/two) No comma before the word "because" (subordinate clause at cnd) Indirect quote Overuse of pronouns ("he" is unclear — use noun)	B - he shouted two conan that the fight should stop because the house would soon be engulfed in flames. C - Harold shouted to Conan that the fight should stop because the house would soon be engulfed in flames.
66. conflagration Paragraph (change of action) Use of "quick" (adjective) and "quickly" (adverb) Comma (compound sentence) Strong verbs (stopped, ran)	B - the fight stopped quick and harold ran to throw water and baking soda on the conflagration. C - The fight stopped quickly, and Harold ran to throw water and baking soda on the conflagration.

100 Caught'ya Sentences: Tales of a Four-eyed Weirdo	**B** – Sentence for the board. **C** – Corrected version of the sentence.
67. stupefied, mesmerized No paragraph (same topic) Antecedent/pronoun agreement (indefinite pronoun is singular—everyone) Commas (adverb phrase, to make pause after "limbs") Simile (like frogs . . .) Use of "who" with people and "that" with animals and things Strong verb (stood)	B - everyone else stood stupefied unable to move their limbs like frogs who have been mesmerized by a flashlight C - Everyone else stood stupefied, unable to move his or her limbs, like frogs that have been mesmerized by a flashlight.
68. complicate, abode Paragraph (introduce new people) Conjunction (Do not begin a sentence with one.) Comma (introductory infinitive phrase) Difference between "further" and "farther" (distance only) Apostrophe (singular possessive) Homophones (to/too/two, their/there/they're)	B - and to farther complicate things at that moment belindas parents returned to there abode C - To further complicate things, at that moment Belinda's parents returned to their abode.
69. irate, faltered No paragraph (same topic) Comma (appositive, quote) Quotation marks (quote) Homophone (it's/its) Apostrophes (contraction, singular possessive) Transitive and intransitive verbs ("rise" has no object and "raise" takes object) No comma (subordinate clause at end) Plural rule (nouns that end in "o" as in "hero")	B - harold the brave hero never faltered. its my fault he told belindas irate parents as he rose up to greet them C - Harold, the brave hero, never faltered. "It's my fault," he told Belinda's parents as he rose up to greet them.

100 Caught'ya Sentences: Tales of a Four-eyed Weirdo	B – Sentence for the board. C – Corrected version of the sentence.
70. renewed Paragraph (change in time) Comma (introductory adverb phrase) Homophone (there/their/they're) Hyphens (four-eyed, middle-school as adjective) Spelling (weirdo) No comma before "since" (subordinate clause at end) Apostrophe (contraction) Plural rule (nouns ending in "o")	B - the next day in school there was a renewed respect for the four eyed weirdo since their werent many middle school heros C -　　The next day in school, there was a renewed respect for the four-eyed weirdo since there weren't many middle-school heros.
71. valiant, bespectacled No paragraph (same topic) Comma (2 adjectives) Homophone (to/too/two) Indirect quote Verb tense shift (story in past tense)	B - cassandra wrote a note to the valiant bespectacled young man to tell him that she is proud of him. C - Cassandra wrote a note to the valiant, bespectacled young man to tell him that she was proud of him.
72. averting, calamity Paragraph (letter) Friendly letter format Commas (city, state; greeting; closing; date) Abbreviation (Ave., state) Capitalizations (address, date, greeting, first letter only of closing, I) Homophone (you're/your) Use of "well" (adverb) and "good" (adjective) Spelling (friend)	B -　　　　1234 main ave 　　　　　　(your town and state 　　　　　　and zip) 　　　　　　march 26 1993 dear harold your super for averting that calamity with the fire. you did so good. i want to be your freind. 　　　　　　affectionately yours 　　　　　　cassandra C -　　　　1234 Main Ave. 　　　_____ , _____ zip 　　　　　　March 26, 1993 Dear Harold, 　　　　You're super for averting that calamity with the fire. You did so well. I want to be your friend. 　　　　　　Affectionately yours, 　　　　　　Cassandra

100 Caught'ya Sentences: Tales of a Four-eyed Weirdo	**B** – Sentence for the board. **C** – Corrected version of the sentence.
73. penned, vision, pulchritude Paragraph (new topic) Transitive and intransitive verbs ("sit" has no object and "set" takes object) Metaphor (vision of pulchritude)	B - harold sat down and hastily penned a letter to his vision of pulchritude C - Harold sat down and hastily penned a letter to his vision of pulchritude.

74. incinerated
 	
Paragraph (letter)
Friendly letter format
Commas (address; city, state,; greeting; closing)
Abbreviation (St., state)
Apostrophes (contractions)
Negatives (no double negatives—"wasn't nothing")
Capitalizations (I, greeting, first letter of closing)
Spelling (truly, weird)
	B - 5678 side st
	                (your town, state, zip)
	                march 28 1993
	dear cassandra
	it wasnt nothing. i didnt want to see you incinerated by the flames or get blamed for something you didnt do.
	                yours very truely
	                harold weird
	
	C - 5678 Side St.
	_____ , _____ zip
	        March 28, 1993
	Dear Cassandra,
	        It wasn't anything. I didn't want to see you incinerated by the flames or get blamed for something you didn't do.
	                Yours very truly,
	                Harold Weird
	
	NOTE: *This, of course, leads right into a friendly letter writing unit. If your class needs more practice in letter writing format, have Harold and Cassandra exchange a few more letters. Some "torrid" love letters might appeal to seventh and eighth graders.*

100 Caught'ya Sentences: Tales of a Four-eyed Weirdo	**B** – Sentence for the board. **C** – Corrected version of the sentence.
75. swinish, a plethora of, repentant Paragraph (new person) Commas (appositive) Verb tense shift (story in past tense) Quotation marks around "cool" (sarcasm) Spelling (friends) Simile (like a repentant dog...) Use of "who" (subject) and "whom" (object) Past perfect tense (had peed)	B - conan the swinish fighter with a plethora of cool friends comes up to harold like a repentant dog who had peed on the rug. C - Conan, the swinish fighter with a plethora of "cool" friends, came up to Harold like a repentant dog who had peed on the rug.
76. shouldering, culpability Paragraph (new speaker) Quotation marks (quote) Commas (interjection, direct address) Capitalization of the word "I" Run-on (2 sentences) Negative Pronouns (correct use and order)	B - hey man i didn't mean nothing by my comment me and my friends are thankful to you for shouldering the culpability for the fire C - "Hey, man, I didn't mean anything by my comment. My friends and I are thankful to you for shouldering the culpability for the fire.

100 Caught'ya Sentences: Tales of a Four-eyed Weirdo	B – Sentence for the board. C – Corrected version of the sentence.
77. leer Paragraph (new speaker) Quotation marks (quote) Apostrophe (contraction) Comma (direct address, quote) Abbreviation (O.K. or okay) Pronouns (correct use and order) Spelling (friend) No comma (appositive is restrictive and thus necessary — which friend) Split infinitives (Do not split them as in *Star Trek* "to boldly go") Incorrect placement of preposition at end of sentence	B - thats ok conan murmured harold with a leer at gnarly. me and my friend gnarly just want to somehow fit in. C - "That's O.K., (OR "That's okay,) Conan," murmured Harold with a leer at Gnarly. "My friend Gnarly and I just want to fit in somehow."
78. toothsome Paragraph (time change) Optional comma after "later" (introductory adverb phrase) Numbers (Write them out.) Colon (list) Semicolons (list with commas to avoid confusion) Commas (appositive, 2 adjectives) Abbreviation (Mrs.) Strong verbs (happened, convinced,spoke, came)	B - a few days later 3 things happened at _____ (put the name of your school here) harold the hero convinced his parents to get him contact lenses the toothsome grateful belinda spoke to him and a substitute came in for mrs keck C - A few days later (,) three things happened at _____ : Harold, the hero, convinced his parents to get him contact lenses; the toothsome, grateful Belinda spoke to him; and a substitute came in for Mrs. Keck.
79. torment, striplings No paragraph (same topic) Conjunction (Do not begin a sentence with one.) Use of "this," "that," "these," "those" Verb tense shift (story in past tense) Metaphor (was a nightmare . . .)	B - and this substitute is a nightmare designed to torment striplings C - This substitute was a nightmare designed to torment striplings.

100 Caught'ya Sentences: Tales of a Four-eyed Weirdo	**B** – Sentence for the board. **C** – Corrected version of the sentence.
80. obdurate No paragraph (same topic) Verb tense shift (twice—story in past tense) Run-on (2 sentences) Commas (adjective series, compound sentence) Ordinal numbers (Write them out.)	B - he is big burly and obdurate and he hates kids and he especially hated _____ (put the grade level of your students here) graders C - He was big, burly, and obdurate. He hated kids, and he especially hated (sixth, seventh, eighth) graders.
81. knavish, thwart Paragraph (change of scene) Transitive and intransitive verbs ("sit" has no object and "set" takes object) Spelling (friends) Difference between "between" (2 things) and "among" (more than 2) Strong verbs (sat, plotted) No comma (not a compound sentence—compound predicate) Use of "this," "that," "these," "those"	B - harold set among his new friends at lunch and plotted to thwart this knavish sub C - Harold sat among his new friends at lunch and plotted to thwart this knavish sub.
82. contrived, ploy No paragraph (same topic) Pronouns (correct use and order) Dash (discuss use) Homophone (their/there/they're) Capitalization of names of countries, titles Titles of books (underline) Commas around title of book (non-restrictive modifier — students only have one English book and title is extra information) Strong verb (contrived)	B - him and gnarly contrived the perfect ploy to get this person—at his signal all of the students would drop there english book boring language on the floor C - Gnarly and he contrived the perfect ploy to get this person — at his signal all of the students would drop their English book, *Boring Language*, on the floor.

100 Caught'ya Sentences: Tales of a Four-eyed Weirdo	**B** – Sentence for the board. **C** – Corrected version of the sentence.
83. loomed Paragraph (change of time and place) Comma (subordinate clause) Abbreviation (Mrs.) Apostrophe (singular possessive) No comma (not a compound sentence—compound predicate) Homophone (their/there/they're) Strong verb (loomed)	B - when harold and his friends arrived in mrs kecks classroom the sub loomed over them menacingly and asked for their homework C - When Harold and his friends arrived in Mrs. Keck's classroom, the sub loomed over them menacingly and asked for their homework.
84. slothful No paragraph (same topic) Commas (adjective phrase in middle, interrupter)) Antecedent/pronoun agreement (indefinite pronoun "everyone" is singular) Collective noun (class) Homophone (its/it's)	B - everyone in the class except the slothful conan of course had their homework C - Everyone in the class, except the slothful Conan, of course, had his or her homework.
85. verbally, pulverize No paragraph (same topic) Commas (subordinate clause, adverb phrase in middle) No comma (not a compound sentence with "so that") Spelling (Discuss rule: If there is a consonant/vowel/consonant in a word, double the final consonant before adding a suffix like "ed," that begins with a vowel.) Strong verb (slipped) Split infinitive "to verbally pulverize" (Do not split infinitives as in the well-known *Star Trek* error — "to boldly go where no man has been before.")	B - as the sub prepared to verbally pulverize conan harold with a wink sliped him a copy of the homework so conan could pretend to find it C - As the sub prepared to pulverize Conan verbally, Harold, with a wink, slipped him a copy of the homework so (that) Conan could pretend to find it.

100 Caught'ya Sentences: Tales of a Four-eyed Weirdo	B – Sentence for the board. C – Corrected version of the sentence.
86. attained No paragraph (still talking about sub incident) Commas (subordinate clause, compound sentence) Apostrophe (singular possessive) Spelling (Discuss the consonant/vowel/consonant plus suffix rule with "dropped.") Antecedent/pronoun agreement ("everyone" is singular) Strong verb (gave)	B - at the moment the sub attained conans desk harold gave the signal and everyone droped their book C - At the moment the sub attained Conan's desk, Harold gave the signal, and everyone dropped his or her book.
87. befuddled No paragraph (same topic) Transitive and intransitive verbs ("lie/lay" has no object and "lay/laid" takes object) Confused spellings (quiet/quit/quite) Verb tense shift (story in past tense) No comma (compound predicate)	B - the befuddled sub lay off conan and is quite for the rest of the period C - The befuddled sub laid off Conan and was quiet for the rest of the period.
88. flabbergasted Paragraph (new incident) Numbers (Write them out.) Colon (list) Quotation marks (something that is not a word—Point out placement of comma after "A's,") Apostrophes (to form plural of single letters) Comma (introductory adverb phrase — optional) Strong verbs (happened, decided, took, asked) Semicolons (complete sentences in a series)	B - after that incident 3 more things happened that flabbergasted harold conan decided that F's were no fun and asked harold to teach him how to get A's belinda and her crowd took harold and gnarly in hand and put them on a diet and cassandra asked harold to sit with her at lunch C - After that incident (,) three more things happened that flabbergasted Harold: Conan decided that "F's" were no fun and asked Harold to teach him how to get "A's;" Belinda and her crowd took Harold and Gnarly in hand and put them on a diet; and Cassandra asked Harold to sit with her at lunch.

100 Caught'ya Sentences: Tales of a Four-eyed Weirdo	**B** – Sentence for the board. **C** – Corrected version of the sentence.
89. cohorts, flourished No paragraph (same topic) Apostrophes (singular and plural possessives) Spelling (a lot) No comma (subordinate clause at end)	B - conans and alot of his cohorts grades improved as their friendship with harold and gnarly flourished C - Conan's and a lot of his cohorts' grades improved as their friendship with Harold and Gnarly flourished.
90. sagaciously No paragraph (same topic) Title of book (underline, capitalize) No comma in appositive (restrictive modifier—which book, movie?) No comma (not a compound sentence with "so that") Comma (compound sentence) Title of movie (underline, capitalize) Title rules (underlining vs. quotation marks) Split infinitive (to sagaciously discuss)	B - harold read the book war and peace so that he could have something to sagaciously discuss with cassandra and they saw the movie always together C - Harold read the book *War and Peace* so that he could have something to discuss sagaciously with Cassandra, and they saw the movie *Always* together.
91. languidly No paragraph (same topic) Verb tense shift (story in past tense) Apostrophe (singular possessive) Split infinitive (to languidly listen) Run-on (2 sentences) Title of long musical work—album (underline) Comparative (good/better/best) Title of song (quotation marks — note placement of comma) Commas (appositive — non-restrictive as he only has one favorite song) Placement of comma within quotation marks	B - harold even goes to cassandras house to languidly listen to her pink floyd album animals it was even better than his favorite song help by the beatles C - Harold even went to Cassandra's house to listen languidly to her Pink Floyd album <u>*Animals*</u>. It was even better than his favorite song, "Help," by the Beatles.

100 Caught'ya Sentences: Tales of a Four-eyed Weirdo	**B** – Sentence for the board. **C** – Corrected version of the sentence.
92. blithe Paragraph (now talking about home) Commas (introductory adverb phrase — optional, interrupter — "too") Splitting of helping verb and main verb (move "also" if it makes sense) Verb tense shift (story in past tense) Quotation marks (popular expression—note placement of period)	B - at home as well harold has also become a blithe camper C - At home as well (,) Harold also had become (or "became") "a blithe camper."
93. elusive No paragraph (same topic) Apostrophe (singular possessive) Use of "who" (subject) and "whom" (object) Commas (adjective clause in middle) Overuse of pronouns (referring to two people so meaning is unclear)	B - his elusive dad who he almost never saw asked him to spend the summer with him C - Harold's elusive dad, whom he almost never saw, asked Harold to spend the summer with him.

100 Caught'ya Sentences: Tales of a Four-eyed Weirdo	**B** – Sentence for the board. **C** – Corrected version of the sentence.
94. convinced, vigilant No paragraph (same topic) Apostrophe (singular possessive) Commas (appositive — non-restrictive as only 1 brother, predicate series) Parallel construction (Discuss in relation to predicate series.) Homophone (their/there/they're) Transitive and intransitive verbs ("lie/lay" has no object and "lay/laid" takes object — although "lay off" is not the same as "lay," you can have the discussion anyway.)	B - harolds big brother marvin helped him with his algebra stopped teasing him and convinced their vigilant mom to lay off harold about his grades C - Harold's big brother, Marvin, helped him with his algebra, stopped teasing him, and convinced their vigilant mom to lay off Harold about his grades.
95. abetted No paragraph (same topic) Apostrophe (singular possessive) Overuse of pronouns (too many for clarity) Homophone (too/to/two) Commas (around "too" meaning also, compound sentence) Verb tense shift (story in past tense) Avoidance of split helping verb and verb (move adverb if it makes sense) Difference between meaning of verbs "lose" and "loose" Spelling (diet, weight)	B - harolds mom abetted him on his diet to and he is rapidly losing weight C - Harold's mom abetted him on his diet, too, and Harold was losing weight rapidly.

100 Caught'ya Sentences: Tales of a Four-eyed Weirdo	**B** – Sentence for the board. **C** – Corrected version of the sentence.
96. relent, flamboyant No paragraph (same topic) Apostrophe (singular possessive) Use of "who" and "whom" (who is subject of "would relent"—this is a hard one) Commas (adjective clause in middle) Plural rule (nouns that end in "y")	B - harolds mom who harold never thought would relent even let him host a flamboyant party C - Harold's mom, who Harold never thought would relent, even let him host a flamboyant party.
97. comely, cronies Paragraph (new person as subject) Conjunctions (Do not begin sentences with them.) Use of dash Comma (compound sentence) Apostrophe (singular possessive) Plural rule (nouns that end in "y")	B - and as for conan—his grades improved and he even attracted one of cassandras comely cronies to go with him C - As for Conan—his grades improved, and he even attracted one of Cassandra's comely cronies to go with him.
98. optimistically Paragraph (new subject) Commas (interrupter) Use of "who" (subject) and "whom" (object) Verb tense shift (story in past tense) Abbreviation (Mrs.) Apostrophe (singular possessive) Ordinal numbers (Write them out.)	B - the year therefore ended optimistically for everyone who is in mrs kecks 5th period class C - The year, therefore, ended optimistically for everyone who was in Mrs. Keck's fifth period class.

100 Caught'ya Sentences: Tales of a Four-eyed Weirdo	**B** – Sentence for the board. **C** – Corrected version of the sentence.
99. ghastly, assailed No paragraph (same topic) Strong verb (assailed) Comma (compound sentence) Homophone (their/there/they're) Spelling (diets, its/it's)	B - the only bad thing was that the lunchroom still assailed students with its ghastly smells but this actually helped harold and gnarly with they're diets C - The only bad thing was that the lunchroom still assailed students with its ghastly smells, but this actually helped Harold and Gnarly with their diets.
100. persevered No paragraph (same topic) Antecedent/pronoun agreement (Collective noun "crew" is singular; avoid use of a possessive pronoun) Abbreviation (Mrs.) Apostrophe (singular possessive)	B - the entire crew even persevered with all their homework in mrs kecks class C - The entire crew even persevered with all the homework in Mrs. Keck's class.
P.S. a plethora of, dearth Paragraph (new subject) Commas (2 noun series) Spelling (a lot) Plural rule (nouns that end in "y")	B - harold conan belinda gnarly and cassandra all wish you a wonderful summer with a plethora of awesome partys alot of fun and a dearth of homework C - Harold, Conan, Belinda, Gnarly, and Cassandra all wish you a wonderful summer with a plethora of awesome parties, a lot of fun, and a dearth of homework.

CAUGHT'YA TEST   Name _____
Middle School   Date _____

DIRECTIONS: Correct all the errors. Mark new paragraphs with the proofreading symbol for a paragraph as we do in the Caught'yas. Note that all periods have been supplied. HINT: There are five spelling errors (mostly homophones), two verb tense errors, and eight paragraphs, as well as missing apostrophes, commas, capital letters, quotation marks, and one hyphen.

the wild party of a former four eyed weirdo

when harolds mom let him host a party for his many new freinds all his friends parents let there children attend it. conan wore his best jeans and everyone else dressed up in good clothes to. the hole group is on their best behavior that evening but they had a wonderful time anyway. well look at the new skinny harold said belinda as she combed her long blond hair back with her hand. i think hes handsome in his new contacts sighed cassandra. the party gets better and better. harold put the song yesterday on the record player so that he could slow dance with cassandra. he spied conan dancing with one of cassandras friends. some kids made popcorn in the kitchen and had a popcorn fight. they did however clean it all up afterwards. gnarly looking skinny in a new outfit danced with every girl in the room. 2 girls sat on the couch reading the magazine seventeen. oh boy harold said gnarly i like your party. harold answered back as he hugged cassandra tightly yes this is great gnarly. conan shouted over the top of the head of the girl with who he was dancing hey harold where did you find all these beautiful girls? harolds only brother marvin the college student kept the crowd supplied with punch cake chips and cookies. the party didnt end until after midnight and everyone had a great time to. harold couldn't wait for other parties! now they all were part of the cool crowd!

CAUGHT'YA TEST KEY
Middle School

NOTE: *Teachers, you may wish to count the errors in Middle School each line and indicate that number to your students. My students say that this helps. Be careful! It is easy to count incorrectly.*

The Wild Party of a Former Four-eyed Weirdo

When Harold's mom let him host a party for his many new friends, all his friends' parents let their children attend it. Conan wore his best jeans, and everyone else dressed up in good clothes, too. The whole group was on its best behavior that evening, but they had a wonderful time anyway.

"Well, look at the new, skinny Harold," said Belinda as she combed her long blond hair back with her hand.

"I think he's handsome in his new contacts," sighed Cassandra.

The party got better and better. Harold put the song "Yesterday" on the record player so that he could slow dance with Cassandra. He spied Conan dancing with one of Cassandra's friends. Some kids made popcorn in the kitchen and had a popcorn fight. They did, however, clean it all up afterwards. Gnarly, looking skinny in a new outfit, danced with every girl in the room. Two girls sat on the couch reading the magazine Seventeen.

"Oh boy, Harold," said Gnarly, "I like your party."

Harold answered back as he hugged Cassandra tightly, "Yes, this is great, Gnarly."

Conan shouted over the top of the head of the girl with whom he was dancing, "Hey, Harold, where did you find all these beautiful girls?"

Harold's only brother, Marvin, the college student, kept the crowd supplied with punch, cake, chips, and cookies. The party didn't end until after midnight, and everyone had a great time, too. Harold couldn't wait for other parties! Now they all were part of the "cool" crowd!

Chapter 9

100 Caught'ya Sentences

for Grades 9 – 12

**"Charlie Excess
Does It Again"**

Important Notes

Because students are required to capitalize the first letter of each sentence, capitalize proper nouns, and supply end punctuation, these are not listed each time as a skill. You probably also will notice that in the sentences destined for the board, there are no contraction errors nor errors with articles. It is assumed that by ninth grade, students no longer have difficulty with these skills. If this is not the case with your students, program in a few errors with articles and contractions to engender discussion.

This story is designed to appeal to the high-school age group. In fact, several tenth and twelfth grade students chose this story from several plots I had given them. Of course, it can be simplified for younger students as well. When I showed the story to my guinea pig high-school students (before I wrote the actual sentences), they laughed over various elements of the plot. I experienced the additional delight of

overhearing one young man retell the story to his younger brother.
I couldn't help but hoot with laughter at his rendition. The parts that he
stressed in his retelling are elaborated upon in the sentences. I trust a
sixteen-year-old better than a middle-aged women (me) to tell me what
sixteen-year-old youngsters prefer.

In all my experience with teaching and raising children, I have
noticed that teenaged children (caught in that delicate stage between
childhood and adulthood) love to read about peers, excesses, sports,
parties, and recalcitrant parents. The girls always enjoy a love element,
and the boys relish an exciting adventure into slightly forbidden
territory even if there is a moral at the end. These elements have been
included in this story.

Since the mother in me always likes to teach my students
morals, kindness, and moderation in all things, this story has a moral.
Please note that, although Charlie tries all sorts of nasty things, he
realizes that there is no substitute for clean living, caring parents, good
grades, love, kindness, friendship, and moderation.

One-hundred Caught'ya sentences are given here, all you need
for a year if you use three a week. If you want to use more each week,
add them based on the deficiencies your students' writing reveals. Some
places where it is easy to add more sentences are noted. In this way a
teacher or a parent painlessly can flesh out the story line to give
students more practice in the skills they need (See the Appendix for an
annotated list of these skills.).

I have tried to use all of the grammar, mechanics, and usage
rules mentioned in the Appendix somewhere among these one- hundred
sentences. Obviously, I couldn't use all the irregular forms of verbs, but I
have attempted to use the ones that students most frequently abuse.
With this age group, you might also wish to do a brief unit on analogies.
For obvious reasons, I couldn't include these in the Caught'ya
sentences.

Those of you who teach eighth or ninth grade may wish to
simplify some of these sentences, retain fewer of the errors in the board
sentences, or discuss a skill such as correcting a misplaced modifier the
first time it appears without making your students correct it by

themselves. Without much trouble, this story probably can be adapted for all high-school grades.

During the current school year, I am using this story with advanced eighth graders in order to "road test" it. Naturally, I simplify some of the sentences. So far, the students like the story. They think that Charlie is crazy. The boys, especially, enjoyed the action scenes for the basketball game. While students complain about the frequency of the misplaced modifiers, they are learning to spot them. About one-fourth of the students now consistently get the sentences correct on their own. They're getting downright smug!

Those of you who teach very astute eleventh and twelfth graders can make the sentences even more difficult by adding errors to the board sentence. For example, if your students need much more practice with antecedent/pronoun agreement and with correctly placing modifiers, you can add a misplaced modifier for them to remove or you can add an antecedent/pronoun problem in another clause that you tack onto the original sentence. For practice in skills such as consistent verb tense, simply switch the tense of the verb.

At this age level, students are capable of editing out errors as well as editing in corrections. You might want to think about putting correct (and incorrect) punctuation into the sentence you put on the board. After all, students need to learn to edit out extraneous punctuation in their own papers.

In the last fifty sentences, I let myself get carried away with vocabulary words. There are so many really fantastic words out there! This was deliberate since tenth and eleventh graders who are college bound have SAT and ACT tests coming up, and they need the vocabulary practice. If more than one difficult word per sentence frustrates your students, swap some of these words for simpler synonyms.

All the skills referred to at the left of each Caught'ya sentence are listed, annotated, and explained with examples in the Appendix. This supplement will be helpful to those of you who did not major in English in college and thus may not be aware of every one of the technical reasons for correct English.

Some of the mechanics rules are debatable. I, for example, always put the comma before the "and" in a series. Others do not. Each of us can usually find a source that substantiates our position. Even the "experts" continue to disagree. A well-known author of over fifty popular books wrote to tell me that every word in English can be every part of speech, depending on how it is used. While I feel that this is a slight exaggeration (how do you use "the" as a verb?), it is a valid point. Another debatable point is the use of conjunctions to begin sentences. Technically this is not allowed, but all modern authors begin sentences with "and," "but," and "yet." Reserve this privilege for proficient students who use them judiciously. Those who teach advanced students at the upper grade levels probably should ignore this restriction, except in formal writing.

Since you explain the "why" of all the corrections when you go over the Caught'ya, you do not want to go beyond what your students can learn. As I have mentioned, you also need to keep in mind that the end result is not to learn the terms, but to write correctly. Who cares if sometime in the future your students can recognize and label subordinate clauses? Future employers do care, however, that their future employees can punctuate them correctly in their writing.

By using the eight parts of speech (terms you do want to teach to your students), you easily can explain all the essential grammar and usage without using the more technical terms. For example, you can explain a participial phrase by identifying it as a phrase that has a verb in it and is used as an adjective. You can follow that up with examples to illustrate the use of commas to set off the phrase. Only English teachers need to know how to recognize participial phrases by name. For further suggestions, consult the "Introductory Notes" to the Appendix or the mini-lessons in Chapter 4.

Those of you who are home-schooling or tutoring only a few children can still use this story even though it is set in a public school. You can use the story as is, or you can modify it to center around your child's neighborhood. The basketball team can be a city league instead of a school team. The rest can be adapted.

Those of you who are teachers in a church-school where there are often mixed grade levels, will find that the story is generic enough to appeal to a wide span of ages of children from thirteen to eighteen. My advanced eighth graders are enjoying it this year even though they are only thirteen years old.

Please note that there are two tests at the end of this chapter. On the upper levels, it is important to document student progress. In addition, in most high schools, semester exams are mandatory.

Use these sentences to forge a partnership with your students, a partnership that will result in improved writing, increased vocabulary, and lots of shared laughs. A summary of this story has been included in Chapter 6.

100 Caught'ya Sentences: Charlie Excess Does It Again	**B** – Sentence for the board. **C** – Corrected version of the sentence.
1. disparate Paragraph (beginning of story) Commas (long introductory adverbs, 2 adjectives — go over rule) Optional comma (after "time") No comma after "man" (non-restrictive modifier) Hyphen (one-sided — see Appendix for explanation)	B - once upon a time in a school not so very disparate from yours a young man named charlie excess led a very dull one sided life C - Once upon a time (,) in a school not so very disparate from yours, a young man named Charlie Excess led a very dull, one-sided life.
2. proboscis **NOTE:** *Warn students of passive verb that needs to be changed.* No Paragraph (continued narration/same topic) Optional comma (short introductory adverb) Strong verbs (correct passive to active) Comma (compound sentence) Use of active vs. passive voice (Active is always better.)	B - all day he attended horribly hard high school and all evening his proboscis was buried in his books C - All day(,) he attended Horribly Hard High School, and all evening he buried his proboscis in his books.

100 Caught'ya Sentences: Charlie Excess Does It Again	**B** – Sentence for the board. **C** – Corrected version of the sentence.
3. naught No paragraph (continued narration) Conjunction (Do not begin a sentence with one.) Quotation marks (around something that is not a real word) Commas (verb series) Parallel construction (Discuss in reference to the verb series.) Use of "who" (subject) and "whom" (object) Adjective clause (who did naught but attend classes . . .) Difference between a clause and a phrase	B - and charlie was a straight A student who did naught but attend class study and sleep C - Charlie was a straight "A" student who did naught but attend class, study, and sleep. NOTE: *Now that you have introduced the difference between a phrase and a clause, you can elicit that difference from your students every time you encounter a phrase or a clause.* *Also, please notice that I always use the "who" form of that pronoun in the board sentence. This makes the children have to think whether to use "who" or "whom" every time. You might want to point this out to your students. Make them think. After I first go over the concept, I always notice an incorrect overuse of "whom" in my students' writings. This quickly corrects itself. You also might want to point out the common error and confusion between the use of "who" or "whom" and "that." "Who" and "whom" refer to people, and "that" refers to anything else. Many people incorrectly use "that" to refer to people.*

100 Caught'ya Sentences: Charlie Excess Does It Again	**B** – Sentence for the board. **C** – Corrected version of the sentence.
4. meretricious No paragraph (continued narration) Commas (predicate series) Parallel construction (Discuss in reference to predicate series.) Use of contractions (avoid except in dialogue) Verb tense shift (story is in past tense) Run-on (too many ideas in one sentence — make 2 sentences) No comma if subordinate clause at end ("since . . . ") Plural of "party" (Discuss plurals of nouns that end in "y.") Title of book (Discuss underlines vs. quotes, capitalization.)	B - he never attended partys did not participate in any sports and doesn't know any girls except suzie meretricious and he isn't even sure what she looks like since her nose is always buried in a textbook such as The joys of boring english. C - He never attended parties, did not participate in any sports, and did not know any girls except Suzie Meretricious. He wasn't even sure what she looked like since her nose was always buried in a textbook such as *The Joys of Boring English.* NOTE: *This is not the only possible correct answer.*
5. a plethora of Paragraph (introduces new characters) Apostrophe (singular possessive) Comma (subordinate clause at beginning) Subordinate clauses Subordinating conjunctions (Go over them all and begin to memorize.) Introduction of simple, compound, and complex sentences (This sentence is complex.) Possibility of a misplaced modifier (after "grades" the next word needs to refer to Charlie's parents) Improper placement of preposition at end of sentence Homophone (their/there/they're)	B - while charlies parents were pleased with his grades they still found a plethora of picky things to nag and torture their only son with. C - While Charlie's parents were pleased with his grades, they still found a plethora of picky things with which to nag and torture their only son. NOTE: *These last two sentences are very complicated and include lots of concepts for discussion. Include in your board sentence and in your subsequent discussion only the ones you feel that your students can handle. Do not overwhelm them. If you teach advanced eleventh or twelfth graders, you hopefully will find*

(continued on p. 235)

100 Caught'ya Sentences: Charlie Excess Does It Again	**B** – Sentence for the board. **C** – Corrected version of the sentence.

that all of this is review. You could also use these two sentences as a pretest to see what your students know.

Whether a sentence is simple, compound, complex, or compound/complex will not be pointed out in the list of skills beside the sentences. If your students still cannot recognize the different types of sentences, you can point them out as they appear until students can spot the differences themselves.

---

6. pondered

No paragraph (still about parents)

Interjection "Wow" (possible punctuations: , or !)

Complex sentence

Strong verb (pondered)

Comma (subordinate clause at beginning of sentence)

Subordinating conjunction

Quotation marks (something that is not a real word)

Apostrophe (to form plural of a letter)

Contraction (avoid except in dialogue)

Run-on

Use of "well" (adverb) and "good" (adjective)

Gerund ("Being good" as subject)

B - wow even though charlie earned all A's his parents pondered why he didn't get all A+'s being good wasn't good enough

C - Wow! Even though Charlie earned all "A's," his parents pondered why he did not get all "A+'s." Being good was not good enough.

100 Caught'ya Sentences: Charlie Excess Does It Again	**B** – Sentence for the board. **C** – Corrected version of the sentence.
7. contention, carping Paragraph (new topic) Difference between "farther" (distance only) and "further" Difference between "between" (comparing 2 things) and "among" (comparing more than 2 things) Quotation marks (idiomatic expression) Subject/verb agreement (bones . . . were) Apostrophes (singular possessives) Comma rules (This is a good place to introduce the comma rules if some of your students tried to insert a comma in this sentence.)	B - further bones of contention between charlie and his carping parents was charlies room and charlies bedtime C - Further "bones of contention" between Charlie and his carping parents were Charlie's room and Charlie's bedtime.
8. squalid, appropriate No paragraph (continuing list of "bones of contention") Commas (predicate series, compound sentence) Parallel construction (Discuss in reference to predicate series.) Verb tense shift (story is in past tense) Strong verbs (made, put, threw, nagged) Coordinating conjunctions (Memorize them — and, or, nor, for, so, but, yet.) Compound sentence Homophone (through/threw) Spelling ("a lot" is 2 words)	B - charlie made his bed daily put his squalid clothing in the hamper and throws all trash in the appropriate place but his parents still nagged alot C - Charlie made his bed daily, put his squalid clothing in the hamper, and threw all trash in the appropriate place, but his parents still nagged a lot. **NOTE:** *It is a good idea to have your students memorize (if they have not already done so) the conjunctions (coordinating and subordinating) and the prepositions.*

100 Caught'ya Sentences: Charlie Excess Does It Again	**B** – Sentence for the board. **C** – Corrected version of the sentence.
9. fretted No paragraph (same topic) Conjunction (Do not begin a sentence with one.) Strong verb (fretted) Commas (appositive) No comma before "because" (subordinate clause at end) Use of prepositional phrase "around the pillow" as an adverb Use of passive verb (active is better) Run-on (solved by semicolon) Use of semicolon in a compound sentence Contractions (Avoid except in dialogue.) Difference between "accept" and "except"	B - and his mom the neat freak fretted because the bedspread wasn't tucked appropriately around the pillow she didn't except any excuses C - His mom, the neat freak, fretted because he didn't tuck the bedspread around the pillow appropriately; she did not accept any excuses
10. primly No paragraph (same topic) Comma (compound sentence) Semicolon (use in compound sentence instead of coordinating conjunction) End punctuation (exclamation mark or period) Homophones (to/too/two, there/their/they're) Interjection (horror of horrors) Comma or exclamation mark (interjection) Use of irony (horror of horrors)	B - his desk was never neat enough too please his mom horror of horrors their were school books piled primly on top C - His desk was never neat enough to please his mom; horror of horrors, there were school books piled primly on top! NOTE: *From this point on I will misspell the common homophones about half of the time. This keeps students guessing. Make sure that you discuss the correct spelling and use of each homophone even if you spell it correctly on the board. Of course, if all of your students no longer experience any difficulty with the common homophones, ignore this comment.*

100 Caught'ya Sentences: Charlie Excess Does It Again	**B** – Sentence for the board. **C** – Corrected version of the sentence.
11. martinet, disciplinarian No paragraph (continuation) Apostrophe (singular possessive) Commas (appositive, before "even" to make sense of sentence) Numbers (Write out numbers of two words or less.) Incorrect placement of preposition at end of sentence	B - charlies dad the disciplinarian and martinet in the family complained if charlies light was on 1 minute after ten o'clock even when charlie had a major test to study for C - Charlie's dad, the disciplinarian and martinet in the family, complained if Charlie's light was on one minute after ten o'clock, even when Charlie had to study for a major test.
12. comestibles No paragraph (same topic) Apostrophe (singular possessive) Commas (noun series, introductory adverb phrase) Parallel construction (Discuss in reference to noun series.) Use of semicolon in compound sentence for effect Verb tense shift (story in past tense)	B - charlies parents nagged him about bedtime laundry comestibles his clothes and his room in short they are never satisfied C - Charlie's parents nagged him about bedtime, laundry, comestibles, his clothes, and his room; in short, they were never satisfied.
13. abhorred Paragraph (quote) Conjunction (Do not begin a sentence with one.) Strong verb (abhorred) Quotation marks (quote) No new paragraph (same speaker) Run-on Use of "good" (adjective) and "well"(adverb), "bad" (adjective), and "badly" (adverb) Use of "as" instead of "like" in a comparison	B - and charlie abhorred it. i'm a good kid he said to himself i don't do bad things like other kids do he muttered C - Charlie abhorred it. "I'm a good kid," he said to himself. "I don't do bad things as other kids do," he muttered.

100 Caught'ya Sentences: Charlie Excess Does It Again	B – Sentence for the board. C – Corrected version of the sentence.
14. groused No paragraph (same speaker) Quotation marks (quote) Placement of question mark inside quotation marks Use of reflexive pronoun ("himself") No comma (subordinate clause at end)	B - why do they always pick on me he groused to himself as he walked to the library to study C - "Why do they always pick on me?" he groused to himself as he walked to the library to study.
15. carrel Paragraph (change of place) Commas (interrupter) Transitive and intransitive verbs ("sit" has no object and "set" takes object) Participial phrase (sitting in a very uncomfortable . . .) No comma after "uncomfortable" (2nd adjective is color)	B - charlie as usual spent the evening setting in a very uncomfortable gray study carrel at the library C - Charlie, as usual, spent the evening sitting in a very uncomfortable gray study carrel at the library.
16. ensconced No paragraph (same place, same action) Use of "that" to refer to animals and objects and "whom" to refer to people Use of "who" (subject of "is") and "whom" (object of "knew") Commas (date, city/state, appositive, compound sentence, adjective clause as a parenthetical expression — "whom Charlie knew . . . ", parenthetical expression — "as usual") 2 Adjective clauses with "who" and "whom" (no need for commas) Verb tense shift (story is in past tense)	B - it was saturday night september 15th 1991 in gainesville florida (put the name of your city and state here) and no one inhabited the library except a few librarians that charlie knew by name and suzie meretricious who is ensconced in a book as usual C - It was Saturday night, September 15th, 1991, in Gainesville, Florida, and no one inhabited the library except a few librarians, whom Charlie knew by name, and Suzie Meretricious who was ensconced in a book, as usual.

100 Caught'ya Sentences: Charlie Excess Does It Again	**B** – Sentence for the board. **C** – Corrected version of the sentence.
17. carped, encumbered, redoubtable Paragraph (new topic) Run-on Strong verb (encumbered) Commas (parenthetical expression — "especially . . . ," appositive) Capitalization of subjects (only languages) Negatives	B - charlie was depressed his parents carped constantly and his teachers especially mrs longpapers his english teacher encumbered him with a redoubtable amount of work and he had no friends and he never had any fun C - Charlie was depressed. His parents carped constantly. His teachers, especially Mrs. Longpapers, his English teacher, encumbered him with a redoubtable amount of work. He had no friends. He never had any fun. **NOTE:** *There are many other ways to correct this run-on sentence. Accept any correct answer from students. Another way to correct this, for example, could be writing a series of compound sentences.*
18. diabolically, pique No paragraph (continuation of lament) Homophones (knew/new, to/too/two) Commas (parenthetical expression — "in order . . . ") Split infinitive (Don't split them as in *Star Trek* — "to boldly go . . . ") Verb tense shift (story is in past tense) Plural rules (review all)	B - charlie just new that his teachers in order to pique the students got together to diabolically plan big assignments that are due on the same day. C - Charlie just knew that his teachers, in order to pique the students, diabolically got together to plan big assignments that were due on the same day.

100 Caught'ya Sentences: Charlie Excess Does It Again	B – Sentence for the board. C – Corrected version of the sentence.
19. ruminated Paragraph (quote) Apostrophes (contractions) Homophone (past/passed) Punctuation (quote, quote with a question) Numbers (Write them out.) Commas (compound sentence, parenthetical expression or interrupter) Use of "good" and "well" (In this sentence, "good" is a predicate adjective.)	B - ive grown 10 inches in the passed year and my mirror tells me that im beginning to look good despite the glasses. where are the girls he ruminated C - "I've grown ten inches in the past year, and my mirror tells me that I'm beginning to look good, despite the glasses. Where are the girls?" he ruminated.
20. apex Paragraph (change in topic) Quotation marks (quote) Commas (direct address, quote) Apostrophe (singular possessive)	B - hi suzie he said to the apex of suzies head C - "Hi, Suzie," he said to the apex of Suzie's head.
21. masticating Paragraph (new speaker) Quotation marks (quote) Commas (interjection, direct address, quote, participial phrase) Transitive and intransitive verbs (lie and lay) Run-on Participial phrase ("masticating . . . ") Book title (underline) No comma (title of book is necessary and thus a restrictive modifier)	B - mmph charles go away i'm studying mumbled suzie masticating the end of her pencil and lying the book equally boring math flat on the table C - "Mmph, Charles, go away. I'm studying," mumbled Suzie, masticating the end of her pencil and laying the book *Equally Boring Math* flat on the table.

100 Caught'ya Sentences: Charlie Excess Does It Again	**B** – Sentence for the board. **C** – Corrected version of the sentence.
22. athenaeum, swine 2 Paragraphs (new speaker) Quotation marks (quote) Participial phrase (shocking all the Saturday-night patrons . . .) Exclamation point (Charlie yelled rather emphatically) Hyphen (Saturday-night) Commas (quotes, direct address, participial phrase — "shocking . . . ") Homophone (you're/your) Run-on Metaphor (You're a crazy swine.)	B - i've had ENOUGH yelled charlie shocking all the saturday night patrons of the athenaeum. shut up stupid whispered suzie your a crazy swine C - "I've had ENOUGH!" yelled Charlie, shocking all the Saturday-night patrons of the athenaeum. "Shut up, stupid," whispered Suzie. "You're a crazy swine."
23. arduous Paragraph (narrator) Conjunction (Do not begin a sentence with one.) Gerund (the use of a verb as a noun — "deciding") Commas (interrupter) Verb tense shift (story is in past tense)	B - but deciding on a course of action though is arduous C - Deciding on a course of action, though, was arduous.
24. cogitating No paragraph (still deciding) Commas (participial phrase, compound sentence) Misplaced modifier (Charlie's foot is not doing the thinking)	B - cogitating for an hour charlies foot went to sleep in the process but he finally came up with a solution C - Cogitating for an hour, Charlie finally came up with a solution, but his foot went to sleep in the process.

100 Caught'ya Sentences: Charlie Excess Does It Again	**B** – Sentence for the board. **C** – Corrected version of the sentence.
25. dullard, perturbing 2 Paragraphs (new speaker) Use of single word sentence for effect Run-on Improper use of conjunction "and" to begin a sentence Quotation marks (2 quotes, 2nd one is interrupted) Apostrophe (contraction of "that is") No hyphen ("middle school" used as a noun, not an adjective) Commas (compound sentence, quotes, interjection, direct address) Use of reflexive pronoun (himself) Homophone (you're/your)	B - basketball! thats the ticket im tall and i used to be good when i was in middle school and i like it he told himself. hush you dullard hissed suzie your perturbing me C - "Basketball! That's the ticket. I'm tall. I used to be good when I was in middle school, and I like it," he told himself. "Hush, you dullard," hissed Suzie. "You're perturbing me."
26. surcease Paragraph (narrator speaking — new speaker) Improper use of conjunction "so" to begin a sentence Optional comma after "month" (introductory adverb phrase) Awkward phrasing of board sentence Numbers (Write them out.)	B - so for the next month charlie practiced every afternoon without surcease for 3 hours C - For the next month (,) Charlie practiced every afternoon for three hours without surcease.

100 Caught'ya Sentences: Charlie Excess Does It Again	**B** – Sentence for the board. **C** – Corrected version of the sentence.
27. staunchly No paragraph (continuation) Strong verb (practiced) Combining of sentences for better writing Run-on No comma (not compound sentence — compound direct object) Hyphen (lay-up) Transitive and intransitive verbs ("rise" has no object and "raise" takes an object)	B - he staunchly practiced his jump shots and he practiced his lay up shots and he has risen his basket average C - He staunchly practiced his jump shots and his lay-up shots. He raised his basket average. **NOTE:** *There are other correct solutions.*
28. goggles, vexatious, spectacles No paragraph (continuation) Strong verb (purchased) Capitalization of name even though used as an adjective No comma after "Jabbar" ("protection goggles" is like "jet plane") Comma (2 adjectives) Use of "that" for objects and "who" for people Use of "good" as adjective and "well" as adverb	B - he purchased karim abdul jabbar protection goggles to cover the thick vexatious spectacles that he hated but which made him see good C - He purchased Karim Abdul Jabbar protection goggles to cover the thick, vexatious spectacles that he hated but which made him see well.
29. abandoned No paragraph (same topic) Strong verb (abandoned) Direct object (studies) Plural rules (Discuss them all, especially the one for nouns that end in "y")	B - charlie entirely abandoned his studys. C - Charlie entirely abandoned his studies.

100 Caught'ya Sentences: Charlie Excess Does It Again	B – Sentence for the board. C – Corrected version of the sentence.
30. gulled, strategies No paragraph (same topic) Strong verb (gulled) Prepositional phrases and their uses (there are 3) Plural rules (words that end in "o")	B - he gulled his parents by reading books at night about basketball heros and strategies C - He gulled his parents by reading books at night about basketball heros and strategies.
31. sanguine No paragraph (same topic) Misplaced modifier (team isn't scared) Commas (introductory adverb — not optional because it is needed to make sense, participial phrase) Correct word order in sentence (for clarity) Apostrophe (singular possessive) Verb tense shift (story is in past tense) Use of exclamation mark for emphasis	B - finally charlie tried out for the schools basketball team scared but strangely sanguine and makes the cut C - Finally, scared but strangely sanguine, Charlie tried out for the school's basketball team and made the cut! **NOTE:** *There are other ways to handle this sentence, but the word "Charlie" has to follow soon after the word "sanguine."* *Example: Finally, Charlie, scared but strangely sanguine, tried out for the school's basketball team and made the cut!*
32. ecstatic, renewed Paragraph (new action) Passive verb (active is better) Misplaced modifier (his devotion is not ecstatic, *he* is) Comma (participle)	B - ecstatic charlies devotion to the sport is renewed C - Ecstatic, Charlie renewed his devotion to the sport.

100 Caught'ya Sentences: Charlie Excess Does It Again	**B** – Sentence for the board. **C** – Corrected version of the sentence.
33. adroit No paragraph (he is reiterating devotion) Spelling of "until" Comma (participial phrase) Possibility of dangling modifier ("Charlie" has to follow "set" since it is he who practiced daily) Verb tense shift (story is in past tense) Numbers (Write out numbers of two or less words.)	B - practicing daily untill the sun set Charlie got so adroit at basketball that he could make the basket from a distance of 30 feet C - Practicing daily until the sun set, Charlie got so adroit at basketball that he could make the basket from a distance of thirty feet.
34. ablest, uncanny, adroitly, purloin No paragraph (same topic) Split verb (Don't split helping verb and main verb unless it is absolutely necessary for clarity Numbers (Write them out.) Colon (list) Hyphen (lay-up) Commas (noun series after a colon without other commas) Parallel construction (Discuss in reference to noun series.) Split infinitive (to adroitly purloin)	B - he became the ablest forward horribly hard high school had ever had for 3 reasons his lay up shots his jump shots and his uncanny ability to adroitly purloin the ball from the other team C - He became the ablest forward Horribly Hard High School ever had had for three reasons: his lay-up shots, his jump shots, and his uncanny ability to purloin the ball adroitly from the other team.
35. flocked Paragraph (new topic) Comma (compound sentence) Homophone (to/too/two) Simile (like mosquitoes . . .) Plural rule (nouns that end in "o")	B - girls flocked to his side like mosquitoes to a bare arm and they asked him for dates C - Girls flocked to his side like mosquitoes to a bare arm, and they asked him for dates.

100 Caught'ya Sentences: Charlie Excess Does It Again	B – Sentence for the board. C – Corrected version of the sentence.
36. basking No paragraph (same topic) Conjunction (Do not begin a sentence with one.) Misplaced modifier (Saturday night is not basking in the attention, Charlie is) Comma (participial phrase)	B - and basking in all the attention every saturday night charlie went out with a different girl C - Basking in all the attention, Charlie went out with a different girl every Saturday night.
37. residuum No paragraph (same topic) Commas (interrupter) Strong verb (spent)	B - the residuum of his time however charlie happily spent practicing at the hoop C - The residuum of his time, however, Charlie happily spent practicing at the hoop.
38. closure Paragraph (different topic and time) Comma (long introductory adverb, compound sentence) Numbers (Write them out.) Subject/verb agreement ("everyone" is a singular indefinite pronoun) Antecedent/pronoun agreement ("everyone" is a singular indefinite pronoun — "their" is a plural pronoun) Collective noun "crowd" (Discuss collective nouns.) Plurals (nouns with irregular plurals)	B - near the closure of 1 game charlie was 30 feet from the basket and everyone in the crowd were on their feet C - Near the closure of one game, Charlie was thirty feet from the basket, and everyone in the crowd was on his or her feet. **NOTE:** *Now that collective nouns and indefinite pronouns have been introduced, it might be a good idea to go over the common ones. Agreement of pronouns with indefinite pronoun antecedents and agreement of verbs with indefinite pronoun or collective noun subjects proves very difficult for students to understand. From now on, whenever a collective noun or indefinite pronoun appears in a sentence, it would be a good idea to go over them. There are lists of the most common ones in the Appendix.*

100 Caught'ya Sentences: Charlie Excess Does It Again	**B** – Sentence for the board. **C** – Corrected version of the sentence.
39. traipsed, establish No paragraph (same topic — the game) Hyphen (giraffe-like) Strong verb (traipsed up) Simile (giraffe-like player from the . . .) Homophone (to/too/two)	B - a giraffe like player from the other team traipsed up too establish a screen C - A giraffe-like player from the other team traipsed up to establish a screen.
40. assayed, wraith **NOTE:** *Warn students of awkward phrasing which needs to be corrected. This sentence is very difficult.* No paragraph (same topic — the game) Misplaced modifier (the ball didn't assay the situation, Charlie did) Comma (subordinate clause) Awkward phrasing (renders sentence unclear) Passive voice (active is better) Simile (wraith-like arms) Hyphen (wraith-like) Use of "who" (subject) and "whom" (object) Incorrect placement of preposition at the end of a sentence	B - after he assayed the situation the ball was knocked out of the wraith like arms of his opponent by charlie who was able to reach in C - After he assayed the situation, Charlie was able to reach in and knock the ball out of the wraith-like arms of his opponent. **NOTE:** *There are other solutions, but just make sure that "Charlie" follows the word "situation."*

100 Caught'ya Sentences: Charlie Excess Does It Again	**B** – Sentence for the board. **C** – Corrected version of the sentence.
41. spheroid No paragraph (same topic) Spelling (Discuss rule: If a noun has a consonant/vowel/consonant, double the final consonant before adding a suffix like "ed" that begins with a vowel.) Commas (predicate series) Parallel construction (Discuss in reference to verb series.) Hyphen (lay-up) Strong verbs (grabbed, ran, dashed)	B - he grabed the bouncing spheroid ran down the court and dashed in for a lay up shot C - He grabbed the bouncing spheroid, ran down the court, and dashed in for a lay-up shot.
42. gambit, harum-scarum (an adverb used as a noun here) No paragraph (same topic) Use of comma or exclamation (after interjection) Strong verb (won) Hyphen (Harum-scarums)	B - whoopee this gambit won the game for the horribly hard high school harum-scarums C - Whoopee! This gambit won the game for the Horribly Hard High School Harum-scarums.
43. stripling Paragraph (new topic, new time) Commas (introductory adverb — optional, appositive, 2 adjectives) Verb tense shift (story is in the past tense) Comparatives and superlatives (more and most) Hyphen (teenager-filled)	B - overnight charlie the hero becomes the most popular stripling in the entire teenager filled school C - Overnight (,) Charlie, the hero, became the most popular stripling in the entire, teenager-filled school.

100 Caught'ya Sentences: Charlie Excess Does It Again	**B** – Sentence for the board. **C** – Corrected version of the sentence.
44. truculent, palled Paragraph (new topic) Commas (introductory adverb and adverb phrase — first comma is optional) Verb tense shift (story is in the past tense)	B - finally in the middle of a particularly truculent game charlie realizes that his life still palled C - Finally(,) in the middle of a particularly truculent game, Charlie realized that his life still palled.
45. deduced, accolades Paragraph (quote) Quotation marks (interrupted quote) Commas (verb series, compound sentence, quote) Parallel construction (Discuss in reference to verb series.) Run-on	B - i live and eat and breathe basketball and i'm not having any fun he deduced and applause and accolades aren't enough." C - "I live, eat, and breathe basketball, and I'm not having any fun," he deduced. "Applause and accolades aren't enough." **NOTE:** *There are other correct answers to this one.*
46. blustered, novice Paragraph (new speaker) Quotation marks (quote) Use of comma or exclamation (after interjection) Commas (direct address, quote, parenthetical expression) Simile (like a complete novice) Misplaced modifier (the shot is not the novice, Charlie is)	B - hey stop mumbling and play ball charlie blustered the coach as charlie missed a shot like a complete novice C - "Hey, stop mumbling and play ball, Charlie," blustered the coach as Charlie, like a complete novice, missed a shot.

100 Caught'ya Sentences: Charlie Excess Does It Again	**B** – Sentence for the board. **C** – Corrected version of the sentence.
47. dolor, lugubrious, heavyhearted Paragraph (about new person) Commas (participial phrase, 2 adjectives, quote) Possible misplaced modifier ("heavyhearted Charlie" has to follow "dolor" because it is he who is lost in it) Homophone (hear/here) Quotation marks (quote with a question) Reflexive pronoun (himself) Question mark (inside quote)	B - lost in his dolor lugubrious heavyhearted charlie didn't hear. what about girls he whimpered to himself C - Lost in his dolor, lugubrious, heavyhearted Charlie didn't hear. "What about girls?" he whimpered to himself.
48. a plethora of, a dearth of No paragraph (still Charlie speaking on same topic) Quotation marks (quote) No comma before "because" (subordinate clause at end) Comma (compound sentence) Homophone (there/their/they're) Subjunctive (if I were)	B - a plethora of girls hang on me because i'm the star of the team but a dearth of them would be their if i was no longer a hero C - "A plethora of girls hang on me because I'm the star of the team, but a dearth of them would be there if I were no longer a hero."

100 Caught'ya Sentences: Charlie Excess Does It Again	B – Sentence for the board. C – Corrected version of the sentence.
49. musings Paragraph (new speaker) Quotation marks (quote) Commas (introductory "yes," direct address, quote, participial phrase) No comma before "when" (subordinate clause at end of sentence)	B - hey watch the ball charlie shouted the coach when charlie lost in his musings missed another shot C - "Hey, watch the ball, Charlie," shouted the coach when Charlie, lost in his musings, missed another shot. NOTE: *From this point on, I really pour on the vocabulary words. If the use of all these unknown words will frustrate your students, substitute a familiar synonym for some of them. All of these words can be replaced by a one-word, simple synonym.*
50. carp, reiterated Paragraph (new speaker) Punctuation (interrupted quote — note no capital in "and") Commas (after "yes" or "no" at the beginning of a sentence, quote, compound sentence) Use of "I" as subject and "me" as object Pronoun order ("my sister and I")	B - yes my parents carp at me all the time he reiterated and me and my sister don't get along either C - "Yes, my parents carp at me all the time," he reiterated, "and my sister and I don't get along either."
51. vociferated, wits Paragraph (new speaker) Quotation marks (quote) Commas (quote, interjection, direct address, compound sentence) Homophone (you're/your) Use of exclamation for effect	B - the coach vociferated from the side hey charlie keep your wits on the game or your out C - The coach vociferated from the side, "Hey, Charlie, keep your wits on the game, or you're out!"

100 Caught'ya Sentences: Charlie Excess Does It Again	**B** – Sentence for the board. **C** – Corrected version of the sentence.
52. disconsolate, limelight Paragraph (new speaker) Quotation marks (quote) Run-on Commas (quote, adverb clause as a parenthetical expression) Gerund ("breathing" as subject) Homophone (no/know)	B - i'm lonely and disconsolate even in the limelight breathing basketball all the time is know fun concluded charlie. C - "I'm lonely and disconsolat,e even in the limelight. Breathing basketball all the time is no fun," concluded Charlie.
53. cretin, bellowed Paragraph (new speaker) Quotation marks (quote) Commas (interjection, direct address, quote, participial phrase) Transitive and intransitive verbs ("sit" has no object and "set" takes object) Possible misplaced modifier ("coach" has to go before "disgusted") Homophone (by/buy/bye) Apostrophe (singular possessive)	B - hey set on the sidelines cretin bellowed the coach disgusted by charlies performance C - "Hey, sit on the sidelines, cretin," bellowed the coach, disgusted by Charlie's performance.

100 Caught'ya Sentences: Charlie Excess Does It Again	**B** – Sentence for the board. **C** – Corrected version of the sentence.
54. ceased, hedonist, amenities Paragraph (back to narrator) Run-on (make a compound sentence) Use of semicolon in a compound sentence Comma (appositive) Metaphor (a pleasure animal) Apostrophe (singular possessive) Use of the noun "pleasure" as an adjective Quotation marks around invented expression	B - charlie ceased to practice basketball at home he became a total hedonist a pleasure animal grooving on lifes amenities C - Charlie ceased to practice basketball at home; he became a total hedonist, a "pleasure animal" grooving on life's amenities.
55. comely No paragraph (same topic) Gerund phrases (finding . . . party) Use of "who" (subject) and "whom" (object) Strong verb (occupied) Verb tense shift (story is in past tense) No commas around the adjective clause "whom he could love" (not an appositive)	B - finding a comely girl who he could love and getting to the next party occupy his every thought C - Finding a comely girl whom he could love and getting to the next party occupied his every thought.

100 Caught'ya Sentences: Charlie Excess Does It Again	**B** – Sentence for the board. **C** – Corrected version of the sentence.
56. rationalizing, moot No paragraph (same topic) Awkward phrasing (makes meaning unclear) Optional use of the word "that" to clarify meaning Indirect quote Comma (participial phrase) Misplaced modifier ("it" is not rationalizing, Charlie is) Homophone (to/too/two)	B - rationalizing that his parents were on to him for everything anyway it was a moot point to study at all charlie thought C - Rationalizing that his parents were on to him for everything anyway, Charlie thought (that) it was a moot point to study at all. **NOTE:** *There are other correct ways to handle this sentence as long as the word "Charlie" is near the modifier.*
57. imbibe, commenced Paragraph (new topic, new time) Spelling ("a lot" is 2 words — Ask students to come up with an alternative.) Plural (nouns that end in "y") Comma (compound sentence) Quotation marks around "cool" (to denote irony — note placement of period)	B - charlie began to imbibe alot of beer at partys and he commenced smoking cigarettes to look cool C - Charlie began to imbibe a lot (great quantities, a plethora) of beer at parties, and he commenced smoking cigarettes to look "cool."
58. covertly No paragraph (same topic) Commas (participial phrase, infinitive series) Possible misplaced modifier ("Charlie" has to be near "window.") Parallel construction (Discuss in reference to the infinitive series.) Homophone (to/too/two)	B - climbing through his bedroom window charlie covertly snuck out almost every night too go to parties drink and to smoke C - Climbing through his bedroom window, Charlie covertly snuck out almost every night to go to parties, (to) drink, and (to) smoke.

100 Caught'ya Sentences: Charlie Excess Does It Again	**B** – Sentence for the board. **C** – Corrected version of the sentence.
59. diminutive Paragraph (introducing new person) Commas (appositive — he only has one younger sister) No commas ("diminutive younger" — 2nd adjective is age, not a compound sentence — compound predicate) Overuse of pronouns (meaning not clear) Apostrophe (singular possessive)	B - his diminutive younger sister melinda smelled the smoke and alcohol on him and blackmailed him for her silence C - Charlie's diminutive younger sister, Melinda, smelled the smoke and alcohol on him and blackmailed him for her silence.
60. pretense Paragraph (new topic) Verb tense shift (story in the past tense) Quotation marks (idiomatic expression) Use of the noun "party" as an adjective Comma (compound sentence — note placement within quotation marks)	B - charlie has become the original party animal and he no longer even makes a pretense of studying C - Charlie had become the original "party animal," and he no longer even made a pretense of studying.

100 Caught'ya Sentences: Charlie Excess Does It Again	**B** – Sentence for the board. **C** – Corrected version of the sentence.
61. a plethora of, appellations, feted No paragraph (same topic) Comma (compound sentence — unless you want to omit the 2nd "he" to avoid redundancy) Use of "this/that/these/those" Use of "who" (subject) and "whom" (object of preposition in this sentence) Improper placement of a preposition at the end of the sentence (You can use the well-known quote, "That is something up with which I will not put," as an illustration of the absurdity of consistently adhering to this rule.)	B - he partied with a plethora of girls but he couldn't remember the appellations of any of these who he had feted with C - He partied with a plethora of girls, but he couldn't remember the appellations of any of them with whom he had feted. Or - He partied with a plethora of girls but couldn't remember the appellations of any of them with whom he had feted.
62. prowess, dissipated Paragraph (new topic) Comma (parenthetical expression) Apostrophe (singular possessive) Use of the noun "basketball" as an adjective Strong verb (dissipated)	B - needless to say charlies basketball prowess dissipated C - Needless to say, Charlie's basketball prowess dissipated.
63. stalwart No paragraph (same topic) Apostrophes (plural possessive, singular possessive) Difference between "affect" and "effect" Homophone (too/to/two) Run-on Comma before "too" (interrupter) Use of semicolon for effect in compound sentence	B - all the other players games were affected too they had come to depend on stalwart charlies moves C - All the other players' games were affected, too; they had come to depend on stalwart Charlie's moves.

100 Caught'ya Sentences: Charlie Excess Does It Again	**B** – Sentence for the board. **C** – Corrected version of the sentence.
64. disport No paragraph (same topic) Commas (subordinate clause, appositive) Complex sentence Contraction (avoid use unless in dialogue) Use of "well" as adverb and "good" as adjective Run-on Difference between "farther" (distance only) and "further" Awkward ending of sentence (incomplete final clause — needs a verb)	B - while charlie showed up for games he did not disport himself good he couldn't throw the ball further than his little sister melinda C - While Charlie showed up for games, he did not disport himself well. He could not throw the ball farther than his little sister, Melinda, could toss it.
65. dissipated No paragraph (same topic) Homophones (too/to/two) Comma (compound-complex sentence) Verb tense shift (story is in past tense) Use of "bad" as adjective and "badly" as adverb No comma before "when" (subordinate clause at end)	B - he was to dissipated from all the partying to show up at all the practices and he plays bad when he did go C - He was too dissipated from all the partying to show up at all the practices, and he played badly when he did go.

100 Caught'ya Sentences: Charlie Excess Does It Again	**B** – Sentence for the board. **C** – Corrected version of the sentence.
66. plummeted, mandatory, ousted **NOTE:** *Warn students of awkward phrasing. Sentence needs to be rewritten.* Paragraph (new topic, new time) Comma (appositive) No comma (subordinate clause at end of sentence in rewritten version) Misplaced modifier (The coach's grades did not plummet; Charlie's did.) Passive voice (Active voice is always preferable — sentence needs to be changed so this is possible.) Overuse of pronouns (Antecedents are unclear.)	B - when his grades plummeted below a 1.5 the mandatory grade point average necessary to participate in sports the coach ousted him from the team C - The coach ousted Charlie from the team when his grades plummeted below a 1.5, the mandatory average necessary to participate in sports.
67. proverbial Paragraph (new characters — parents) Apostrophes (singular possessive, plural possessive) Comma after"yes" (introductory word at the beginning of sentence) No comma (subordinate clause at end) Use of "out" as an adverb (where they came)	B - yes charlies parents blood pressure hit the proverbial roof when report cards came out C - Yes, Charlie's parents' blood pressure hit the proverbial roof when report cards came out.

100 Caught'ya Sentences: Charlie Excess Does It Again	**B** – Sentence for the board. **C** – Corrected version of the sentence.
68. belligerent, slothful No paragraph (same topic) Homophone (their/there/they're) Commas (series of adjective phrases) Parallel Construction (Discuss in reference to adjective phrases.) Prepositions and prepositional phrases (a good place for a review)	B - there son had become belligerent to adults slothful around the house and neglectful of his homework C - Their son had become belligerent to adults, slothful around the house, and neglectful of his homework.
69. livid, choleric Paragraph (new topic) Abbreviations (Mr. and Mrs.) Commas (adjective series) Single present participle as adjective (raging) Parallel construction (Discuss in relation to adjective series.) Metaphor (parents as creatures)	B - mr and mrs excess became livid choleric and raging creatures C - Mr. and Mrs. Excess became livid, choleric, and raging creatures.
70. acrimony, iniquitous No paragraph (describing what they did in their anger) Spelling of "disappointment" Comma (long introductory adverb phrase) Possibility of misplaced modifier ("they" are grounding Charlie) Strong verb (grounded) Homophone (their/there/they're)	B - with much disappointment and acrimony they grounded their iniquitous son within an inch of his young life C - With much disappointment and acrimony, they grounded their iniquitous son within an inch of his young life.

100 Caught'ya Sentences: Charlie Excess Does It Again	**B** – Sentence for the board. **C** – Corrected version of the sentence.
71. clandestinely No paragraph (same topic) Apostrophes (singular possessive) Overuse of pronouns (meaning unclear) Use of "his son's" instead of "Charlie's" to avoid redundancy Strong verb (slept)	B - charlies father even slept in his room in order to keep him from clandestinely sneaking out at night C - Charlie's father even slept in his son's room in order to keep Charlie from clandestinely sneaking out at night.
72. sinewy, hedonistic, "fair-weather" Paragraph (now discussing Charlie) Parallel construction ("his" and "friends" — otherwise the sentence is not indicating two different types of friends) Comma (2 adjectives) Quotation marks around idiomatic expression Split verb (had all been) Hyphen (fair-weather)	B - charlie found out that his sinewy athletic and partying friends from his hedonistic days had all been of the fair weather type C - Charlie found out that his sinewy, athletic friends and his partying friends from his hedonistic days all had been of the "fair-weather" type.
73. associated, forsook **NOTE:** *Warn students to rephrase this awkward sentence.* No paragraph (same topic) Quotation marks around "partying dudes" (idiomatic expression) Use of "whom" as object and "who" as subject Antecedent/pronoun agreement ("group" is a collective noun and singular) Awkward sentence structure Strong verb (forsook) Homophone (their/there/they're) Plural rules (Review plural rules, especially the "i" before "e" one.)	B - the group of partying dudes who charlie had associated with forsook their new freind C - The group of "partying dudes" with whom Charlie had associated forsook its (or the) new friend.

100 Caught'ya Sentences: Charlie Excess Does It Again	**B** – Sentence for the board. **C** – Corrected version of the sentence.
74. feigned No paragraph (still about "fair-weather" friends) Apostrophes (singular possessive) Strong verb (feigned) Antecedent/pronoun agreement ("team" is a collective noun and singular) Difference between "its" and "it's"	B - charlies former basketball team feigned ignorance of their former mates name C - Charlie's former basketball team feigned ignorance of its former mate's name.
75. vexatious No paragraph (same topic) Apostrophe (singular possessive) Commas (appositive) No comma (2 adjectives — but 2nd adjective indicates age) Verb tense shift (story is in past tense)	B - even charlies vexatious little sister melinda has nothing to do with her big brother for a few days C - Even Charlie's vexatious little sister, Melinda, had nothing to do with her big brother for a few days.
76. hapless, ostracised, woebegone Paragraph (new topic) Commas (2 adjectives, adjective series) Parallel construction (Discuss in reference to adjective series.)	B - hapless ostracised charlie was miserable lonely and woebegone C - Hapless, ostracised Charlie was miserable, lonely, and woebegone.

100 Caught'ya Sentences: Charlie Excess Does It Again	B – Sentence for the board. C – Corrected version of the sentence.
77. vapid, repetitive No paragraph (same topic) No comma (not a compound sentence because of "and that" — compound direct object) Plural (nouns ending in "y") Optional comma before "except" (for clarity) Use of parallel construction ("that . . . that") Plural rules (consonant "y" to "ies" rule) Indirect quote	B - he realized that the alcohol had dulled his mind and that he couldn't remember much from the partys except that the conversation had been repetitive and vapid C - He realized that the alcohol had dulled his mind and that he couldn't remember much from the parties (,) except that the conversation had been repetitive and vapid.
78. inhaled, rendered, No paragraph (same topic) Strong verb (rendered) No comma (subordinate clause at the end) Verb tense shift (story in past)	B - the cigarette smoke he had inhaled rendered him breathless when he tries to run C - The cigarette smoke he had inhaled rendered him breathless when he tried to run.
79. lamented, solicited Paragraph (new speaker) Quotation marks (quote) Question mark (within a quote) Use of parentheses Apostrophe (singular possessive) Placement of period inside parentheses	B - what am i going to do he lamented to his sister. he had sunk so low that he even solicited his little sisters advice C - "What am I going to do?" he lamented to his sister. (He had sunk so low that he even solicited his little sister's advice.)

100 Caught'ya Sentences: Charlie Excess Does It Again	**B** – Sentence for the board. **C** – Corrected version of the sentence.
80. propitiously Paragraph (new speaker) Quotation marks (quote) Homophone (your/you're) Commas (quote, participial phrase) No comma before "and" (compound imperative sentence does not take a comma because subjects are not stated)	B - go get help and bring up your grades melinda suggested propitiously trying to be sympathetic C - "Go get help and bring up your grades," Melinda suggested propitiously, trying to be sympathetic.
81. alienated, estranged Paragraph (new speaker) Quotation marks (quote) Run-on Commas (direct address, compound sentence, 2 adjectives) Capitalization of the word "I" No comma (subordinate clause at end)	B - where melinda charlie asked i feel alienated and estranged from everyone and i have disappointed our parents and they really are nice caring people and i wont go to college if i can't improve my grades C - "Where, Melinda?" Charlie asked. "I feel alienated and estranged from everyone. I have disappointed our parents, and they really are nice, caring people. I won't go to college if I can't improve my grades." **NOTE:** *This sentence also can be corrected by using a few compound sentences.*

100 Caught'ya Sentences: Charlie Excess Does It Again	**B** – Sentence for the board. **C** – Corrected version of the sentence.
82. interjected, ensure **NOTE:** *Point out awkward phrasing that needs to be corrected.* Paragraph (new speaker) Quotation marks (quote) Capitalization of "Mom" (name used by children for their mother — proper noun) Homophones (to/too/two, there/their/they're) Commas (quote, subordinate clause with "when") Run-on	B - melinda interjected talk to mom when mom follows you to school to ensure that you get their that will be a start C - Melinda interjected, "When Mom follows you to school to ensure that you get there, talk to her. That will be a start."
83. sage, progenitor **NOTE:** *This is a good point to review all pronouns.* Paragraph (time change) Comma (subordinate clause) Optional comma (short introductory adverb of time) Correct pronoun use ("he" is subject, "him" is object) Correct pronoun order Abbreviation (Mrs.) Apostrophe (singular possessive) Capitalization of languages	B - the next day as his mother and him stood outside mrs longpaperss english class charlie asked his sage progenitor for suggestions C - The next day (,) as he and his mother stood outside Mrs. Longpapers's English class, Charlie asked his progenitor for suggestions. **NOTE:** *You must be sure that the following Caught'ya and the Caught'ya after that (#84 and #85) are on the board together. You want to show how to handle a paragraph change within a quote. Ask your students to consider both Caught'yas when they punctuate the first one.*

100 Caught'ya Sentences: Charlie Excess Does It Again	**B** – Sentence for the board. **C** – Corrected version of the sentence.
84. queried, hedonist Paragraph (new person) Quotation marks (quote that is continued in next paragraph) Commas (direct address, compound sentence) Run-on Gerund ("Playing" and "being" as subjects) No end quotation mark (a quote that is continued into the next paragraph)	B - mom what can i do he queried i'm so confused and i hate studying all the time and playing basketball constantly is no fun and being a total hedonist just isn't for me C - "Mom, what can I do?" he queried. "I'm so confused. I hate studying all the time. Playing basketball constantly is no fun, and being a total hedonist just isn't for me. (No end quotation mark; see #85.) **NOTE:** *There are other correct ways to rewrite this run-on sentence.*
85. lugubriously Paragraph (same quote but different topic — show how to punctuate) Quotation marks (quote) Capitalization of the word "I" Parallel construction (infinitives "to find" and "to play" — 2nd "to" can be eliminated to avoid redundancy and to correct split infinitive) Split infinitive (to . . . occasionally play) Run-on Homophone (too/to/two) Comma before "too" (used as interrupter) Comma (quote)	B - all i ever wanted was to find a close friend my age and to occasionally play basketball having a girlfriend would help to he concluded lugubriously C - "All I ever wanted was to find a close friend my age and (to) play basketball occasionally. Having a girlfriend would help, too," he concluded lugubriously.

100 Caught'ya Sentences: Charlie Excess Does It Again	**B** – Sentence for the board. **C** – Corrected version of the sentence.
86. sagaciously, objective, mediator Paragraph (new speaker) Punctuation (interrupted quote) Abbreviation (Mrs.) No comma between "objective" and "party" ("third party" is like one word) Comma before simile (parenthetical expression) Simile (like an independent mediator)	B - why don't you go see the guidance counselor mrs excess suggested sagaciously. she would be an objective third party sort of like an independent mediator C - "Why don't you go see the guidance counselor?" Mrs. Excess suggested sagaciously. "She would be an objective third party, sort of like an independent mediator."
87. tactfully No paragraph (same speaker even though indirect quote) Indirect quote Pronouns ("she" is subject, "her" is object) Homophone (too/to/two) Comma (before "too" meaning "also")	B - she added tactfully that maybe it would be a good idea for her husband and she to go see a counselor too. both her and charlie felt much better after this conversation C - She added tactfully that maybe it would be a good idea for both her husband and her to go see a counselor, too. Both she and Charlie felt much better after this conversation.
88. ascertain, astute Paragraph (new topic) Verb tense shift (story in past) Run-on No comma with 2 adjectives ("gray-haired" indicates color) Hyphen (gray-haired) Use of "who" for people and "that" for things Apostrophe (plural possessive)	B - charlie goes to ascertain whether the guidance counselor can help him and she was an astute gray haired lady that had seen her share of teenagers problems C - Charlie went to ascertain whether the guidance counselor could help him. She was an astute gray-haired lady who had seen her share of teenagers' problems.

100 Caught'ya Sentences: Charlie Excess Does It Again	**B** – Sentence for the board. **C** – Corrected version of the sentence.
89. temperance, jocularly Paragraph (new speaker) Quotation marks (quote) Strong verb (advised) Run-on Commas (direct address, quote) Homophone (too/to/two)	B - moderation charlie she advised temperance is the clue to your happiness you try to hard to live up to your last name she added jocularly C - "Moderation, Charlie," she advised. "Temperance is the clue to your happiness. You try too hard to live up to your last name," she added jocularly.
90. proffer, entreated Paragraph (new speaker) Quotation marks (quote) Homophone (to/too/two) Simile (like that of a small child) Comma ("too" meaning "also") Question mark (inside quote)	B - would you proffer that advice to my parents to charlie entreated in a voice like that of a small child C - "Would you proffer that advice to my parents, too?" Charlie entreated in a voice like that of a small child.
91. articulated Paragraph (new speaker) Quotation marks (quote) Commas (quote, 2 adjectives, participial phrase)	B - i'd be delighted articulated the kind understanding counselor smiling at charlie with a friendly grin C - "I'd be delighted," articulated the kind, understanding counselor, smiling at Charlie with a friendly grin.

100 Caught'ya Sentences: Charlie Excess Does It Again	**B** – Sentence for the board. **C** – Corrected version of the sentence.
92. tempered, bouts, clamoring Paragraph (new topic) Apostrophes (singular possessive, plural possessive, plural of single letters) Adjective/noun agreement (adjectives indicate more than one life) Plural (nouns ending in "fe" or "ve") Run-on Comma (2 adjectives) Quotation marks (something that is not a word)	B - charlies and his parents life changed charlie tempered his studying with short daily bouts of basketball his parents stopped clamoring for all A+'s and settled for A's and B's C - Charlie's and his parents' lives changed. Charlie tempered his studying with short, daily bouts of basketball. His parents stopped clamoring for all "A+'s" and settled for "A's" and "B's."
93. waxed No paragraph (same topic) Conjunction (Do not begin a sentence with one.) Apostrophe (singular possessive) Comma (subordinate clause) Strong verbs (waxed, rejoined)	B - and when charlies grades waxed to a 3.5 average on the next report card he rejoined the basketball team C - When Charlie's grades waxed to a 3.5 average on the next report card, he rejoined the basketball team.
94. perambulated, proboscis, tome Paragraph (time change) Commas (introductory adverb — optional, participial phrase, parenthetical expression "as usual") Strong verb (perambulated) Homophone (there/their/they're)	B - one saturday night charlie perambulated to the library. there was suzie proboscis buried as usual in a tome C - One Saturday night(,) Charlie perambulated to the library. There was Suzie, proboscis buried, as usual, in a tome.

100 Caught'ya Sentences: Charlie Excess Does It Again	**B** – Sentence for the board. **C** – Corrected version of the sentence.
95. preempted, spectacles No paragraph (same topic) Strong verbs (preempted, took, removed) No commas (not compound sentences — compound predicates) Run-on	B - charlie preempted her book and took her chin gently in his hand he removed her spectacles and looked her in the eye C - Charlie preempted her book and took her chin gently in his hand. He removed her spectacles and looked her in the eye. **NOTE:** *There are other correct ways of writing this sentence.*
96. supplicated Paragraph (person speaking) Quotation marks (quote) Commas (compound sentence, quote) Spelling rule ("i" before "e" except after "c")	B - you've not been my friend because weve never talked but you have been my library companion for years. please be my friend he supplicated C - "You've not been my friend because we've never talked, but you have been my library companion for years. Please be my friend," he supplicated.
97. orbs Paragraph (new person) No comma after "big" (2nd adjective is color) Quotation marks (interrupted quote) Use of "who" as subject, "whom" as object, "that" for things Comma (quote) Capitalization of the word "I" Run-on	B - suzie looked at him through big green orbs filled with tears. you are the only boy who i like she whispered i could use a friend C - Suzie looked at him through big green orbs filled with tears. "You are the only boy whom I like," she whispered. "I could use a friend."

100 Caught'ya Sentences: Charlie Excess Does It Again	B – Sentence for the board. C – Corrected version of the sentence.
98. quivered Paragraph (new topic) Commas (interrupter — "too") Run-on Strong verbs (told, quivered) Homophone (to/too/two) No comma before "since" (subordinate clause at end)	B - charlie told suzie about learning to live a life of moderation suzie quivered with joy since she to had been lonely and unhappy C - Charlie told Suzie about learning to live a life of moderation. Suzie quivered with joy since she, too, had been lonely and unhappy.
99. inaugurated, commenced No paragraph (same topic) Run-on Strong verbs (inaugurated, commenced, gave) Comma (compound sentence) Verb tense shift (story in past) Quotation marks around "dates" (not usual meaning of word)	B - suzie and charlie inaugurated study groups with other students and they commenced dating each other and charlie gives suzie his class ring they had study dates where they studied between kisses C - Suzie and Charlie inaugurated study groups with other students. They commenced dating each other, and Charlie gave Suzie his class ring. They had study "dates" where they studied between kisses. **NOTE:** *There are other ways to correct this passage.*
100. commiserating No paragraph (same topic) Quotation marks around "paper parties" (made-up term) Comma (participial phrase) Verb tense shift (story in past) Collective noun "group" (Discuss collective nouns being singular or plural.)	B - charlie and suzie give paper parties where a group of kids got together and wrote their papers for school commiserating over the hard work C - Charlie and Suzie gave "paper parties" where a group of kids got together and wrote their papers for school, commiserating over the hard work.

100 Caught'ya Sentences: Charlie Excess Does It Again	**B** – Sentence for the board. **C** – Corrected version of the sentence.
P.S. palatable, tempered, sage Paragraph (new topic) Commas (adjective series, compound sentence) Run-on Homophones (to/too/two, their/there/they're)	B - life was palatable tempered and even fun and charlie realized how nice and helpful his parents were and he frequently went to them for there sage advice C - Life was palatable, tempered, and even fun. Charlie realized how nice and helpful his parents had been, and he frequently went to them for their sage advice.
P.P.S. beckoned Paragraph (new character, new topic, new place) Optional comma after "office" (introductory adverb phrase) Strong verbs (smiled, beckoned) No comma before "and" (not a compound sentence — compound predicate)	B - in her cheerful office the guidance counselor smiled and beckoned in the next student C - In her cheerful office(,) the guidance counselor smiled and beckoned in the next student.

MID-YEAR CAUGHT'YA TEST   Class _____
High School   Name _____
                              Date_____

DIRECTIONS: Write in all corrections. When a paragraph is needed,
put a paragraph sign to indicate the need for a paragraph. There
are six paragraphs in this test. All but one period (in the one run-
on sentence) have been provided. Only one sentence, the one with
the misplaced modifier, needs rewriting. There are two verb tense
shift errors. Remember all the comma rules (two adjectives before
a noun, compound sentences, subordinate clauses, appositives,
participial phrases, series, interrupters, direct addresses). All of
the comma rules we have gone over so far this year have been
included on this test!! Check for correct spelling of homophones.
Watch out for the split verb. Good luck!

the king of excess

when charlie the kid who did everything to excess plunged
himself into the world of basketball he ignored his studies his
family and his only friend suzie. charlie convinced himself that
he was doing the right thing because hed never felt healthier
in his life. he jogged 5 miles a day and he practiced at the
basket for at least 3 hours a day. abandoning his work
charlie angered mrs longpapers. since he no longer did his
long boring math homework charlie also annoyed his math
teacher mr calculus. charlie however was living on borrowed
time his parents are soon bound to find out what is happening.
what are you doing too yourself charlie suzie queried one day
in the halls of school. flexing his muscles charlies pride in his
prowess showed in his voice. im devoting myself to a
worthwhile endeavor and im feeling wonderful he said. why
asked suzie puzzled at charlies turnabout. im doing this
because i want to become a hero and get all the pretty girls
charlie replied. oh charlie sighed suzie hurt by this statement. i
miss you in the library.

MID-YEAR CAUGHT'YA TEST KEY
High School

TEACHERS: *You may wish to help your students by counting the errors in each line and listing them in the margin before you photocopy the test for your students. It also helps to read the test out loud to your students before they begin to work.*

The King of Excess

When Charlie, the kid who did everything to excess, plunged himself into the world of basketball, he ignored his studies, his family, and his only friend, Suzie. Charlie convinced himself that he was doing the right thing because he'd never felt healthier in his life. He jogged five miles a day, and he practiced at the basket for at least three hours a day. Abandoning his work, Charlie angered Mrs. Longpapers. Since he no longer did his long, boring math homework, Charlie also annoyed his math teacher, Mr. Calculus. Charlie, however, was living on borrowed time. His parents were bound to find out soon what was happening. (OR "parents soon")

"What are you doing to yourself, Charlie?" Suzie queried one day in the halls of school.

Flexing his muscles, Charlie showed in his voice his pride in his prowess. "I'm devoting myself to a worthwhile endeavor, and I'm feeling wonderful," he said.

"Why?" asked Suzie, puzzled at Charlie's turnabout.

"I'm doing this because I want to become a hero and get all the pretty girls," Charlie replied.

"Oh, Charlie," sighed Suzie, hurt by this statement. "I miss you in the library."

END-OF-THE-YEAR	Class _____
CAUGHT'YA TEST, page 1	Name _____
High School	Date _____

DIRECTIONS: Be very careful. You will receive no hints for this test, except that there are eleven (11) paragraphs, only one misplaced modifier, and one run-on sentence. Other than in the run-on sentence, all end punctuation has been provided. Edit this story as best you can. Use the paragraph sign to indicate the need for a paragraph. Write in all corrections. Write in corrections of misspelled words. Rewrite sentences where the meanings are unclear. When you reach the end of the test, do the following: write the numbers 1 to 20 on the back of your paper and tell the part of speech of each word in the last sentence of the story. After you have finished the entire test, go back and check your work several times. Good editors always do. Good luck! This is an extremely difficult test with almost two hundred errors to find.

the party of the year

when the end of the school year arrived charlie and his freinds wanted to celebrate. charlies parents let him host the event at there house and they even promised to remain out of sight for the evening. charlie the nice kind person that he was invited every student who he knew. he didnt however invite any teachers. charlie why not invite mrs longpapers and mr calculus asked suzie as she contemplated the invitation list. i like them and there fun. besides they both gave me an A for the semester she concluded. no i dont think so suzie said charlie. if we invited teachers we would feel inhibited. let them have there own partys he added feeling a little guilty. all right charlie your probably right. its not good to mix grown ups and teenagers said suzie giving in gracefully. suzie the more organized of the 2 planned the food and charlie sends the invitations. suzie buys popcorn cold cuts cheeses small pizzas and alot of cola charlie wrote addressed and mailed out

(continued)

53 invitations. the long awaited day of the party finally arrives. everyone dressed in their best pair of jeans and looked forward to a evening of celebration. charlies parents living room was soon filled with loud music dancing teens and much laughter. annoyed by the loud music the tv was kept at top volume in the bedroom by charlies father. charlies mother who always was able to tune out teenagers buried her nose in a long romantic novel lovely loving lovers by her favorite author. melinda the little sneak peered stealthily into the living room for a view of the festivities. her favorite teddy bear and her were curious. some day me and my friends will have a party like this melinda promised herself as she crawled under the table to watch for a chance to snatch a slice of pizza. she laid there listening to the music and watching dancing feet shuffle. she couldn't see further than 3 feet because the tablecloth blocked her view. many hours later as they were cleaning up from the very successful party charlies parents found melinda sound asleep pizza in her hand under the table. even the teddy bear had its slice of pizza. charlie who was happy at the success of his first party carried his sister to bed. alls good that ends good sighed charlies mother as she cleaned pizza off the floor. they didnt act to bad for teenagers said mr excess charlies father. oh charlie is a very good kid but his taste in music is horrible he concluded tiredly to his wife.

END-OF-THE-YEAR
CAUGHT'YA TEST KEY, page 1
High School

TEACHERS: *This is an extremely difficult test. It covers a year's worth of material. You might want to have a review before the test. On the day of the test, read the test out loud to your students to give them hints of where to paragraph. Remind students to number their papers from 1 to 20 on the back and write the part of speech of each word in the last sentence. Since there are almost two hundred errors in this test, depending on how you count the misplaced modifier, you might want to grade it on a percentage basis. Those of you who teach lower grades (eighth, ninth, and tenth) might want to help out students by counting the possible errors in each line and writing these numbers in the margin before you photocopy the test for your students. Because it is so difficult to count errors correctly, you might want to triple-check your figures.*

The Party of the Year

When the end of the school year arrived, Charlie and his friends wanted to celebrate. Charlie's parents let him host the event at their house, and they even promised to remain out of sight for the evening. Charlie, the nice, kind person that he was, invited every student whom he knew. He didn't, however, invite any teachers.

"Charlie, why not invite Mrs. Longpapers and Mr. Calculus?" asked Suzie as she contemplated the invitation list. "I like them, and they're fun. Besides, they both gave me an 'A' for the semester," she concluded.

"No, I don't think so, Suzie," said Charlie. "If we invited teachers, we would feel inhibited. Let them have their own parties," he added, feeling a little guilty.

"All right, Charlie, you're probably right. It's not good to mix grown-ups and teenagers," said Suzie, giving in gracefully.

Suzie, the more organized of the two, planned the food, and Charlie sent the invitations. Suzie bought popcorn,

(continued)

cold cuts, cheeses, small pizzas, and a lot of cola. Charlie wrote, addressed, and mailed out fifty-three invitations.

The long-awaited day of the party finally arrived. Everyone dressed in his or her best pair of jeans and looked forward to an evening of celebration. Charlie's parents' living room was soon filled with loud music, dancing teens, and much laughter.

Annoyed by the loud music, Charlie's father kept the T.V. on top volume in the bedroom. Charlie's mother, who always was able to tune out teenagers, buried her nose in a long, romantic novel <u>Lovely Loving Lovers</u> by her favorite author. Melinda, the little sneak, peered stealthily into the living room for a view of the festivities. She and her favorite teddy bear were curious.

"Some day my friends and I will have a party like this," Melinda promised herself as she crawled under the table to watch for a chance to snatch a slice of pizza. She lay there, listening to the music and watching dancing feet shuffle. She could not see farther than three feet because the tablecloth blocked her view.

Many hours later, as they were cleaning up from the very successful party, Charlie's parents found Melinda sound asleep, pizza in her hand, under the table. Even the teddy bear had its slice of pizza. Charlie, who was happy at the success of his first party, carried his sister to bed.

"All's well that ends well," sighed Charlie's mother as she cleaned pizza off the floor.

"They didn't act too badly for teenagers," said Mr. Excess, Charlie's father. "Oh, Charlie is a very good kid, but his taste in music is horrible," he concluded tiredly to his wife.

**END-OF-THE-YEAR
CAUGHT'YA TEST KEY, page 3
High School**

**Key for parts of speech
of last sentence**

1. interjection
2. noun (subject)
3. verb
4. adjective (noun marker)
5. adverb (modifies an adjective)
6. adjective
7. noun
8. conjunction
9. possessive pronoun
10. noun
11. preposition
12. noun (object of preposition)
13. verb
14. adjective (predicate)
15. pronoun (subject)
16. verb
17. adverb
18. preposition
19. possessive pronoun
20. noun (object of preposition)

Everything You Never Wanted
to Know about

Grammar, Mechanics, and Usage

But I'm Going to Tell You Anyway

Introductory Notes

Those of us who are familiar with some topic or idea sometimes forget that not everyone else has the same knowledge. This is why I included the Appendix. Until you have taught English for a year at eighth-grade level or higher — unless you have had a teacher somewhere along the way who has successfully taught you all the terms or unless you have studied a grammar book from cover to cover and keep up with all the changes — there is no way that you can know the rules of English grammar and usage and its many technical terms.

Complex as the language is, even we English teachers have trouble with some of the picky mechanical points of the language. We also disagree!

English is a fluid language. It changes with use. Thirty years ago we strewed commas with near abandon. Now we are eliminating many of them. People begin sentences with conjunctions. I have real trouble with this. Conjunctions are for joining ideas, not starting them. What teachers once called a dependent clause is now lumped under the heading of subordinate clause, and so on. Because of this, we all do not follow identical rules and terms, yet all of us can still be officially correct at the same time.

Do not be afraid to disagree with me. Many points of mechanics, especially the use of some commas, are highly debatable, extremely personal, and sometimes linked to a particular generation. When I participated in writing the English curriculum for the middle schools in my county, seven English teachers sat around a table and argued various points. Each of us always could find a book that would support a specific opinion. After a few hot debates, we finally had to agree to use one standard book for reference.

When Maupin House asked me to include a section that could serve as a reference for the grammar, mechanics, and usage terms, frankly, I was apprehensive. It seemed to be a dangerous task for one person to attempt. Grammar books are usually written by committees and still have errors in them. I solicited the help of my mother and several of my colleagues, all excellent grammarians, to ensure accuracy.

Parents, do not feel inadequate or undereducated if you find yourself frequently referring to this Appendix. Most of you, like me, probably did not major in English in college and do not read grammar textbooks for pleasure. This Appendix will help you understand the whys and wherefores of a sentence so that you can explain it to your children in a way that makes sense to them. Once students understand the underlying concept of a rule, they can apply that rule to their own sentences when they write.

The terms are listed in alphabetical order for easier reference. If you do not fully understand a term used in one explanation, you can look it up under its own heading. All the terms that a non-English major might need for clarity are cross-referenced. Also included in the Appendix are some tips for teaching some of these concepts. I hope you find these suggestions useful. All of these teaching tips have proven successful with students.

Examples are included for each concept. If, after reading the explanation of a concept, you still do not feel comfortable with it, study the examples. Right here, I feel the need to apologize for the truly uninspired examples. The majority of them concerns my two dogs and one cat. They are always present when I write, like furry muses.

While I am aware that the current trend is to abandon the teaching of certain concepts and terms such as the parts of speech, as a foreign language teacher I know that students need to know these terms to learn the new language. If a student is aware of the difference, for example, between a subject pronoun and an object pronoun, then French pronouns do not hold much horror.

In my French classes, I often find myself having to teach the parts of speech just so my students and I can have a common frame of reference. It is hard enough to learn a different vocabulary in another language. If, in addition, students have to learn basic grammar terms as well, it makes the task much more difficult. The grammar of languages based on Indo-European is basically similar. The verb may come at the end of a sentence in German or at the end of a subordinate clause in Dutch, or there may be an extra verb tense to learn in Spanish and French. The basic concepts and parts of speech, however, are the same in all these languages.

I believe, too, in the teaching of sentence diagramming to help teach students to think and to use logic. Diagramming reaches some left-brain students who otherwise might never understand sentence structure.

After teaching rudimentary sentence diagramming through the Caught'yas (see the mini-lessons in Chapter 4), I almost can see the light bulb go on in some students' eyes. I do not believe, however, in teaching all the picky points of English like infinitive phrases, gerund phrases, etc., unless there is a reason for learning them, like learning the appropriate placement of commas.

Even then, when teaching the picky points is unavoidable, I advise trying to avoid using the abstruse, esoteric grammar terms. Instead, explain these points in simpler terms, using the eight parts of speech for reference. I don't say to students, for example, "If a participial phrase begins or interrupts a sentence, you need to set it off by commas. You need to know that a participial phrase is . . . " Even after you explain what a participial phrase is, your students probably are gazing out the window, minds elsewhere.

Try something like this instead. "See this phrase. What part of speech is it? An adjective? Right! You know the parts of speech! Well, look at it. It contains a form of a verb. If you see a group of words like this at the beginning of a sentence or in the middle of a sentence, you need to put commas after it or around it." That gets their attention because it is something that makes sense to them. I do mention the words "participial phrase" so that students may recognize the term in the future in case other English teachers use it,

but I stress the concept and not the specific term.

For further example, instead of talking about "gerunds," you can teach your students to use a verb or a verb phrase as a noun. In teaching verbs like "lie" and "lay," "sit" and "set," and "rise" and "raise," a teacher can explain the use of each verb by talking about verbs that take direct objects and verbs that do not, instead of introducing new labels "transitive" and "intransitive."

Basically, the bottom line is to write correctly, not to memorize the names for everything or to identify certain phrases or clauses. When a student writes a sentence, the labels are useless. The task of English teachers is not to teach rules and technical terms, but to teach correct writing and editing skills.

Those of you who teach younger children will want to avoid the more complicated concepts anyway. Use your own judgement as to how much your students can comprehend and transfer to their writing. Each class is different. Each group has different needs. You know them best.

If you are writing your own sentences, you will want to keep this book open to the Appendix as you write. Make certain that you include in your story the grammar, mechanics, and usage that you know your students can comfortably grasp. The list is comprehensive so that this book can be used at any level. I hope that all of you find this Appendix a useful tool in teaching this beautiful language of ours.

ABBREVIATIONS
Most abbreviations are followed by a period.

Examples: Mr., Mrs.

If, however, all the letters of the abbreviation are capitals, a period is not used.

Examples: NATO, USSR, USA

Usually abbreviations begin with a capital letter. Abbreviations of units of measure, however, do not begin with capital letters. They also do not require periods. The only exception is the abbreviation for inch.

Examples: mph, hp, l, km, and so on.

Exception: in.

Common abbreviations: Mr., Mrs., Ms., Dr., St., Rd., Ave., Co., Inc., days of the week, months of the year, A.M., P.M., O.K.,etc.

State abbreviations: The United States Postal Service now uses special abbreviations for each state. These are always two letters, both capitalized, without any periods. The postal code of twenty-nine states is the first two letters of the state. If the state has two words, the first letter of each word is used.

States that follow this rule: AL, AR, CA, CO, DE, FL, ID, IL, IN, MA, MI, NE, NH, NJ, NM, NY, NC, ND, OH, OK, OR, RI, SC, SD, UT, WA, WV, WI, and WY

Exceptions: Alaska (AK), Arizona (AZ), Connecticut (CT), Georgia (GA), Hawaii (HI), Iowa (IA), Kansas (KS), Kentucky (KY), Louisiana (LA), Maine (ME), Maryland (MD), Minnesota (MN), Mississippi (MS), Missouri (MO), Montana (MT), Nevada (NV), Pennsylvania (PA), Tennessee (TN), Texas (TX), Vermont (VT), and Virginia (VA).

ACCEPT/EXCEPT
These two words often are confusing for students since they are so close in sound. Every time one of them appears in a Caught'ya, you can explain the difference.

1. Accept is a verb that means "to receive willingly."

Example: The fat Rottweiler surely **will accept** the bone.

2. Except is a preposition that means "excluding" or "other than." It can also be used as a verb that means "to leave out" or "exclude."

Examples: The fat Rottweiler eats everything **except** onions. (preposition)

The fire department will **except** men over seventy-two inches from that kind of duty. (verb)

ACTIVE VS PASSIVE VERB VOICES
1. **Active:** In the active voice, the subject does the action. Active voice is always better for more effective writing.

Example: The owner **pets** the happy dog on the head.

2. **Passive:** In the passive voice, the subject **receives** the action. Encourage students to try to avoid passive voice if at all possible. It weakens writing and often muddies the meaning in a sentence.

Example: The happy dog **was petted** on the head by the owner.

ADJECTIVE
An adjective describes a noun; it gives information about a noun.

Examples: ugly, pretty, big, little, this, four

An adjective answers one of the following three questions about a noun:
1) which one?
2) what kind?
3) how many?

Example: **The amazing** teacher taught **two** grade levels. (which teacher? **the** teacher; what kind of teacher? an **amazing** teacher; how many grade levels? **two** grade levels.)

ADJECTIVE CLAUSES
An adjective clause is any subordinate clause (a complete sentence made into an incomplete sentence by the addition of a subordinating conjunction) that acts as an adjective in a sentence.

Example: The house **where she lives** is filled with animals. ("She lives." would be a complete sentence without the addition of "where." "Where she lives" modifies the noun "house.")

Adjective clauses also can begin with a relative pronoun: who, whom, whose, which, that, where, or when.

Examples: The oven **which was small and dirty** could not be used.

This is the school **where my child is a student.**

The school **that my child attends** is a good one.

The teacher **who loves to laugh** has more fun.

Monday is the day **when we always write in our journals.**

The teacher **whom we admire** is retiring.

Jane Kiester, **whose dogs are obese,** teaches middle school.

ADVERB

An adverb is any word, phrase or clause that tells more about a verb; many of the single word adverbs end in "ly."

An adverb also tells to what extent an adjective or another adverb is true (very, extremely, and so on). This is called an intensifier.

Examples: a **very** hungry dog, an **extremely** sleepy cat

An adverb answers one of the following six questions about a verb, an adjective, or another adverb: where, when, why, how, how often, or to what extent it happened.

Examples: Where? The students learned grammar **at home.** (phrase)

When? **Yesterday** the teacher was absent.

How? The students **quickly** intimidated the substitute.

How often? The student yawned **four times** during class. (phrase)

To what extent? The teacher was **very** angry. (modifies the adjective "angry")

Why? She yelled **because she was angry.** (clause)

ADVERB CLAUSES

In the "olden days," an adverb clause was called an adverbial clause.

An adverb (or adverbial) clause is a subordinate clause that cannot stand on its own in a sentence. It acts as an adverb in a sentence.

Adverb clauses begin with a subordinating conjunction (see list under "Subordinating Conjunctions")

Examples: **Whenever the teacher taught grammar,** the students groaned. (When did the students groan? "Whenever the teacher . . .")

The students went home **when the last bell rang.** (When did the students go home? "when the bell rang.")

AFFECT/EFFECT

"Affect" and "effect" are two more words that many people confuse. If students have trouble with the correct use of these two words, use them in the Caught'yas and discuss their meanings.

1. **Affect** is a **verb** that means "to influence." It cannot be used as a noun.

Example: The eating habits of the fat Rottweiler will **affect** her girth.

2. **Effect** can be a **noun or a verb.** As a noun it means "the result of an action." As a verb it means "to cause to happen."

Examples: The **effect** of overeating is obvious in the width of the dog's belly. (noun)

The fat dog's owner **will effect** a new rule this week — no more scraps. (verb)

AGREEMENT

1. **Antecedent and pronoun:** It is important that everything agrees in a sentence. If the subject is singular, than the pronoun used later in the sentence also must be singular. If the subject is plural, the pronoun should be plural.

Example of incorrect agreement: **Everyone** ate **their** pizza. (The indefinite pronoun "everyone" is singular and thus the possessive pronoun which refers to it must also be singular.

Examples of correct agreement: **Everyone** ate **his** or **her** pizza.

Each finished **his** or **her** lunch.

The **teachers** ate **their** lunch.

The **teacher** ate **his** lunch.

2. **Subject and verb:** If the subject is singular, then the verb must also be singular. If the subject is plural, then the verb must be plural.

Examples: The **dog bays** at the full moon. (singular)

The **dogs bay** at the full moon. (plural)

3. **Verbs in a story:** When writing a story an author must keep all the verbs in the same tense. If the story starts in the present tense, it must continue in the present tense (unless, of course, there is a flashback or a reference to something general). If a story begins in the past, it must remain in the past and so on.

AMONG AND BETWEEN
"Among" and "between" are two prepositions that students often confuse, but they cease to be a problem very quickly after you point out the difference.

1. **Between** refers to two people, things, or groups.

Example: The cat slept **between** the two huge dogs.

2. **Among** refers to more than two people, things, or groups.

Example: The foolish cat slept **among** the four dogs.

ANTECEDENTS (*See also* COLLEC-TIVE NOUNS)
These are the words that come before a given word in a sentence, as in "antecedent/pronoun agreement," and are referred to by the given word. Thus, they must agree with each other. If one is singular, the other must also be singular, etc.

Example: The **pack** (antecedent) of dogs forsook **its** (pronoun) mistress. ("**Pack**" is singular and thus must be followed by a singular pronoun.)

APOSTROPHES
1. **Contractions** always contain apostrophes. A contraction comprises two words that are combined into one by omitting one or more letters. (*See* CONTRAC-TIONS for more information and examples.)

Common contractions: I'm, I've, can't, don't, haven't, isn't, it's, let's, they're, we're, we've, won't, you're

2. **Possessive nouns** always contain apostrophes. A possessive noun is a noun that shows ownership of something.

Singular: Always add 's to the noun.

Examples: The **dog's** growl is ferocious. (The growl belongs to the dog.)

The **glass's** rim is dirty. (The rim belongs to the glass.)

Plural: Add ' after the noun if the noun ends in "s."

Add 's to the noun if the plural does not end in "s."

Examples: The **dogs'** growls are fero-cious. (Several dogs "own" their growls.)

The **children's** laughter fills the room. (Several children "own" the laughter.

3. **Plurals of letters:** Form the plural of single letters by adding apostrophe "s."

Examples: You will find more **"E's"** in words than any other letter.

She received all **"A's"** on her report card.

APPOSITIVE
An appositive is a noun or a noun phrase that means the same thing as the noun that comes before it.

Appositives are set off by commas if they occur in the middle or end of a sentence and are not necessary to the meaning of the sentence.

Examples: Dino, **the Doberman with the floppy ears**, loves to eat bananas.

The dog who craves bananas is Dino, **the Doberman with the floppy ears.**

Appositives are set off by commas if the appositive is extra information and is not needed to complete the meaning of the sentence.

Examples: Jane Kiester, **an English teacher at Westwood**, loves dogs.

Always by her side are her two dogs, **a wimpy Rottweiler and an oversized Doberman.**

Appositives are not set off by commas if the information given is needed to identify the noun.

Example: Mrs. Kiester's son **John** loves to tease his mother.

(There are no commas to set off this appositive because Mrs. Kiester has more than one son. The name is necessary to determine to which son the sentence refers. Technically, this is called a restrictive modifier. If Mrs. Kiester has only one son, the comma is needed because the information is *not* necessary. This is called a non-restrictive modifier.)

(*See* MODIFIERS AND MISPLACED MODIFIERS for more information and examples of restrictive and non-restrictive appositives.)

ARTICLES

These are simply the three most commonly used adjectives. They are also called noun markers since they signal the arrival of a noun.

List of articles: a, an, the

1. Use "a" before a word that begins with a consonant.

Example: There is **a** lazy dog and **a** sleepy cat on the floor.

2. Use "an" before a word that begins with a vowel.

Example: **An** obnoxious black and white cat howled until someone let him out the door.

These three adjectives answer the question "which one?" (*See* NOUN MARKERS.)

BAD AND BADLY

These words often cause confusion. "Bad" is the adjective and should modify a noun. "Badly" is the adverb and should tell about a verb.

Examples: The **bad** dog begged for forgiveness. (adjective tells what kind of dog)

The poor dog **badly** wanted a bone. (adverb tells to what extent it wanted the bone)

When a sense verb such as "feel" functions as a verb of being, it is often followed by a predicate adjective. Thus, one would use the adjective form after such a verb.

Example: I feel **bad**. (Not "I feel badly," since one would not say "I am badly.")

BECAUSE AND SINCE

If you never put a comma before "because" and "since," you will be right 98 percent of the time. While there are some exceptions to this, they are rare. The words "because" and "since" begin adverb clauses. An adverb clause that begins a sentence needs a comma, but an adverb clause that follows the independent clause usually does not need a comma. Saying the sentence aloud is a good test.

About the only exceptions to this would be with a quotation or a series, in the case of "since" acting as a coordinating conjunction in a compound sentence, or in one of the few subordinate clauses that takes a comma for clarity.

Examples: **Because I like books about cats,** I read *The Literary Cat.* (adverb clause at the beginning of the sentence)

I read *The Literary Cat* **because I like books about cats.** (adverb clause that follows the independent clause)

BETWEEN (*See* AMONG AND BETWEEN)

BIBLIOGRAPHICAL FORMS

These do vary. Use the Modern Language Association form, and you will be safe. Most traditional grammar books have a large list explaining how to write any reference you may need in correct bibliographical form. Just make sure that you insist that students list the books, articles, etc. in their bibliographies in alphabetical order.

BUSINESS LETTERS (CORRECT FORMAT)

> Sender's address
> Sender's city, state   zip
> Date

Receiver's name
Receiver's address
Receiver's city, state   zip

Dear Sir or Madam:

The bulk of the letter should be written in block style, skipping lines between paragraphs.

> Sincerely yours,
> Write name here in cursive.
> Print or type name here.

CAPITALIZATION

Capitalize the following:

1. Abbreviations (See ABBREVIATIONS for the exceptions.)

2. Beginnings of sentences

3. First word in the greeting and closing of a letter

4. I

5. Names of months and days and holidays

6. Proper nouns and proper adjectives

7. Titles of long works (see TITLES)

– Capitalize first and last words.

– Capitalize all other words in title except prepositions, noun markers (a, an, the), and short conjunctions.

CHRONOLOGICAL ORDER

In writing stories and paragraphs, it is important to narrate the action in a logical order. Chronological order maintains a sequence of time.

CLAUSES AND PHRASES

1. **Phrase:** Simply stated, a phrase is a group of words that serves as one part of speech (like a noun or an adjective or an adverb). It lacks a subject or a verb or both. Prepositional phrases are the most common. These are phrases that begin with a preposition and end with a noun (in the dog house).

Examples: in the dog house, to the store, filled with anger, rubbing his ears

2. **Clause:** A clause, on the other hand, is a group of words that contains a subject *and* a verb. With the removal of a subordinating conjunction that begins it, it could stand on its own as a sentence.

Example: because the dog is lazy (The subject is the word "dog." The verb is the word "is.")

COLLECTIVE NOUNS   Collective nouns are nouns that take a group of something (many) and make that group one thing.

Common collective nouns: crew, class, orchestra, chorus, committee, family, flock, herd, fleet, jury, group, team, majority.

1. Most collective nouns are singular and therefore require the singular form of the verb. Also, any pronoun that refers to such a collective noun must be singular.

Examples: A **flock** of big birds **flies** over her house every autumn. ("Fly" would be the plural form of the verb)

The **group** applauded **its** leader. "Its" is the singular pronoun; "their" is the plural pronoun and thus is incorrect. This is one of the most common mistakes that people make in speech and in writing.

The girl's **family** took **its** vacation in June.

2. A few collective nouns are plural.

Example: The **people** took **their** dogs to the veterinarian.

COLONS

1. Use a colon before a list but never after a verb or a preposition.

Example: It is important to remember to bring the following to class: pencil, paper, and a big grin.

2. Use after the greeting in a business letter.

Examples: Dear Sir or Madam:

To Whom It May Concern:

3. Use a colon to separate the hour from the minute in telling time.

Examples: 5:45 P.M., 6:24 A.M.

4. If the wording that follows a colon forms a complete sentence, do not capitalize the first letter of the sentence.

Example: The question is as follows: do Dobermans like to eat broccoli?

COMBINING SENTENCES FOR CLEARER, MORE CONCISE WRITING

Combine two related sentences into one by making a compound subject and/or a compound verb or by adding an appositive. There are other ways to combine sentences. These are the most common.

Example: Change "The teacher hated spelling. Her students hated spelling." to "The teacher and her students hated spelling." (compound subject).

Change "The Rottweiler loved to sleep. She liked to lick her owner's face in the morning." (compound verb) to "The Rottweiler loved to sleep and liked to lick her owner's face in the morning."

Change "The Doberman had floppy ears. He also had a sweet disposition." to "The Doberman, who had floppy ears, had a sweet disposition." (adding an adjective clause)

COMMA RULES

1. Use commas to separate items in a series. There are many different kinds of series, one for each part of speech except conjunctions.

Examples: The teacher **entered** the class, **wrote** on the board, and **sat** down at her desk. (verb series)

The teacher ate **apples**, **bananas**, and **cherries**. (noun series)

The **nice**, **kind**, and **beautiful** teacher assigned no homework for the weekend. (adjective series)

The teacher sat down **quickly**, **quietly**, and **with great dignity**. (adverb series)

He went **to the store**, **down the aisle**, and **into the vegetable section**. (prepositional phrase series)

She sat with **him**, **her**, and **them**. (series of pronouns)

Oh boy, **wow**, and **whoopee**, the teacher had a great class! (series of interjections)

You also can have a series of predicate nouns and adjectives. (These are just nouns and adjectives that are located after the predicate.)

2. Use commas between two or more adjectives that precede a noun unless one of the adjectives expresses a single idea with the noun (jet plane) or the last adjective tells color (green, etc.) or age (old, young).

Comma needed: The **cute**, **fuzzy** dog barked at everyone.

Comma omitted: The **cute brown** dog barked at everyone. (color adjective)

The **noisy jet** plane flew overhead. ("Jet plane" is one idea. The adjective is really part of the noun.)

The **ugly young** dog wolfed down its food. (age adjective).

The general "rule of thumb" in this comma rule is to use a comma if it sounds right to use the word "and" instead of a comma.

Examples: The **old oaken** bucket was covered with **wet green** moss. (No commas needed as it would be awkward to say "The old and oaken bucket was covered with wet and green moss.")

The **floppy-eared**, **lazy** Doberman slept all day. (Here you use a comma because it makes sense to say "The floppy-eared and lazy Doberman slept all day.")

3. Use commas to separate the simple sentences included in a compound sentence. (See COMPOUND SENTENCES)

Example: The teacher wrote the sentence, and she put in a comma because the sentence was compound.

4. Use commas after words, phrases, and clauses that come at the beginning of sentences. "No" and "yes" are included here. They always are followed by a comma.

Examples: **No,** you may not turn in your homework late.

Yes, you may do extra work if you wish.

Wow, the student earned an A+ on his test!

At the end of the phrase, there should be a comma.

If a subordinate clause is at the beginning of a sentence, you have to put a comma after it.

Suddenly, the teacher yelled. (This comma is often debated. Put a comma if a breath or a pause would help clarify the sentence or if you want to accentuate the adverb.)

Well, she said that she would come.

5. Use commas to separate interrupters such as parenthetical expressions, direct addresses, and unnecessary appositives in a sentence.

Examples: Parenthetical expression — The big dog, **of course,** was a wimp.

Direct address: You know, **parents,** it is important to write correctly.

Parents, you know it is important to write correctly.

Unnecessary appositive: My cat, **Skeeter,** likes to sit on my lap as I write. (I have only one cat; therefore his name is not necessary for the meaning of the sentence to be clear.)

My dog Dino has floppy ears. (No commas are needed because I have two dogs, and I need to identify to which dog I refer.)

6. Use commas to separate the month and the day from the year.

Example: September 15, 1945

7. Use commas between the city and the state and after the state as well if the address is within the sentence.

Example: The animal lover lives in **Gainesville, Florida,** and teaches English at a middle school.

8. Use commas after the greeting in friendly letters and after the closing in both friendly and business letters.

Examples: Dear Jane,

Sincerely yours,

9. Use commas with quotation marks to set off what is being said out loud.

Examples: "Get off my foot," she whimpered to the heavy dog.

She whimpered to the heavy dog, "Get off my foot."

"If you don't get off my foot," she said, "I'll step on yours."

COMPARISONS

Adjectives

1. If you are comparing two or more things and the adjective has less than three syllables, add "er" to the adjective.

Example: Florida is **warmer** than Maine in the winter.

2. If you are stating that something is the best (or worst), add "est" to the adjective if it has less than three syllables.

Example: Florida is the **warmest** state in the union.

3. Using "more" and "most"

Adjectives of three or more syllables almost always use the words more" or "the most" to state comparison.

Examples: The Rottweiler is **more obnoxious** than the Doberman.

The black and white cat is **the most obnoxious** of all of the animals in her menagerie.

4. When comparing persons or things in the same group, use the word "other."

Example: Jesse can run faster than **any other** boy in his club.

A few adjectives with irregular forms of comparison must be memorized: good-better-best; bad-worse-worst; many, much-more-most; little (quantity only)-less-least; far-farther-farthest.

Adverbs

1. If you are comparing two things, add "er" to the adverb. If you are saying that something is done better than anything else, add "est" to the adverb.

Examples: Planes travel faster than cars.

Rockets travel fastest of all.

2. Using "more" and "most"

There is no steadfast rule as to when you add "er" or "est" or when you use "more" or "most." The best suggestion I can make is to go with what sounds correct. Most adverbs of two or more syllables form comparisons with "more" or "most."

Example: comprehensively, more comprehensively, most comprehensively

COMPLEX SENTENCES (*See also* SUBORDINATE CLAUSES)

A complex sentence is a sentence that has one or more independent clauses (a group of words that makes sense by itself) and a subordinate clause (a group of words with a subject and a verb but which does not make sense by itself).

The important thing to remember about a complex sentence is that if the subordinate clause begins the sentence, a comma must follow it.

Example: Although the dog sat on her foot, she did not say a word. (subordinate clause, independent clause)

COMPOUND SENTENCES

A compound sentence is composed of two complete sentences (related ideas only) joined together with a comma and a coordinating conjunction (and, or, nor, for, so, but, yet) or a semicolon.

Examples: The big dog sat on her foot, **and** she gazed up at her mistress with love. "The big dog sat on her foot" is a complete sentence. "She gazed up at her mistress with love" is a sentence.

I tell my students to put their finger over the coordinating conjunction and check whether there is a complete sentence on either side of the finger. If there are two sentences, a comma has to precede the conjunction because the sentence is compound.

Examples: The big dog licked his paw, **or** he licked his leg.

The big dog did not lick his paw, **nor** did he lick his leg.

The big dog sat on her foot, **for** he loved her.

The big dog ate too much, **so** he was rotund.

The big dog sat on her foot, **but** he didn't put his full weight on it.

The big dog sat on her foot, **yet** he still felt insecure.

Sometimes a compound sentence does not have a coordinating conjunction joining the two sentences. Instead, it has a semicolon.

Example: The big dog sat on her foot; it then licked her knee.

A compound sentence does not occur when the word "that" is included or implied after the word "so." "So that" is a subordinating conjunction of a subordinate clause. If a subordinate clause comes at the end of a sentence, there is no comma.

Examples: She grabbed the bone **so that** the other dog could not get it. (**"So that"** the other dog could not get it, she grabbed the bone.)

She gobbled her food **so** the other dog could not get it. ("That" is implied)

A compound imperative sentence **does not** take a comma because the subjects, while implied, are not stated.

Examples: Get off my feet and go lie down elsewhere. (to the dog)

Stop clawing my legs and settle down. (to the cat)

COMPOUND SUBJECTS AND COMPOUND PREDICATES

These should be recognized if only to ensure that the students know the meanings of the words "compound," "subject," and "predicate." These words appear on the standardized tests. I usually teach these in my diagramming unit. Diagramming makes compound subjects and predicates much clearer.

1. A compound subject is simply more than one thing or person doing the action.

Example: **Rottweilers** and **Dobermans** make wonderful pets.

2. A compound predicate is more than one verb supplying the action.

Example: Rottweilers **love** to eat and **enjoy** being petted.

CONJUNCTIONS

A conjunction is a word that joins words or groups of words together. Do not capitalize a conjunction in a title.

Example: The dog **and** the cat are friends.

1. **Coordinating conjunctions:** These are the conjunctions (joiners) which join two complete thoughts (independent clauses) together to form a compound sentence.

List of coordinating conjunctions: and, or, nor, for, so, but, yet.

It is a good idea to chant these with your students every time you encounter a compound sentence in a Caught'ya.

Example: She loves ice cream, **and** she loves candy, too.

Do not begin a sentence with a coordinating conjunction since they are supposed to join, not begin. Many authors of fiction ignore this rule. This is fine, and it can make for very effective writing. I have to enforce this rule with those students who begin almost every sentence with a conjunction.

2. **Correlative conjunctions:** These are used to join words or word groups. They appear in pairs.

Examples: **Either** you do your homework, **or** your grade will suffer.

Both Dobermans **and** Rottweilers make good companions.

List of correlative conjunctions: either/or, neither/nor, not only/but, both/and, just as/so.

3. **Subordinating conjunctions:** These conjunctions make a clause that was a complete sentence into a clause that cannot stand on its own. In other words, if a subordinating conjunction is placed before an independent clause (complete sentence), the clause becomes a dependent clause (subordinate clause).

Complete sentence: The dog licks the rug.

Dependent clause: **When** the dog licks the rug (no longer a complete sentence)

Subordinating conjunctions begin subordinate clauses. Always set off an introductory adverb clause (another word for a subordinate clause since subordinate clauses act as adverbs) with a comma.

Examples: **After the cat fell asleep,** he twitched his whiskers.

As the man shouted, the two dogs cringed.

Common subordinating conjunctions: after, although, as, as if, as long as, as soon as, as though, because, before, even though, if, in order that, provided that, since, so that, than, till, unless, until, when, whenever, where, whereas, wherever, while.

CONTINUED QUOTE
This is a sentence in a quote that is interrupted by identifying the speaker. It is important to recognize that when the quoted sentence continues, quotation marks are necessary, but the first letter should not be capitalized. This is also called an interrupted quote.

Example: "My Doberman is a lazy dog," she said, "but my Rottweiler is even lazier."

CONTRACTIONS
A contraction is a word made by the shortening of two words into one, eliminating some letters in the process. The two words are then joined by an apostrophe.

1. Contractions can be made by shortening "not" to "n't" and adding to a verb. Sometimes the spelling of the verb changes as in when "n't" is added to "shall," "will," or "can."

Examples: is not/isn't; does not/doesn't; cannot/can't; shall not/shan't; will not/won't.

2. It's and its

"Its" is a possessive pronoun that shows that "it" owns something.

Example: The dog ate **its** food.

"It's" is a contraction for "it is."

Example: **It's** a shame that she has so many animals to feed.

3. Contractions are also formed by joining nouns or pronouns with verbs.

Examples: I am/I'm; he is/he's; he had/he'd; you are/you're; she has/she's; let us/let's, they are/they're.

Avoid contractions in formal writing. Contractions render writing informal, and unless a writer is using dialogue or a truly informal style, the use of contractions should probably be avoided.

DANGLING PARTICIPLE
A dangling participle is a participle (present or past form of a verb) used as an adjective that is not adjacent to the noun that it modifies. Dangling participles should be avoided.

Example: **Snoring, the dog's nose** twitched. (The dog's nose did not do the snoring, the dog did. The word "dog" needs to follow the participle "snoring.")

Snoring, the dog twitched his nose.

DASHES A dash can be used to show a break or a shift in thought or structure. It also can signal an afterthought.

Examples: Now, when I was a boy — (break)

I found her most — well, I didn't like her manner. (shift in structure)

The big Doberman — the one with the floppy ears —leans against walls and people. (break)

My floppy-eared Doberman often leans — you know, all Dobermans lean like that. (shift in thought)

It is important to limit the use of dashes when writing. Too many dashes make the writing seem confused and jerky.

DIAGRAMMING SENTENCES

Sentence diagramming takes every word in a sentence and places it, according to its use, in a diagram-like chart. It is a graphic picture of a sentence. Diagramming sentences is a good skill for students to learn because it forces them to think logically. Diagramming sentences also teaches students good puzzle-solving techniques and makes them practice their knowledge of the eight parts of speech.

If you want students to diagram a few Caught'yas for practice, look at the section on diagramming sentences in any traditional grammar text.

The example below shows how a diagram works for a compound sentence:

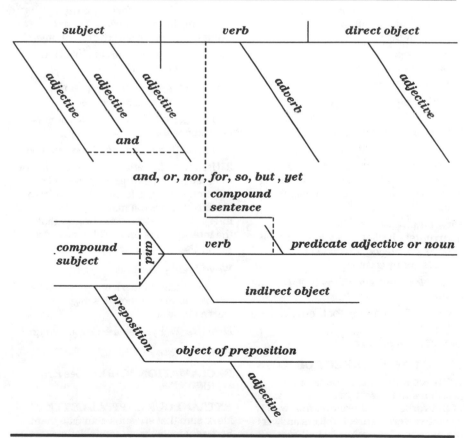

Basic example of a diagram for a compound sentence

DIALOGUES

Begin a new paragraph *every* time a different person speaks. If a person's speech includes more than one paragraph at a time, do not put quotation marks at the end of the first paragraph. Begin the next paragraph with quotation marks.

Example: (end of paragraph) " . . . and the teacher is always there."

(new paragraph) "Students, on the other hand . . . "

Punctuation of quotes: Put quotation marks around what is said aloud. Capitalize the first letter of a quote unless the quote is a continued one. Set off the quote by commas or by end punctuation. Always put all punctuation inside the quotation marks.

Examples: "Close the window, you outdoor fanatic," she whimpered. "I'm freezing in here."

"Please close the window," she said, "or I'll become an icicle."

She pleaded again, "Close that window."

"Will you please close the window?" she asked.

"Close that window!" she yelled.

DIRECT ADDRESS

A direct address occurs when the writer is speaking directly to someone, telling someone something, and naming that someone.

Direct addresses are also called interrupters because they interrupt the flow of a sentence. Always set a direct address off by commas.

Examples: **Dog,** get off my foot. (talking to the dog)

If you don't get off my foot, **dog,** you are in big trouble.

Get off my foot, **dog.**

DIRECT AND INDIRECT OBJECTS

1. **Direct objects** are nouns or pronouns that directly receive the action of the verb. They, therefore, follow only transitive verbs. Direct objects answer the question "whom" or "what" receives the action of the verb.

Examples: The dog licked the **teacher.** ("teacher" answers the question "whom")

Students should do all their **homework.** ("homework" answers the question "what")

The dog licked **me.** (whom)

2. **Indirect objects** are nouns or pronouns that indirectly receive the action. The action happens to them or for them, but the indirect object does not receive the action. This is an important concept to learn if anyone wants to learn a second language. Indirect objects follow only transitive verbs. You must have a direct object before you can have an indirect object. An indirect object answers the questions "to whom" or "for whom" the action is done.

Examples: The teacher gave **the children** (indirect object) **a short homework assignment.** (direct object)

The dog gave **me** (indirect object) **his paw.** (direct object)

END MARKS (PUNCTUATION)

Make sure each sentence has one!

1. Use a period at the end of a statement (a sentence that tells something).

Example: Dobermans can be sweet dogs.

2. Use an exclamation mark at the end of a sentence that expresses powerful emotion or strong feeling. You can also use an exclamation mark after an interjection of strong emotion so that the interjection stands all by itself.

Examples: Get out of here!

Wow! I really like that.

3. Use a question mark at the end of an interrogative sentence (a sentence that asks a question).

Example: Will you please get out of here?

EXCEPT (*See* ACCEPT/EXCEPT)

EXCLAMATION MARKS (See END MARKS)

EXTRANEOUS CAPITAL LETTERS

Make sure that students eliminate them. Some students throw capital letters around in their writing without any rhyme or reason. If any students do this, put a stop to it.

FARTHER/FURTHER

These two words are sometimes used incorrectly, but it is really very easy to tell the difference between the two and, therefore, an easy mistake to correct. Farther talks about physical distance. Further talks about everything else.

Examples: Mark can throw a ball **farther** than Jesse can.

We will discuss this **further** after dinner.

FEWER AND LESS

Few, fewer, and fewest should be used with things that can be counted. Little, less, and least should be used with things that cannot be counted.

Examples: **Fewer** students are interested in literature these days. (You can count students.)

I have **less** interest in Poodles than I do in Dobermans. (You cannot count an abstract concept like interest.)

FINDING AND IDENTIFYING

It is extremely important that students be able to find and identify the following:

1. **Eight parts of speech:** Noun, verb, adjective, adverb, conjunction, inter-jection, preposition, pronoun. (See each part of speech under its own heading.)

2. **Predicates**

Simple — The main verb or the main verb with a helping verb

Complete — the verb and its complements or modifiers (adverbs, adverb phrases).

3. **Subjects**

Simple — the noun or pronoun that does the action

Complete — the noun or pronoun that does the action and its modifiers (adjectives, adjective phrases)

4. **Synonyms for better writing**

Encourage students to use in their writing the vocabulary words of the Caught'yas and encourage them to use a thesaurus when they write.

FOOTNOTES

Most people do not use footnotes or endnotes (footnotes at the end of a paper) any more. The trend is to list all sources in the bibliography and when a quote from one is used or referred to in the body of the paper, to follow that quote or reference with parentheses containing the author's last name and the date of publication. When an author has published two sources within one year, list the title.

Example: The section on footnotes in Kiester's book says that the trend is not to have footnotes or endnotes in a paper. **(Kiester, 1992)**

FRAGMENTS

A sentence fragment is an incomplete thought (either lacking in subject or verb) that is used and punctuated incorrectly as a complete sentence. This is an egregious error. Help students overcome this habit. If students write fragments, then they probably don't understand what a subject and verb are. Frame your discussions accordingly.

Examples: A rather chubby dog on the floor. (no verb)

Slept on the floor by her side. (no subject)

Sticking his paws into the air. (no verb or subject)

FRIENDLY LETTERS (CORRECT FORMAT)

Sender's address
Sender's city, state   zip
Date

Dear Jane,
  The bulk of the letter goes here written without skipping lines between paragraphs.

With love,
Sign name here

FURTHER   (*See* FARTHER AND FURTHER)

GERUND

A gerund is a verb form that ends in "ing" and is used as a noun. A gerund can be used in any way that a noun can be used. Sometimes a gerund serves as the simple subject, direct object, or as the object of a preposition.

Examples: **Snorkeling** is my favorite sport. (subject)

I like **snorkeling**. (direct object)

I think of **snorkeling** a lot when I daydream. (object of the preposition)

GERUND PHRASES
Depending on your point of view, gerund phrases are either fun or useless to learn. I believe that the understanding and recognizing of them serves no purpose since no placement of commas is involved. One of my colleagues, on the other hand, maintains that gerunds and gerund phrases are fun. She uses art work to teach the concept to her students. She may well be right.

A gerund phrase is a group of words that includes a gerund and other words that complete its meaning. It can be accompanied by an adjective, an adverb, a direct object, or a prepositional phrase.

A gerund phrase functions as a noun in a sentence. The gerund phrase can be a subject or an object.

Examples: **Speaking softly** was one of the rules. (subject)

She made **speaking softly** a requirement in her class. (object)

GOOD AND WELL
These two words often are confused.

1. "Good" is an adjective; it tells about the noun that must follow it.

Example: The **good** dog sat at her feet instead of on them. (adjective — tells what kind of dog)

2. "Well" is the adverb that modifies a verb; it often appears at the end of the sentence.

Examples: He did it **well**. (adverb — tells how he did it)

He did **well** on the test. (adverb — tells how he did)

You can, however, "feel good" because "feel" acts as a verb of being and thus "good" is a predicate adjective.

Example: I **feel good** when I pet my cat.

HELPING VERBS
These verbs accompany a past or present participle in a sentence. My students and I call them "dead verbs" or "weak verbs." Help students limit them in their writing.

Common helping verbs: am, are, be, is, have, had, had been, has been, have, have been, was, were, will, and any form of "be" (such as could be, would be, might be, etc.).

Good writing uses strong verbs ("screamed" instead of **"was screaming"**). Look at literature!

Sense verbs (look, see, smell, feel, taste) can function as verbs of being or as action verbs.

Example: I **feel** loving today. (verb of being)

The boy **felt** the dog's broken leg. (action verb)

When a sense verb functions as a verb of being, it is often followed by a predicate adjective.

Example: I **feel** bad. (Not "I feel badly" since one would not say "I am badly.")

HOMOPHONES
Students need to be able to correctly use the most common ones.

Common homophones: there/their/they're; to/too/ two; your/you're; no/know; its/it's; right/rite/write; threw/through; quiet/quit/quite; all ready/already; all together/ altogether; hole/whole; pair/pare/pear; whose/who's

HYPHENS
1. Use a hyphen to divide a word at the end of a line. Divide only at syllables. Check a dictionary for syllables.

Example: The two huge dogs ran a-round the yard and terrified the little girl.

2. Use a hyphen to separate the words in compound numbers from twenty-one to ninety-nine and in fractions that are used as adjectives.

Examples: The teacher had **thirty-five** pupils in the class.

They ate ten and **one-half** pizzas for lunch.

3. Use a hyphen in a compound noun that serves as an adjective. More simply stated, use with two or more words that express one thought and serve as one adjective. To test whether a hyphen is needed, simply see if each word alone makes sense in describing the noun.

Examples: an **up-to-the-minute** report

two **star-crossed** lovers

a very **well-known** man

bell-bottom trousers

4. Use a hyphen after the following prefixes: all-, ex-, self-.

Examples: all-knowing, ex-husband, self-deprecating

5. Use a hyphen to separate any prefix from a word that begins with a capital letter.

Example: **pre-Civil** War

IMPERATIVES

Imperatives are sentences that are orders. The subject is omitted.

Examples: Get off my feet. (The subject of the dog has been left out.)

Do your homework now! (Again, the subject has been omitted.)

Compound imperative sentences do not take a comma because the subjects are not stated.

Example: Get off my feet and go lie down elsewhere.

INDEPENDENT CLAUSES

An independent clause is a sentence within a sentence.

Example: **She pet the dog,** and **she kissed the cat.**

INDIRECT AND DIRECT OBJECTS

(*See* DIRECT AND INDIRECT OBJECTS)

INDIRECT QUOTE

An indirect quote is really a reference to a direct quote. The use of the word "that" turns a direct quote into an indirect one. In an indirect quote, no quotation marks are necessary because a direct quote is being paraphrased. No comma is necessary either

Examples: The student said **that she was hot.**

He told me **that he had a lot of homework to do.**

We shouted to her **that we didn't want to walk the dogs.**

INFINITIVE

An infinitive is formed from the word "to" together with the basic form of a verb.

Examples: to go, to snore, to eat, to type

Do not split an infinitive with the adverb as in the introduction to the television show *Star Trek.*

Example of what to avoid: " . . . **to** boldly **go** where no one has been before." (*Star Trek*)

Correction: " . . . **to go** boldly where no one has been before."

You might want to explain the use of "to" as a part of a verb. Most students think it functions only as a preposition.

INFINITIVE PHRASE

This is a group of words with an infinitive and the words that complete the meaning. An infinitive phrase can serve as a noun, an adjective, or an adverb.

Examples:

Noun — To teach grammar is sometimes fun. (noun, subject)

Most students hate **to study grammar.** (object)

The goal of my first book was **to make grammar fun.** (predicate noun)

Adjective — It is now time to learn your grammar.

Adverb — The dog turned around six times to get ready for his nap.

INTENSIFIER

An intensifier is an adverb that tells to what extent an adjective or another adverb is true. The most common intensifiers are "very" and "extremely."

Examples: an **extremely** angry (adjective) cat

a **very** placid (adjective) dog

The cat wanted to sit on his mistress's lap **very** badly.(adverb)

She spoke **extremely** softly (adverb) because she was afraid to awaken the cat.

INTERJECTION

An interjection is a word or group of words that expresses feeling (anger, surprise, happiness, pain, relief, grief).

Common interjections: ah, aha, awesome, bam, boom, bravo, good grief, goodness, hey, hooray, hurrah, oh, oh boy, oh dear, oh my, oh yes /no, okay, ouch, ow, phew, pow, shhh, ugh, uh oh, well, whee, whoopee, whoops, wow.

Interjections that are at the beginning of the sentence can be followed either by a comma or by an exclamation mark. If an interjection is followed by an exclamation mark, the next word must begin with a capital letter.

Examples: **Well,** what are you doing there?

Okay, let's finish going over your homework.

Wow! Those dogs are big.

INTERRUPTED QUOTE (*See* CONTINUED QUOTE)

INTERRUPTERS

An interrupter is any word, expression or phrase that interrupts the flow of a sentence. These can be appositives, direct addresses, parenthetical expressions, or any word, phrase, or clause that breaks the flow of a sentence.

Examples: The dog, **however,** refused to get off her foot.

The dog, **I think,** is stubborn.

The black and white cat, **by the way,** is obstreperous.

She loved her only cat, **Skeeter,** very much.

INTRANSITIVE VERBS

An intransitive verb never has a direct object. In a sentence where the verb is intransitive, the subject does the acting and does not do anything to anything or anyone else.

Examples: Dogs **bark**.

The teacher **sits** in the chair.

The class **sleeps** during long messages on the loud speaker.

The class **rises** with respect (dream on, fellow teachers) when the teacher enters the room.

The dog **lies** on the floor.

INTRODUCTORY WORDS AND PHRASES

These are simply words and phrases that begin a sentence. The comma after some of these is hotly debated. Using commas makes sentences easier to understand because they signal a separation or a pause between parts. It sounds better to put a comma after an adverb that comes at the beginning of a sentence if that adverb has to do with time. It also helps clarify a sentence if one puts a comma after an introductory prepositional phrase that acts as an adverb and refers to time that has passed in some way.

1. **Adverb** (one-word adverbs): We commonly use a one-word adverb that indicates when the action (the verb) took place. Put a comma after it if you hear a pause when the sentence is spoken aloud.

Examples: **Meanwhile,** the dog's stomach growled.

Tomorrow, she will be fed again.

2. **Adverbial clauses** (subordinate clauses): A comma is needed after an adverbial clause that introduces a sentence.

Example: **After I feed the chubby Rottweiler,** I will feed the rotund Doberman.

3. **Participial phrases**: A comma is needed after a participial phrase that comes at the beginning of a sentence.

Example: **Traveling away from the city,** you can tour some of the beautiful antebellum homes in the country.

4. **Prepositional phrases:** The comma after these, too, is debatable. Many old-fashioned people, like my mother and I, put a comma after a longish prepositional phrase that comes at the beginning of a sentence, particularly if the phrase refers to time. This also can be called an "adverbial phrase."

Examples: **In about two weeks,** she will need to get her shots.

For a very long time, he will be able to exist on the food on the shelves.

A comma is needed after two or more prepositional phrases that follow each other at the beginning of a sentence.

Examples: **At the end of the day,** the fat dog tries to curl up on her "blankey" to go to sleep.

In one hour in the kitchen, the hungry dog will receive a dog biscuit.

In the fall of 1992, a presidential election was held in this country.

5. **Words:** A comma is needed to show a pause after an introductory word. The most common introductory words are "yes" and "no."

Examples: **Yes,** it is necessary to have a comma after introductory words.

No, many dogs do not receive five dog biscuits a day.

IRREGULAR VERB FORMS
Instead of forcing students to memorize a list which somehow never transfers to their writing, I teach each verb as it comes up in students' writing. This makes it real to them. They know they made a mistake in a verb and are more receptive to learning the forms of that verb. Plus, overkill (there are so many irregular verbs) only confuses students.

Verbs to stress in Caught'yas: be, do, have, lay, lie, raise, rise, see, set, sit. If you want to teach a unit on irregular verbs, any traditional grammar book will have a complete list for you.

LAY/LIE Few adults use these verbs correctly. Think about the trouble students must have with them!

1. **lay:** Lay means to place. Lay always has an object. You lay something on the table. You can't "lay" yourself on the table, that would be awkward as well as ungrammatical.

Principal parts of "lay":
lay (present)
laid (past)
laid (past participle)

Examples: The dog **lay** his head in his owner's lap. (present)

The dog **laid** his head on the rug yesterday. (past)

The dog always **has laid** its bone beside its bed. (past participle)

2. **lie:** Lie means to recline. Lie never takes a direct object. You lie on a bed, but you can never "lie" something on that bed.

Principal parts of "lie":
lie (present)
lay (past)
lain (past participle)

Examples: The dog **lies** on the floor today. (present)

The dog **lay** on the floor yesterday. (past)

The dog **is lying** on the floor right now. (present participle)

The dog **has lain** on the floor every day of its life. (past participle)

LESS AND FEWER (See FEWER AND LESS)

METAPHORS
A metaphor is a comparison of two unlike things without using "like" or "as."

Example: The tree **is a ballerina in green.**

Use metaphors in Caught'yas. Have your students write a "Metaphor Paper." (See the writing ideas in Chapter 5.) Encourage students to write metaphors. They make for beautiful writing. Emily Dickinson used metaphors in almost every poem. Metaphors are a wonderful tool to improve writing and to make it more sophisticated.

MODIFIERS AND MISPLACED MODIFIERS

1. Modifiers: A modifier is simply another word for an adjective. A modifier may be classified as non-restrictive (non-essential) or restrictive (essential). A modifier can be a word, a phrase, or a clause.

An adjective, adjective phrase, or adjective clause is non-restrictive/non-essential when it is not necessary to the meaning of the sentence. The clause gives additional information. Use commas to set off non-restrictive modifiers.

Example: Dino, **who has floppy ears,** won a prize in obedience class. (The name of the dog has been identified, and it is not necessary to add more information about him.)

An adjective, adjective phrase, or adjective clause is restrictive/essential when it is necessary to the meaning of the sentence. Do not set off a restrictive modifier with commas.

Example: The dog **who won a prize in obedience class** has floppy ears. (This information is necessary since there are millions of dogs in the world.)

2. Misplaced modifiers: These are simply adjective phrases or clauses that are in the wrong place in a sentence so that they seem to modify the wrong noun. When you use modifiers in sen-tences, make sure that they are properly placed. The general rule to follow is this: place modifiers as close as possible to the sentence parts they modify.

Examples: The lady was watching her dog **driving down the road**. (The dog is not driving down the road; the lady is.)

Corrected sentence: Driving down the road, the lady was watching her dog.

After purchasing a skirt, her money was all gone. (The clause "her money was all gone" does not tell more about the skirt. It tells about the **person** "her" refers to and therefore should not come immediately after "skirt.")

Corrected sentence: **After purchasing a skirt,** she had no more money.

NEGATIVES

A negative is a word that expresses the lack of something.

Common negatives: no, not, neither, never, nobody, none, no one, nothing, nowhere, barely, scarcely, hardly.

All you need to stress about negatives is the importance of avoiding the use of two negatives in the same sentence like "don't got no" or "don't have nobody." There should be only *one* negative word per sentence unless you are using "neither . . . nor," (but then "nor" is not considered a negative).

Only one negative word is necessary to convey the meaning. There are two ways to correct a sentence with a double negative.

Example: The telephone **isn't no** new instrument.

Corrected sentence: The telephone is **no** new instrument. Or, The telephone is **not** a new instrument.

NOUN

A noun is a person, a place, a thing, or an idea. It is important for students to recognize this part of speech and its function as a subject or object. Teach the difference between common and proper nouns.

Common nouns are terms for persons, places, things, or ideas.

Proper nouns are the names of particular persons, places, or things.

Examples:

Common nouns — girl, school, city

Proper nouns — Jane, Westwood School, Gainesville

Nouns have several functions in a sentence.

Subject — the person, place, or thing doing the action

Example: The **dog** yawned.

Direct object — the person, place, or thing who receives the action

Example: She stroked the **cat**.

Object of preposition — the person, place, or thing affected by the preposition

Example: He gave the bone to the **dog**.

Indirect object — the person, place, or thing for whom or to whom the action is done

Example: She gave the **dog** a big bone.("to" is implied)

NOUN CLAUSE

A noun clause is a subordinate clause which is used as a noun. It can be used as a subject, direct object, indirect object, predicate noun, or object of a preposition in a sentence.

Noun clauses usually begin with the following words: how, if, that, what, whatever, where, when, wherever, whether, which, whichever, who, whom, whoever, whomever, why.

Noun clauses take the place of a noun anywhere in a sentence that a noun can be used (subject, direct or indirect object, object of a preposition, predicate noun).

Examples:

Subject — What the dog intended was obvious.

Direct object — I still don't know **why he did it.**

Indirect object — Please give **whichever dog comes up to you** a pat under the chin.

Object of preposition — She tells her stories **to whoever will listen.**

Predicate noun — That is not **what the dog** intended to do.

NOUN MARKERS

This is the term for the three adjectives "a," "an," and "the." When I introduce these to the students, I first make my hand into a trumpet, "Toot-te-toot," and then announce, "Noun coming!!!!!!" Students quickly get the idea, and we move on to other things. Young students especially love the drama of the hand trumpet and seem to remember these three little words when they are presented in this fashion.

Example: The lady gave **an** old bone to **a** hungry dog.

Use "a" before a word that begins with a consonant and "an" before a word that begins with a vowel. These adjectives are also called "articles." (*See* ARTICLES)

OBJECTS

There are two kinds of objects, direct and indirect. Objects are nouns, noun clauses, or noun phrases that receive the action of the verb either directly or indirectly. They answer the following questions:

1. whom? (direct object)
2. what? (direct object)
3. to or for whom? (indirect object)
4. to or for what? (indirect object)

For further information about objects and for examples, *see* DIRECT AND INDIRECT OBJECTS.

PARAGRAPHS

Discuss the need for a paragraph each time you do a Caught'ya. Correct paragraphing can be learned only through constant practice. While various writers may disagree as to the exact placement of a paragraph, there are some general rules.

1. In general, a new paragraph is needed if there has been a lapse of time, a change of subject, or a change of place. A paragraph is supposed to be about one basic idea. It needs a topic sentence and a concluding sentence (unless it is a quotation).

2. Use a new paragraph in conversations each time a new person speaks. This seems like such a simple thing to grasp, but students have a hard time learning this.

Example:

"Get out of here, you beastly dog!" cried the lady to the big brown Doberman cowering in the kitchen. "You're messing up my floor!"

"Rowrf, Rowrf!" barked back the dog as it slinked sheepishly away.

"Oh, come back here, you poor thing," called the lady. "I'm sorry I yelled at you."

"Rowrf!"

"I like you, too," said the lady.

PARALLEL CONSTRUCTION

Parallel structure are forms that use similar grammatical constructions. Similar forms of phrases, words, and clauses are used for items that are alike in a sentence.

Parallel construction means that if you begin with a word or a certain part of speech, you have to continue it if you have a series. It can, however, be implied, as in a series of infinitives.

Examples: The big Doberman likes **bananas, tomatoes,** and **broccoli.** (words — these are all nouns)

The two dogs liked **sleeping** and **eating.** (words — gerunds)

The chubby Rottweiler went **to her bowl, to her water dish,** and then **to her bed.** (phrases — prepositional)

She felt **that she was unloved** and **that she was unwanted** because there was no food in her bowl. (clauses)

He likes **to eat,** (to) **sleep,** and (to) **play.**

PARENTHESES

(As you may have noticed, I abuse these.)

Parentheses enclose information that isn't vital to the meaning of a sentence, but that is nevertheless important to include. Parentheses can also contain information that some of the readers of the sentence already know.

Examples: The author of this book (Jane Kiester) has a thing about dogs.

Emily Dickinson (1830-1886) is his favorite poet.

Frequent use of parentheses is not desirable. (Do as I say, not as I do.)

PARENTHETICAL EXPRESSIONS

Parenthetical expressions are phrases that are thrown into sentences as asides to the reader. They are not necessary to the meaning of the sentence and often interrupt a sentence's flow. Parenthetical expressions are also called interrupters.

Common parenthetical expressions: of course, however, for example, on the contrary, on the other hand, I suppose, in fact, by the way, in my opinion, to tell the truth, nevertheless, I believe, I think, etc.

Parenthetical expressions are always set off by commas no matter where they occur in a sentence.

Examples: The dog, **in fact,** was too chubby for her collar.

To tell the truth, two faithful dogs are a handful.

The cat, **however,** is quite a dapper fellow.

Cats are smarter than dogs, **of course.**

PARTICIPIAL PHRASES (also called PARTICIPLE PHRASES)

These are groups of words that have the "ing," the "ed," or the special past form of the verb in them. In other words, they are phrases that contain a participle and its complement and modifiers. Participial phrases can come before or after the word that they modify and can give more information about a noun or an adjective. The participle will be present or past.

1. A **present participle** is the "ing" form of a verb. It can be used as an adjective by itself or in a participial or gerund phrase.

Examples: The **snoring** (adjective) dog **sleeping on the floor** (participial phrase) is the gentlest of animals.

Cramming before a test is a poor practice. (gerund phrase)

2. A **past participle** is the past tense form of a verb which usually ends in "ed." It can be used with a helping verb or can be used as an adjective or in a participial phrase.

Examples: The chef served the fish **fried in butter.**

That **trained** (adjective) dog who didn't learn anything has barked all morning long.

Participial phrases act as adjectives

Examples: **Rapidly gaining confidence,** the new teacher taught about participial phrases. (more about "teacher")

The new teacher, **feeling more sure of herself,** taught about participial phrases.

If the participial phrase begins the sentence or comes in the middle of the sentence, it is usually set off by commas. If, however, it is at the end of the sentence, it requires no comma.

Examples: **Groaning softly,** the dog kicked out in his sleep.

The dog, **groaning softly,** kicked out in his sleep.

She spied a dog **groaning softly in its sleep.**

PARTICIPLE

A participle is just a fancy name for a verb form that is used as an adjective. It can be the present participial form of the verb ("–ing") or the past participial form of the verb (usually "–ed").

Examples: The **sleeping** dog blocked the doorway. (present)

A **trained** dog supposedly obeys better than an **untrained** one. (past)

(*See* PARTICIPIAL PHRASES. *See also* DANGLING PARTICIPIAL)

PARTS OF SPEECH

The eight parts of speech are the eight functional categories into which we can divide words. It is important that students learn the eight parts of speech to have a frame of reference and to have a way to understand the finer points of grammar.

The eight parts of speech: adjectives, adverbs, conjunctions, verbs, interjections, nouns, prepositions, pronouns.

PASSIVE VOICE (*See* ACTIVE VS. PASSIVE VERB VOICES)

PERIODS (*See* END MARKS)

PLURAL

A plural is more than one of a noun. In the Caught'yas I covered the common mistakes students make. This is another skill that should be taught individually. When one of your students makes a mistake with the plural of a word, include that word or a similar word in a Caught'ya and teach it.

Basic plural rules.

1. Add "s" to most singular nouns.

Examples: dog-dogs; piano-pianos; monkey-monkeys; cat-cats.

2. Add "es" to singular nouns that end in ss, x, ch, sh, or z.

Examples: church-churches; mix-mixes; glass-glasses; buzz-buzzes; wish-wishes.

3. Most nouns that end in "o" add "s" in their plural form, but a few that end in "o" and are preceded by a consonant form their plurals with "es." Some can end in either one.

Examples: tomato-tomatoes, potato-potatoes; BUT hero-heros or heroes

4. Change singular nouns that end in a consonant and a "y" to plural by changing the "y" to an "i" and adding "es." This rule does not apply to proper nouns that end in a consonant and a "y."

Examples: party-parties; baby-babies; BUT Mary-Marys

5. To form the plural of some nouns that end in "f" or "fe," change the "f" to a "v" and add "es."

Examples: calf-calves; knife-knives

6. To form the plural of any proper name, no matter what the end letters, add "s."

Examples: Brady-Bradys; Finch-Finchs

7. There are so many exceptions to these rules that it boggles the mind. If you want a complete list, see a traditional grammar text. Few people can memorize a list one day and then apply it to their writing a month later. Plurals are best taught on the spur of the moment, at the time they are written incorrectly.

Examples: foot-feet; mouse-mice; deer-deer; child-children

PLURALS VS. POSSESSIVES

For some reason, this is a skill many students find beyond them. No general explanations seem to clear up this problem. Only specific focuses help. I tell my students who put apostrophes on plural nouns to eliminate every apostrophe in their writing for a month. We then slowly put them back in possessives and in conjunctions. This works better than anything else I have tried. I also keep plugging away in the Caught'yas by frequently inserting apostrophes correctly and incorrectly in the sentence that is put on the board. This forces students to think each time– "Does that apostrophe belong there? Is the word plural or possessive?" This way, students eventually get the hang of it.

POSSESSIVE NOUNS

A possessive noun is a noun (a person, place, or thing) that shows ownership of something. Ownership is shown by the use of an apostrophe.

Examples: the dog**'s** bone, the dogs**'** bones

The rules of possessive nouns are quite simple for something that gives students such anguish.

1. **Singular possessive nouns:** Add "'s" to any singular possessive noun no matter what letter ends it.

Examples: glass's, dog's, cat's, box's, church's, calf's, child's

2. **Plural possessive nouns:** Add an apostrophe to all plural possessive nouns that end in "s."

Examples: glasses', dogs', cats', boxes', churches', calves'

Add "'s" to any plural noun that does not end in "s."

Examples: children's, men's, mice's

PREDICATE

A predicate is the verb in a sentence and all the words that modify it.

Example: The black and white cat **sat on his mistress's lap**.

PREPOSITION

A preposition is a little word that, with its object, acts either as an adjective or as an adverb in a sentence.

Examples: in the doghouse, on the roof, under the bed

List of prepositions: aboard, about, above, across, after, against, along, among, around, at, before, behind, below, beneath, between, beyond, by, down, during, except, for, from, in, into, like, of, off, on, onto, over, past, since, through, throughout, to, toward, under, underneath, until, up, upon, with, within, without.

Students should memorize the basic list for quick reference. Repeated daily in class, these prepositions are learned in about three weeks. Teach the prepositions early in the year, write poems where every line has to begin with a different preposition, and refer to them often. Once students have memorized the prepositions, they can begin to use them more effectively and capitalize (or not) them correctly in titles.

Do not end a sentence with a preposition. It is uncouth! Do not capitalize a preposition in a title unless it is the first word of that title.

PREPOSITIONAL PHRASES

A prepositional phrase is a preposition and a noun or pronoun plus the adjectives that modify it. It is a group of words that functions as a single word. Prepositional phrases can serve as adjectives to modify a noun or as adverbs to modify a verb.

Examples: I gave a bone **to the dog**. (adverb)

The dog **with the floppy ears** ate the bone. (adjective)

An adjective phrase usually follows the word it modifies.

Example: The dog **on the right** is snoring.

An adverb phrase, like adverbs, may shift position.

Examples: **In the middle,** lies the cat.

The cat lies **in the middle**.

PRONOUNS

Pronouns are words that take the place of nouns and cause much trouble. They are hateful but necessary. If you think these are bad, try teaching French pronouns!

Especially stress the difference between subject and object pronouns.

Subject pronouns: I, you, he, she, it, we, they

Object pronouns: me, you, him, her, it, us, them.

Include in many Caught'yas "My friend and I did something." and "Someone did something to my friend and me."

Students experience much difficulty differentiating subject and object pronouns. They misuse them because they hear them misused all the time in common speech. Model the correct use as often as you can.

Examples of common errors: My friend and **me** went . . .

It is **me**.

She is better than **me**.

Correct examples: My friend and **I** went . . . ("I" is the subject of "went.")

It is **I**. (Implied here is "It is I who does something." "I" is a subject.)

She is better than **I** . . . (Again, something is implied. The word "am" has been left out. "I" is the subject of "am.")

Teach the correct use of the different kinds of pronouns. It is not the name of each that is important; it is recognizing the differences among them.

1. **Personal pronouns:** These are the subject and object pronouns listed above.

2. **Possessive pronouns:** These are pronouns that show ownership of something.

Singular possessive pronouns: my, mine, your, yours, his, her, hers, its

Plural possessive pronouns: our, ours, your, yours, their, theirs

3. **Interrogative pronouns:** These pronouns ask questions: why, what, which, who, whom.

4. **Demonstrative pronouns:** These pronouns point out people, places or things and highlight them: this, that, these, those.

5. **Indefinite pronouns:** These are pronouns that refer to a person or a thing that is not identified. Some indefinite pronouns are singular. Some are plural. Some can act either way.

Singular: another, anybody, anyone, anything, each, either, everybody, everyone, everything, neither, nobody, no one, nothing, other, one, somebody, someone, something

Plural: both, few, many, ones, others, several

Either: all, any, most, none, some

It is important to teach agreement with indefinite pronouns. Many students find it difficult to make a verb or another pronoun agree with the indefinite pronoun.

6. **Reflexive and intensive pronouns:** These usually end in "self" or "selves" and refer to the subject of the sentence. For your trivia information of the day, you need to know that reflexive pronouns are necessary to the meaning of a sentence and cannot be left out. Intensive pronouns, on the other hand, are not necessary and can be left out without hurting the meaning of a sentence.

Examples: The teacher knows **herself** very well. (reflexive)

The teacher **herself** washed the blackboard. (intensive)

7. **Relative pronouns:** These are the pronouns that modify a noun: who, which, that.

There are two big problems with pronouns — using the correct one and making the rest of the sentence agree with it.

PUNCTUATION

Each kind of punc-tuation is listed under its own heading.

QUESTION MARKS (*See* END MARKS)

QUOTATION MARKS (IN USES OTHER THAN CONVERSATIONS)

Use quotation marks around words referred to or letters referred to in the context of a sentence. Use them also with words that are meant tongue-in-cheek.

Periods and commas always go inside quotation marks.

Examples: If you wish to make plural the word "party," take off the "y" and add "ies."

He loves the poem "Mother to Son."

The corpulent Rottweiler has been nicknamed "Miss Tub."

Exclamation marks and question marks go outside the quotation marks unless they are part of the words in quotation marks.

Examples: She got an "A"!

Did he give an extra bone to "Miss Tub"?

Quotations can be avoided with the use of the word "that." Instead of quotation marks, refer to what has been said with the word "that." *See* INDIRECT QUOTES for more information.

Examples: She said **that** she was hungry and needed refreshments.

Despite her pleas, I told her **that** she was too chubby to get any more ice cream.

(*See also* DIALOGUES, COMMA RULES, INDIRECT QUOTES, and TITLES)

RAISE/RISE

These are two more verbs that confuse students. Again, as in "lie" and "lay" and "sit" and "set," one takes an object and the other does not.

1. Raise means "to lift or to grow." It requires an object that has to be "raised."

Example: The cat **raised** his tail and stormed off when no food was offered.

2. Rise means "to get up." It does not take an object.

Example: All students **rise** with a bow of respect when their English teacher enters the room.

RUN ONS

A run on is a sentence that contains more than one thought. It goes on and on.

1. Sometimes run-on sentences simply lack punctuation.

Example: The dog lay on the floor she snored loudly.

Corrected: The dog lay on the floor. She snored loudly.

2. Sometimes run-on sentences are a group of sentences joined by coordinating conjunctions into one very long sentence.

Example: She lay on the floor, and she snored, but she didn't groan, and she wiggled her ears.

Corrected: She lay on the floor. She snored, but she didn't groan. She wiggled her ears.

Help your students avoid run ons. I have included many of them in the Caught'ya sentences at the upper levels.

SEMICOLONS

A semicolon is a punctuation mark (;) that is used to separate parts of a sentence.

1. Use semicolons in compound sentences instead of using a conjunction and a comma.

Example: The black cat nuzzled the big dog; it is either very friendly or very stupid.

2. Use semicolons in lists where the use of a lot of commas makes meaning difficult.

Example: Learn the meanings of these homophones: there, their, they're; to, too, two; your, you're; no, know; and hear, here.

3. Use a semicolon to join two independent clauses (two sentences within a sentence) when the second clause begins with however, nevertheless, consequently, besides, therefore, moreover, or furthermore.

Example: The Rottweiler may lick faces; **however,** she is charming.

4. To avoid confusion, use a semicolon to separate two independent clauses that have many commas within one or both of them.

Example: My Rottweiler likes to eat tomatoes, broccoli, and cucumbers; my Doberman likes to eat fruit, dog food, and cookies.

SIMILES

A simile compares two unlike things and uses "like" or "as" in the comparison.

Examples: The cat sprawled on the rug **like a furry throw pillow.**

The leaves, **as agile as ballerinas,** seemed to dance in the wind.

Encourage students to use similes. I have included a plethora of them in the middle and high school Caught'yas so that students can learn to recognize and use them. Point them out to students. Practice coming up orally with other similes.

SIMPLE SENTENCE

A simple sentence is a sentence with one subject and one predicate. In a simple sentence, the subject and/or the verb can be more than one thing, as in a compound subject or a compound predicate, but only one idea is expressed.

Examples: The wimpy **Rottweiler sat** on her owner's foot.

The wimpy **Rottweiler** and the brown **Doberman sat** by their owner's feet and **gazed** adoringly into their mistress's eyes. (Two subjects and two verbs, but it is still a simple sentence.)

SINCE (*See* BECAUSE AND SINCE)

SET/SIT

These are two more verbs that students often use incorrectly.

1. Set means to put down. Set always takes an object. You **set** the sleeping cat in the chair or the milk on the table, but you never **set** yourself down anywhere. Tell students to think about it. You can't put your hands under your feet and lift your entire body up and set it down on something.

Example: The dumb Doberman set his bone down on the floor, and the chubby Rottweiler grabbed it from under his nose.

2. Sit means to place yourself in a seated position. Sit does not take an object. You **sit** down, but you never **sit** something down.

Example: The stupid dog always **sits** on its owner's foot.

SPELLING ERRORS, THE MOST COMMON

1. All words with "ie" or "ei"

Examples: thief, relief, believe

weird, neighbor, receive

2. Plurals of nouns that end in "y"

Examples: parties, monkeys, babies

3. "A lot" (students write as one word)

Some teachers forbid the use of this in their classrooms. I agree. There are always ways to avoid the use of "a lot."

4. Doubling consonants in words that end in consonant/vowel/consonant plus a suffix that begins with a vowel (like "ed").

Examples: dropped, stopped, petted

5. Any grammar or spelling book will have a long list of commonly misspelled words, but very few people can memorize a long list of words and then remember the spelling of those words when they use them in their writing at a later date. It is better to attack these misspelled words as they appear in students' writings.

SPELLING RULES

There are too many spelling rules and exceptions to the spelling rules to list here. See any standard spelling book for a discussion of this subject. The most common ones have been listed by the individual Caught'yas in which they appear.

STRONG VERBS

These are verbs that are not helping verbs or sense verbs. They show rather than tell what is going on in a sentence. Use of these verbs fosters better writing. You will find the use of strong verbs in literature. There is even a language called E-Prime that is English minus the verb "to be." Try speaking or writing in E-Prime. The results are amazing, and the verb "to be" is only one of the "telling" verbs.

Examples: The dog **stretched** and **rolled** his big brown eyes at me.

He **ambled** to the door and **peeked** outside.

Dead verbs to avoid: to be — be, am, is, are, was, were; to have — has, have, had; become, became.

Sense verbs: sees, looks, feels, sounds, smells.

Any verb ending in "ing"

SUBJECTS

A subject is the noun that performs the action in a sentence and everything that modifies it.

Example: **The big black cat and his mistress** like to snooze late on Saturday mornings.

SUBJECT-VERB AGREEMENT

Subject-verb agreement is very important to the coherence of a sentence. The subject of a sentence must agree as to whether it is singular or plural with the verb of the sentence.

If the subject is singular, then the verb should be singular. If the subject is plural, the verb should be plural.

Examples: **He think** he is right. (incorrect)

We goes to the circus every year.

Corrected examples: **He thinks** he is right.

We go to the circus every year.

SUBORDINATE CLAUSE

A subordinate clause is a part of a sentence that has a subject and a verb but cannot stand on its own to express a complete thought. A subordinate clause begins with a subordinating conjunction — a conjunction that makes the clause not a complete sentence. *See* SUBORDINATING CONJUNCTIONS for a complete list them.

Examples: **When the teacher was funny,** the students laughed. ("The teacher was funny" is a complete sentence with a subject and a verb. If you add the subordinating conjunction "when," it can no longer stand on its own, and it needs the addition of an independent clause to form a complete sentence.)

While we sit here, I shall tell you my story.

I shall tell you my story **while we sit here.**

Subordinate clauses serve in a sentence as adverbs or adjectives. Subordinate clauses that are adverbs (adverb clauses) tell more about the verb and answer one of the following questions about a verb: when it happened, where it happened, how it happened, how often it happened, why it happened.

Examples: See ADVERB CLAUSES.

Subordinate clauses that are adjectives (adjective clauses) tell more about a noun and answer one of the following questions about it: which one, what kind, how many.

Examples: See ADJECTIVE CLAUSES.

Punctuation of subordinate clauses is easy. Put a comma at the end of the clause if the clause begins the sentence. Do not put any commas if the clause does not begin the sentence.

Examples: **If you pet the dog,** you will get hairs on your suit.

You will get hairs on your suit **if you pet the dog.**

SUBORDINATING CONJUNCTIONS

These are words that make something that was a complete sentence into an incomplete sentence. Subordinating conjunctions begin subordinate clauses (see above).'

Example: **After** the cat fell asleep, he twitched his whiskers.

Common subordinating conjunctions: after, although, as, as if, as long as, as soon as, as though, because, before, even though, how, if, in order that, provided that, since, so that, than, till, unless, until, when, whenever, where, whereas, wherever, while.

SUMMARIZING

To summarize something you write a condensed version of it. This is a skill that is necessary in almost any job. A repair man has to summarize each house call. A doctor has to summarize each patient's problems, and so on. It is a skill that is easily practiced with the Caught'yas. (See #9 of the General Writing Ideas in Chapter 5 for ideas to teach summarization skills.)

THAT

"That" is a relative or a demonstrative pronoun (depending on how it is used). Use "that" in an indirect quote to avoid the use of quotation marks.

Example: She said **that** she was going to feed the dogs.

Do not use "that" as a substitute for "who" or "whom." "That" refers to an object or a thing. "Who" and "whom" refer to people. This is an extremely common mistake.

Example: She is the one **whom** (not "that") I love.

Is feeding two hungry dogs **that** complicated?

She gave the dog the bone **that** seemed the biggest.

TITLES

1. Underline titles of long works — books, magazines, newspapers, plays, movies, paintings, and long musical works.

2. Put quotation marks around short works — short stories, poems, chapters of books, magazine articles, songs. It also is important to recall that if a comma or a period follows the quoted work, it must be placed inside the quotation mark. If a question or an exclamation and the end punctuation is not a part of the cited work, then the question mark or the exclamation point goes outside the quotation mark.

Examples: Although she read the article "Sentence Diagramming," she still didn't understand the concept.

She read the article "Sentence Diagramming."

Did she read the article "Sentence Diagramming"?

3. Do not capitalize prepositions, noun markers, or conjunctions in a title unless they are the first word of the title.

Example: The (noun marker) Dog under (preposition) a (noun marker) Human Roof and (conjunction) the (noun marker) Cat on (preposition) the (noun marker) Lap

The Dog under a Human Roof and the Cat on the Lap

TRANSITIVE VERBS

A transitive verb takes a direct object. In other words, it always has to do something to something or someone.

Example: The dog **lay** his **head** on the carpet today.

The cat **set** his **paw** on the table before attacking the plate.

The dog **raised** his **paw** for inspection.

VERB TENSE SHIFT IN A STORY

Make sure that students stick to the same tense they begin with in any story or paragraph they write. If a story starts in the present tense, it should remain in the present tense. If it begins in the past tense, it should continue in the past tense.

To practice this skill, I frequently have changed the verb tense in the Caught'ya sentences. All of the stories have been told in the past tense, so I sometimes put the verb in the present tense. In the margin I warn the teacher to make sure that the students practice correcting "verb tense shift."

VERBS

For lists of verbs and appropriate forms of regular and irregular verbs, please refer to a traditional grammar text. Otherwise, just correct students as they make the mistakes in their writing. The latter is more effective.

Try to keep students from splitting helping verbs and the participles that follow.

Example: The cat also **has lain** on the carpet all day. (Not "**has** also **lain**") all day.

While splitting helping verbs and the participles that follow is sometimes unavoidable, it is not correct English. Although more rigid grammarians disagree with me on this point, many of my colleagues and I believe that if avoiding the split creates an awkward sentence, the rule should be ignored.

WELL (*See* GOOD AND WELL)

WHO, WHOEVER, WHOM, WHOMEVER

These are relative or interrogative pronouns that are used to refer to people. These four pronouns are so misused in general parlance that to some students the correct form sounds incorrect! Simply correct students every time you hear an error in the use of these four pronouns. You may be making verbal corrections until students feel "grammatically abused," but the more students hear the correct way to use these pronouns, the more they will use them correctly.

Here's a general rule of thumb that works about 95 percent of the time. I tell my students to use "who" and "whoever" if the word after it is a verb. If the word is not a verb but a pronoun or a noun, then they must use "whom" or "whomever."

Another rule that often works even better is to substitute "he" or "she" for "who" and "him" or "her" for "whom" and see if it makes sense. These rules fail when you have one of those weird sentences or phrases that can be turned around like "Who I am" or when you have something else like "I think" between the subject and the verb. (She is the one who **I think** did it.)

1. **Who and whoever:** Used as interrogative pronouns, "who" and "whoever" are the subject of a simple or compound sentence. They should be followed by a verb, the thing that "who" does. Tell students, in they are in doubt, to try substituting "he" or "she" for "who" to see if it makes sense.

Examples: **Who is** that?

Who is sitting on my foot?

All right, **who ate** the dog food?

Whoever broke into the bag and ate the dog food is in big trouble.

Whoever is sitting on my foot had better get off.

Used as a relative pronoun, "who" and "whoever" may be the subject or the predicate noun of a clause.

Examples: **Whoever finishes first** will get extra ice cream for dessert. (subject)

We shall serve **whomever arrives first**. (predicate)

2. **Whom and whomever:** Whom and whomever are relative pronouns that serve as objects of sentences or clauses. They can be direct objects of a verb, indirect objects, or objects of a preposition. Tell students to try substituting "him" or "her" for "whom" to see if it sounds correct.

Examples: He is the one **whom** I love. (object of verb)

With **whom** did you go out last night? (object of preposition)

I will pick the one **whom** I want. (object of verb)

For **whom** does the lady buy diet dog food? (object of preposition)

3. **That:** Do not use "that" instead of "who" or "whom." "That" refers to objects or things. "Who" and "whom" refer to people.

Examples: (*See* THAT)

To reinforce the correct use of "who" and "whom," I tell students that I will give them one point extra credit (three of them erase a zero in my grade book) if they catch someone at home making a "who/whom" error. Students write down the offending sentence, coerce the person into adding a note that he/she did, in fact, make the error, and bring the paper to me. At first I was afraid that I would have angry parents, but it turned out that I received only positive phone calls from grateful parents who were delighted to see their children taking an interest in correct English grammar.

Bibliography

1. Atwell, Nancie. *In the Middle - Writing, Reading, and Learning with Adolescents*. Portsmouth: Boynton/Cook Publishers, 1987.

2. Caplan, Rebakah, and Deech, Catherine. *Showing Writing - A Training Program to Help Students Be Specific*. Berkeley: University of California Press, 1980.

3. Elgin, Suzette Haden. *The Great Grammar Myth*. National Writing Project Occasional Paper #5. Berkeley: University of California Press, 1982.

4. Haley-James, Shirley, and Stewig, John Warren. *Houghton Mifflin English*. Boston: Houghton Mifflin Company, 1988.

5. Kiester, Jane. "Burying Dead Verbs and Reviving Live Ones or All's Fair in Love, War, and the Teaching of Writing in Middle School English." *Visions of Teaching: 100 Innovative Middle Level Projects*. North Carolina State University Press, 1989.

6. Kiester, Jane. *Caught'ya! Grammar with a Giggle*. Gainesville: Maupin House Publishing, 1990.

7. Kiester, Jane. *Language and the Newspaper*. Gainesville: The New York Times Publishing Company, 1981.

8. Laird, Charlton, preparer. *Webster's New World Thesaurus*. New York: Simon and Schuster, Inc., 1985.

9. Macrorie, Ken. *The I-Stand Paper*. Portsmouth, HH: Boynton Cook, 1988.

10. Vail, Neil, and Papenfuss, Joseph. *Daily Oral Language Level 7*. Racine: D. O. L. Publications, 1982.

11. Warriner, John, and Graham, Sheila Laws. *Warriner's English Grammar and Composition*, Complete Course. New York: Harcourt Brace Jovanovich, 1957.

12. Warriner, John, and Graham, Sheila Laws. *Warriner's English Grammar and Composition*, Third Course. New York: Harcourt Brace Jovanovich, 1977.

13. *The World Almanac and Book of Facts*. New York: Newspaper Enterprise Association Inc., 1985.